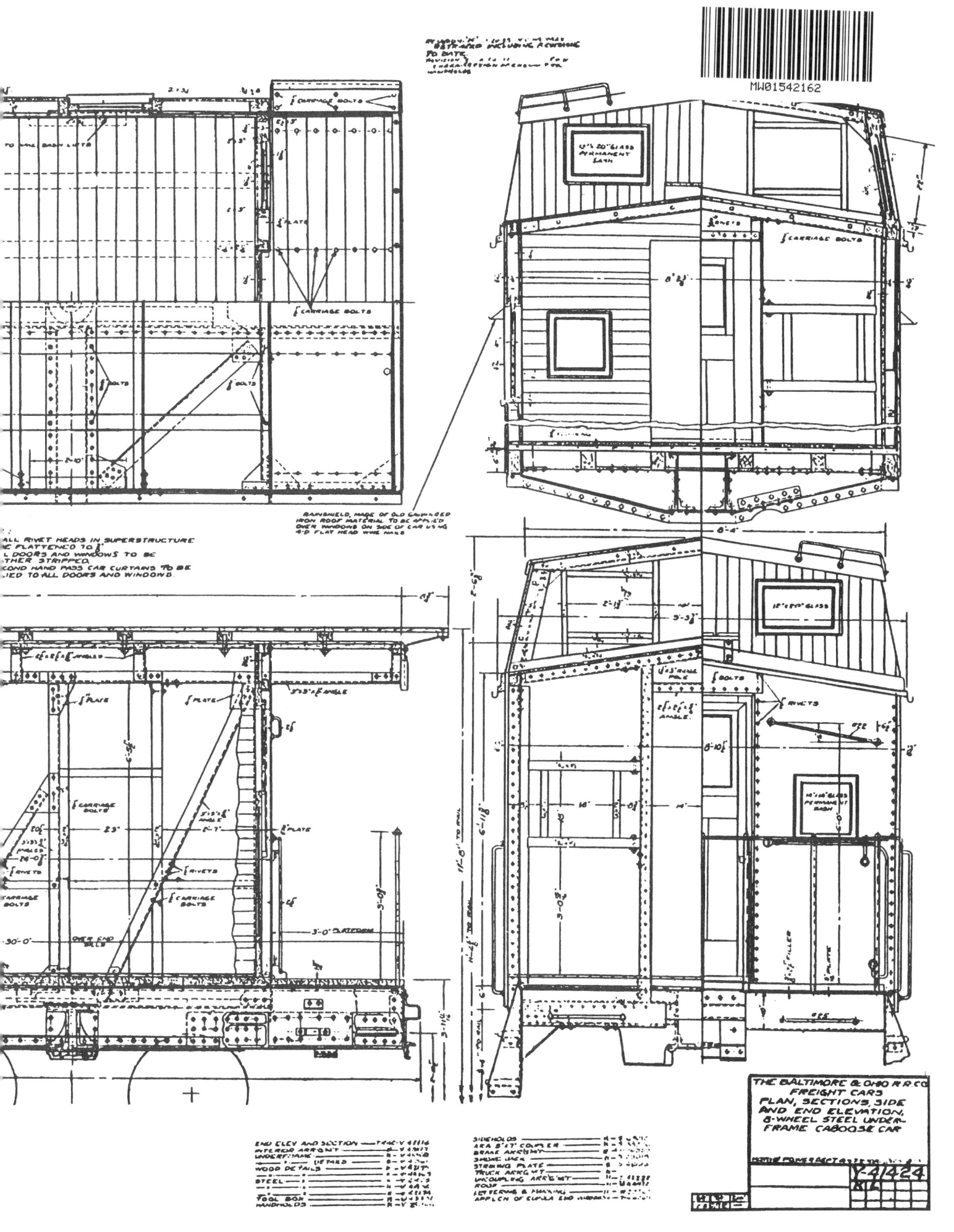

CABOOSES
of the
BALTIMORE & OHIO
RAILROAD

Robert Hubler
with Contributions by
John P. Hankey
Edited by
Gary W. Schlerf

CABOOSES
of the
BALTIMORE & OHIO RAILROAD

by
Robert Hubler

with Contributions by
John P. Hankey

Edited by
Gary W. Schlerf

Copyright © 1994
The Baltimore and Ohio Railroad Historical Society

All rights reserved under International and Pan American Copyright Conventions. No part of this book may be reproduced in any manner whatsoever without written permission from the publisher, except in the cases of brief quotations embodied in reviews or articles.

First Edition
Manufactured in the United States

For information write to:
The Baltimore and Ohio Railroad Historical Society
P. O. Box 13578
Baltimore, MD 21203-3578

Layout and Design by: D. A. McFall
Typesetting by: Old Line Graphics

**Library of Congress Catalog Card Number 94-73254
ISBN 0-9644733-0-5**

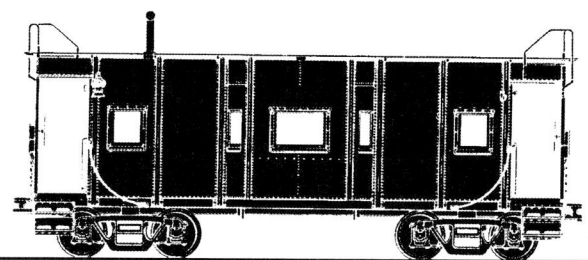

TABLE OF CONTENTS

Foreword 4
Editor's Preface 6
Acknowledgements 7
I. An Historical Perspective 8
II. History and Description
    A. Historical Overview 24
    B. Roster 27
    C. Class Descriptions
        I 29
        K-1 31
        I-1 35
        I-2 40
        I-3 43
        C&C 45
        M&K 46
        I-4 47
        I-1A 47
        I-5 51
        I-5A / I-5B / I-5BA 56
        I-5C 61
        I-5D 63
        I-6 66
        I-7 68
        I-8 / I-9 70
        I-10 73
        I-11 76
        I-12 77
        I-13 81
        I-14 / I-14A 84
        I-16 87
        I-17 / I-17A 89
        I-18 94
        C-15B 96
        C-5 / C-8 / C-9 98
        C-26 / C26A 102
        C-28 106
        C-27 / C27A 106
III. Painting and Lettering 112
    A. Paint Schemes 115
    B. Lettering Schemes 146
Index of Photographs 175

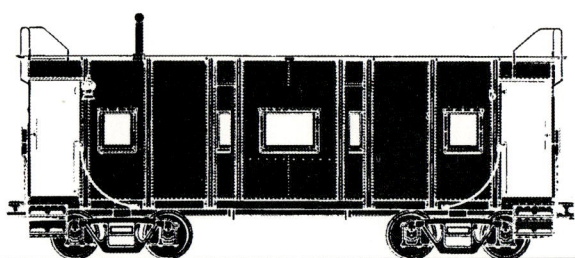

FOREWORD

Cabooses are a subject about which many people know a little, and a few know a great deal. Even so, everyone might agree that they were vital to railroading and deserve serious study today. That is especially true of the cabooses of the Baltimore and Ohio Railroad. When studied closely, they reveal a great deal about railroad life, railroaders themselves, and the intangible aspects of a company which consistently made virtue of necessity and idiosyncracy a de facto corporate policy. Few of us, however, have the time or resources to become experts in railroad technology in general, much less one kind of freight car equipment like the caboose. We rely on people such as Bob Hubler to gather data and make sense of the complex technological history of these unique and colorful cars.

How will we use this book? I suspect in a surprising number of ways. Modelers will use the photographs, diagrams and data to accurately reproduce the cars in miniature. While vestiges of the B&O Railroad and its caboose fleet remain, both are essentially extinct, and recede farther into our collective memory with each passing year. Crafting a model of some part of the B&O thus becomes an act of remembrance and preservation. Having the right caboose, in the correct color and lettering scheme, for the time and place being modeled is a kind of homage to the memory of the B&O.

We might have enjoyed a personal association with the cars. Like railroaders themselves, cabooses were highly mobile. Sometimes, however, they could be found on regular assignments or in predictable places where we had an opportunity to become personally acquainted with a car and its crew. As photographers, no matter what our interests, we tended to take pictures of the front of the train, and less often of the rear. Even if we did not record them, cabooses provided a satisfying sense of closure to the passage of a train—especially if you got a friendly wave from the fellows who spent most of their working lives on the hind end.

The railroad caboose was fascinating precisely because men (and later, a few women) worked and lived aboard in what seemed to be a continuing adventure. The caboose was a distinct kind of car in use for over a hundred years, and through this one type of car we can follow changes in the railroad work experience, car building techniques and operating practices. As Bob Hubler long ago discovered, cabooses offer an interesting and manageable sort of intellectual puzzle. At their most numerous, cabooses were counted in the hundreds, unlike the tens of thousands of coal cars used by the B&O.

After the turn of the century, cabooses were reasonably well documented, but after the rise of popular railroad history in the 1920s, they began to enjoy scrutiny by a select group of devotees. Cabooses offer a nicely bounded topic which, like botany, or entomology, depends on describing, classifying, and relating different types of physical things.

What the B&O lacked in standardization and numbers (compared with the Pennsylvania Railroad, for instance), it made up in variety and sheer creativity. The B&O's resolute individuality manifested itself in numerous caboose classes, sub-classes, and distinctive cars, many of which survived to the end of the company in 1987. As you will see through Bob Hubler's painstaking research, the B&O simply could not leave its cabooses alone, any more than it could its locomotives, stations, or anything else it owned. That fact can bedevil model manufacturers and historians alike. How many windows, in what pattern, should a Class I-5D car have; what were its truck centers; and what variation of a supposed "standard" paint scheme did it wear? Without the kind of documentation provided by a book like this, few outsiders would believe the modeler who operated cabooses with as many variations in construction and lettering as were found on the B&O.

Describing such a complicated fleet is only the first step in understanding why and how cabooses were used in the first place. Therein lies yet another purpose for this work. People interested in railroad operations, labor history, popular culture, folklore, and many other fields will find this data valuable. For all we know about railroading in general and the B&O in particular, we have surprisingly little insight into how the railroad actually operated and the lives and experiences of the men and women who made it their work. Functionally, cabooses changed remarkably little during the more than 125 years of their use. Even with modern stoves, electric lights, and safety appliances, a ride in the latest C-27A car could be as jolting, uncomfortable, and potentially hazardous as an 1870 trip in a caboose converted from a boxcar.

At museums and tourist railroads across the country, familiar cupola and bay window cars represent the B&O. In some places, like the Whitewater Valley Railroad in Indiana, you can still ride Class I-5s; at other places such as the Florida Gulf Coast Railroad Museum, a very much out-of-place I-12 gives visitors a taste of mountain railroading in northern Florida. The B&O Railroad Museum in Baltimore continues to add representative B&O cabooses to its permanent collection, while others are scattered throughout the United States in back yards and parking lots. Of course, thousands of B&O cabooses remain in service in miniature form in countless basements.

I am grateful to Bob Hubler for the thousands of hours of hard work and the dedication that he brought to this book. It represents the results of research in the history of technology but also a starting point for future investigations. Like the previous edition, this is a work in progress, growing as we carefully mine the past for additional clues. The B&O Railroad Historical Society remains unstinting in its efforts to gather and present all aspects of the railroad's rich history. This is the Society's first major book project, and it will be useful for many people doing many kinds of research. I hope that it is but the first of many detailed studies. The company, its railroaders, and the B&O's rich historical legacy deserve no less.

John P. Hankey
Chicago, Illinois
July, 1994

Above: A new Class I-17 caboose at the B&O's Mt. Clare shops in Baltimore on April 15, 1953. (B&O Railroad Museum Collection)

Front Cover: B&O Class I-5D caboose C-2101 in fresh paint at Baltimore, Maryland on January 21, 1967. Years after the C&O takeover and contrary to "official" lettering instructions, the painters at Mt. Clare created a timelessly traditional B&O caboose. (C. G. Parsons, Robert Hubler Collection)

Back Cover: B&O Class I-12 C-2413 stood in front of the twin water tanks at Glenwood yard in Pittsburgh, Pennsylvania in the fall of 1956. (Walter Teskey, Rawdon E. Rambo Collection)

Title Page: B&O Class I-12 C-2437 in its original paint scheme circa 1945. (B&O Railroad Historical Society Collection)

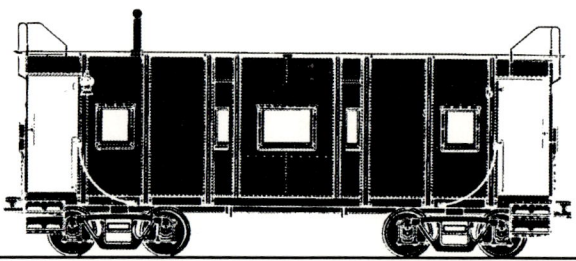

EDITOR'S PREFACE

The Baltimore and Ohio Railroad Historical Society is gratified to present "Cabooses of the Baltimore and Ohio Railroad" by Robert Hubler. It is first in a series of historical monographs covering B&O Railroad subjects. This long awaited work provides the most frequently requested information concerning B&O cabooses and much more.

Society member Robert Hubler spent many years researching the history and mechanical evolution of the B&O's extensive caboose fleet. His scholarship and diligent effort is demonstrated by the tremendous difference in scope between this current work and his first effort published by the Society in 1982. The "B&O Caboose Diagram Book" was just that: a 34-page overview of the B&O caboose fleet from Classes K-1 and I to Class I-18. It included one photograph and one diagram for each class and sub-class known to have existed, and concluded with a general 2-page roster. The limited information sources available during the Society's early years placed severe restraints on the detail and completeness of Bob's earlier work.

After 12 years of additional research in the Society's expanding archival collection, the corporate records of the B&O, and other primary sources, Bob Hubler has produced a substantial book of major significance. He surveyed thousands of photographs and selected over 200 of the best to illustrate this book. Bob photographed and developed many of the images himself during years of field research. Despite his digging out nuggets of information from mountains of paper, many questions remain unanswered as the result of missing company records for certain eras and classes. Until these records can be found, recreated from existing data, or made available to the Society, this study remains a preliminary work.

As it stands, this monograph provides a great deal of useful information. It covers all B&O caboose classes known to have existed, including the last cars purchased for the railroad in 1980 and several classes acquired from the C&O in the mid-1960s and early 1970s. Hubler's history and description of the caboose roster of the B&O begins with an introduction by his friend and fellow B&O historian John P. Hankey. This opening chapter provides a framework for placing the caboose, and B&O cabooses in particular, in a historic perspective. It addresses why and when the caboose became an identifiable type of railroad car; how and why the design improved; and why so many caboose have disappeared.

A word of caution is necessary about the B&O clearance diagrams which illustrate the caboose class descriptions. Users should be aware that these equipment drawings can be misleading. They were issued by the B&O Mechanical Department to disseminate dimensional data and basic mechanical information, and to assist railroad personnel in identifying specific equipment types. Often, diagrams do not represent the true appearance of specific cars, and in some cases may be nothing more than a sketch. Although the B&O employed a specific scale and the recorded measurements are usually accurate, the drawings were not intended to show precise details and were often inaccurate in areas not related to their purpose. For the modeler, the most practical solution to this problem is to use a combination of diagrams and photographs of the particular car to be modeled. What one source does not show, the other may. Also, each reference represents the equipment on a specific date only. A caboose was modified many times during its service life.

All drawings and diagrams in this publication are from the B&O Historical Society Archives unless otherwise noted. They have been restored by hand to publishable condition by Society archivist Walter C. Figiel. To fit the large drawings into the format of this book, it has been necessary to reduce them. In the case of the painting and lettering diagrams this reduction has been considerable - to the point that some written information is no longer readable. Anyone desiring large format copies of any of the drawings in this book may order them from the Society. Please write for a list and ordering information.

The B&O Historical Society Publications Committee hopes you will find this publication an interesting and useful reference. A second Society book, the first in a series on B&O passenger cars, is well underway and can be expected in 1995.

Gary W. Schlerf
Baltimore, Maryland
October, 1994

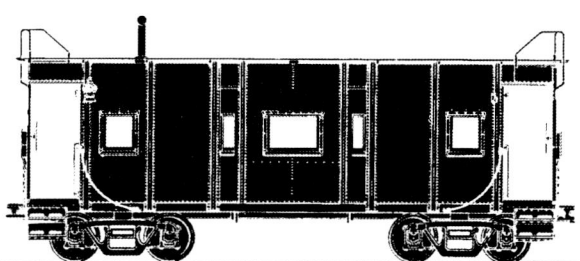

ACKNOWLEDGEMENTS

This book was made possible with the gracious and generous assistance of many people. At the risk of overlooking someone, the author would like to thank Stanley R. Ames, Ralph L. Barger, Lars O. Byrne, Bob Chapman, Charlie's Slides, Dan Finfrock, J. M. Gruber, John P. Hankey, Charles Houser, John R. King, Jr., Roger Kirkpatrick, Edwin C. Kirstatter, John C. LaRue, Jr., Charles T. Mahan, John Malone, Louis A. Marre, Dr. Rawdon E. Rambo, Gary W. Schlerf, John Schletzer, and Andy White for supplying their own photographs or photographs from their collections. Many photographs came from the author's own collection, which has been augmented over the years with images purchased from J. R. Quinn, C. G. Parsons, Dick Fullerton, and George McKay. Special thanks to Steve Davidson, C. W. Abbott, and Dave Oroszi who allowed the use of photographs from their collections, including their own works and those by John Woodbury, C.E. Helms, Jim Henry and Wilson Jones. Thanks also to Al Chione who graciously permitted the use of several of his slides. A large number of photographs have been obtained over the years from Paul Dunn and J. W. Brauner. Regrettably, neither of these gentlemen are still living to see the publication of their work.

Many individuals and organizations contributed to this project. Thanks to John Ott, Dennis Fulton, and Anne Calhoun of the B&O Railroad Museum for allowing the author access to the museum archives and permitting the use of diagrams and photographs from the museum's B&O Railroad photograph collection. From the Baltimore Chapter NRHS came several photographs by Carl Gerber. The B&O Railroad Historical Society supplied photographs by J. W. Barnard and Eileen Wolford Barnard, E.L. "Tommy" Thompson, George Nixon, and Carl Stillwell from collections owned by the Society. Photographs from the collections of Charles A. Brown, R. L. Long, L. W. Rice and George Votava provided by the Society also appear in the book. Most of the caboose diagrams are from the Society's collections. Also, Carstens Publications, Inc., Railfan & Railroad for the use of caboose art.

Special thanks to Wally Figiel who laboriously retouched the diagrams used in the book. Also making a signifigant contribution were Dennis T. Fulton and Robert F. Holzweiss, who provided critical and skillful technical editing. Lastly, the author owes a great debt of gratitude to Ralph and Lois Barger, John P. Hankey, and Gary Schlerf of the Society Publications Committee for the many hours of editing, advice, and assistance during the preparation of this work. Any errors in this work are solely the fault of the author and should not reflect on these individuals or the Society in any way.

Robert Hubler
June 1994

**This Book is
Dedicated
To
My wife, Liz.
For all her support and encouragement.**

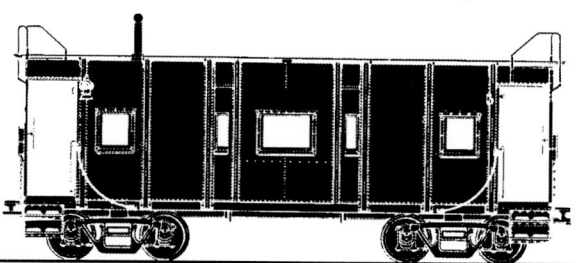

AN HISTORICAL PERSPECTIVE

By John P. Hankey

The Caboose in Context

For almost a century, a caboose was the last car of virtually every freight train operated by the Baltimore and Ohio Railroad. The caboose was distinctive, durable, visible, common, and integral to railroad operations. Its form and use made an indelible impression on the public and railroaders alike, although for quite different reasons. Summarizing the history of the B&O's caboose fleet and presenting a brief description of each class of car are the first, and most straightforward, objectives of this book. However, the history of the caboose on the B&O is not simply the story of the cars themselves, for there are additional ways to frame and understand the history surrounding them. Too often, we forget or disregard the fact that railroad men and women built and used these cars, and that every change made to them was the result of some human action or need.

Many people regard a caboose as a symbol or cultural icon. Like the red barn, red schoolhouse, or red fire truck, the red caboose evokes a range of responses in our popular culture. Because they powerfully evoke a past, great age of railroading, many cabooses are preserved in railroad towns along the length of the B&O, as parts of commercial developments, and in the back yards of people who may not be serious railroad enthusiasts. Others were adaptively reused as boutiques, motel rooms, snack bars, and other "quaint" interpretations. No matter what the circumstances of its preservation, a classic caboose is as much a symbol of "the past" as the steam locomotive, cowboy, or great sailing ship.

For anyone willing to look past its obvious symbolism, the caboose offers a window into the B&O's cultural, social, business, and work history, as well as the history of its equipment and technology. Both the need for the caboose and its basic form remained essentially the same for 125 years, while the railroad grew and changed. Although that holds true for box cars and other kinds of equipment, the caboose had special attributes and existed at the intersection between the company, its employees, and railroad work itself. If one is so inclined, the study of the caboose can reveal a great deal about the entire B&O Railroad, either at a point in time or through its long history. Ironically, historians do not yet know enough about the operation of cabooses, their costs, labor aspects, physical evolution, or even precisely how many there were to be able to write that history in the detail it warrants.

As a first step, this Introduction and its photographs will outline general themes and present tentative conclusions which place these cars in a historical context. It will describe at least some of the ways in which conscious choices made by working railroaders shaped the form and evolution of the caboose. Placing the crews back on their cars and considering the everyday issues they faced helps make sense of the physical design of the caboose, and the ways in which the B&O operated and modified the fleet. By noting and understanding the small details which make the caboose interesting as a vehicle, it becomes possible to expand that insight out to the B&O and railroading in general. Finally, the text and photographs pose questions for further study. This is a complex and rewarding topic, and a great deal of research remains to be done.

This photo epitomizes railroad transportation as the B&O practiced it throughout most of the twentieth century. from the early 1900s, when railroading attained its modern form, through the 1980s, when a series of technological and philosophical revolutions swept through the industry, one could expect every main line freight train to end with a caboose. When this eastbound merchandise train paused at Willard, Ohio, on February 27, 1965, the B&O was still building its own cabooses. It would continue purchasing them for another fifteen years. Nevertheless, between 1985 and 1990, the caboose virtually disappeared from the main line as a consequence of the almost complete reinvention of the industry. Like the private refrigerator cars and the cab unit diesels probably pulling this train, the traditional B&O vanished quickly. (Julian W. Barnard, Jr., The B&O Historical Society Collection)

The history of the caboose is made more interesting and complex by the fact that the cars present a number of paradoxes. Flat cars were more numerous on the B&O and made the company a great deal more money than cabooses, but the story of B&O flat cars does not engage our curiosity in the same way. The caboose was a utilitarian, functional piece of railroad equipment, and neither the B&O (nor any other railroad) intended the car to be anything but a workplace for the conductor and brakemen. Yet through time, the car became part of American folklore and an emblem of traditional railroading. The caboose itself was visible, widely dispersed, and public in the sense that it "represented" the B&O to the outside world, while the interior of the caboose was a very private space "owned" by the crew to which it was assigned.

As common and important as the cars were to everyday railroading, their physical forms, service lives, and conditions of use are poorly documented. To the Mechanical, Accounting, and Operating Departments, a caboose existed in the abstract as an asset or unit. The reality of an individual car sometimes was very different from what the office clerk at Mt. Clare or the Central Building carried on paper. A caboose could be a comfortable haven, or it could be a terrifying, hazardous place to be. Long after other composite wood and steel cars had disappeared from the railroad, wood-bodied I-5 cars could still be found in service with GP40-2s and the early manifestations of computerized twenty-first century railroading. Paradoxes like these suggest a few of the many ways the B&O Railroad's fleet may be interpreted.

As a case study in car construction, operation, and management, a caboose fleet may provide object lessons in how one railroad built and used specific types of cars in a particular service. The B&O's experiences in building, maintaining, and operating the cars represent a fascinating and under-appreciated aspect of railroad history. On the B&O, as on other railroads, cabooses assumed distinctive shapes and characteristics in response to such disparate factors as operating requirements, state politics, federal law, and the tastes and whims of the Mechanical Department.

The technological history of the caboose shares many themes and processes found in the history of locomotives, signal systems, or any other aspect of railroad technology. However, because the demands on the cars were relatively modest and unchanging, cabooses did not show dramatic increases in size or essential changes in form, as did locomotives over the same time period. So long as a car was capable of withstanding in-train forces while providing a minimal level of crew safety and comfort, it fulfilled its mission. That is one reason why cabooses built at the same time as 40-ton cars and World War I-era steam locomotives were in use five decades later with 100-ton cars and 3000 horsepower diesel-electric locomotives. The technological history of the caboose is thus more subtle, and more idiosyncratic, than almost any other piece of rolling stock.

Like most railroads, the B&O regarded cabooses as a necessary evil. They were expensive to build, buy, and maintain. Unlike locomotives, which seemed to earn their keep, cabooses just went along for the ride as dead weight. In railroad operating terminology, cabooses were "non-revenue" equipment, which meant that while they were necessary for the conduct of transportation, no direct income could be attributed to them. Their operation required caboose tracks, laborers and carmen to service them, extra switching moves to handle them, and the need to coordinate supply and demand. Without a suitable caboose, a yardmaster could not dispatch a train, sometimes forcing desperate officials into using a spare passenger car as a caboose.

Like the railroad station, roundhouse, or locomotive cab, the caboose was a distinctive work environment with specific tasks, physical conditions, and occupational folkways. Men and women rode, worked, and rested in cabooses. Aside from William Knapke's *The Railroad Caboose*, few railroad histories describe the actual conditions experienced by train crews.

When a B&O photographer was making a systematic record of the bridges on the Pittsburg & Connellsville Railroad in the late 1880s, he produced this image of a P&C work train at 8th Street in Braddock, Pennsylvania. The caboose is lettered P&C, but appears to be similar to B&O Class K-1. This car is noteworthy for its small steps, which would have made it a challenge to mount at night or while it was in motion. In the middle is B&O 24-foot flat car 18431, and on the right is P&C service car 19201, one of 54 such cars carried on the 1888 roster. Note that the service car has steps, windows, a stove, end doors, and many other attributes of the earliest converted cabooses. On the track behind are several B&O iron pot hopper cars. The scene is utterly typical of B&O operations in the 1880s, and suggests how cabooses had become part of the landscape. This caboose - and its crew - would not have seemed out of place on many parts of the B&O six decades later. (The B&O Railroad Museum Collection)

On the whole, railroad work is poorly represented in the literature, but good narrative or interpretive accounts of life aboard B&O cabooses are almost nonexistent.

Train crews regarded the cars with a mixture of affection and contempt, reflecting the contrast between the pleasant aspects of caboose life and the fact that they might spend 16 hours a day aboard or experience physical discomfort during a bad run. The cars provided a degree of shelter, comfort, and safety in what could be a harsh operating environment. Before the pooling (the generally shared use of a group of equivalent cars) and system-wide assignment of cabooses, they often provided cheap lodging at away-from-home terminals together with a measure of personalized, home-like space in the midst of an otherwise vast and impersonal industrial system. However, cabooses also could be dirty, uncomfortable, and hazardous. A careless engineer's poor train handling technique or a train of mixed heavy and light cars in undulating territory could cause such violent slack action that riding in the caboose was dangerous. Men were injured or killed while aboard cabooses in the ordinary course of their jobs.

The men who made the caboose their work place—conductors, brakemen, flagmen—unionized early. By 1900, the Brotherhood of Railroad Trainmen (BRT) and the Order of Railroad Conductors (ORC) had become two of the strongest and most effective railroad labor organizations. Consequently, the caboose figured prominently in specific railroad labor issues. Physical changes in caboose forms and furnishings were often the result of dispute and negotiation between organized railroad labor and the B&O's management. Indeed, it was only after federal review, lengthy negotiations, and the conclusion of a new national contract between the United Transportation Union (successor to the BRT and the ORC) that railroads, including CSX Transportation, were legally able to substitute "End-of-Train" (EOT) devices for fully manned cabooses.

A few caboose cars remain in service on the former B&O portions of CSX Transportation. Certain operating circumstances, such as work trains or switching runs which involve long backing movements, require the continued use of the caboose as a platform from which to direct train movements. But for the most part, technological and structural changes in the conduct of railroad operations rendered the caboose as obsolete as the steam locomotive and the 40-foot boxcar. Ironically, perhaps symbolically, the conventional main line caboose disappeared from railroading at about the same time as the B&O ceased its corporate existence. The same processes of change and innovation that brought both the B&O Railroad and the caboose into being eventually rendered them expendable. We are left with history, archeology, industrial anthropology, and our personal store of memories.

The Origins of the Caboose on the B&O Railroad

Unlike the First Stone, Peter Cooper's locomotive, or the Carrollton Viaduct, the B&O did not celebrate the first caboose or even note the creation of its first sizeable fleet of the cars. The origins and early evolution of the caboose on the B&O Railroad must be inferred from scraps of evidence and an understanding of the changing nature of railroad freight transportation in the mid-nineteenth century. General questions help define, in broad terms, why the company decided that it needed a new type of car for efficient operations. What were the functional requirements for the first cabooses? What roles did train crews have in the initial designs and subsequent changes to early cabooses? What were the operating conditions at the time of introduction, and how quickly did the use of cabooses diffuse across the system? Was their adoption an indicator of some shift in philosophy or operating practice?

Long before the adoption of the caboose, custom and rules required the conductor to inspect his train, direct the actions of the crew, remain in contact with the locomotive, carry flagging and safety equipment, and "protect" his train against following and opposing movements. B&O rule books and operating timetables from the 1840s and 1850s explicitly directed the conductor to ride atop the last car in the train, prepared to dismount when the train stopped. He was admonished to carry a red flag or lantern in one hand and a bell cord in the other. The cord stretched over the tops of the cars to a gong in the locomotive cab, affording the conductor a primitive means of communication with the head end. Whenever the train stopped, the conductor (or someone he designated) immediately had to walk back (or sometimes, forward) along the track with flagging equipment to warn other trains of the presence of the stopped train. The conductor and crew were also responsible for detecting hot journals, equipment defects, and what we would recognize today as the full range of potential hazards to a train in motion.

Clearly, the caboose existed functionally and conceptually before it took on distinctive physical characteristics. Indeed, it could be regarded as a technologically determinant form: sooner or later, the caboose would have emerged as an operating necessity with substantially equivalent characteristics. Just as there was one basic arrangement of components to which most steam locomotives conformed, the function of the caboose dictated its form, which changed relatively little from the time of its development in the 1850s. The B&O was not the first railroad to use cabooses, but it probably adopted them early and made their use widespread across the system.

The Civil War emerges as the historical pivot, accelerating and intensifying change throughout the railroad industry. Partly due to its wartime experiences and partly due to the new competitive environment of the immediate post-war period, the B&O of 1865 was a very different railroad from what it was only a decade before. Expanding traffic, accelerating change, and a legacy of innovation facilitated the adoption of the caboose as a new car type. There is no evidence that the B&O used cabooses before the war, and abundant evidence that the company did shortly thereafter.

At some point, and for many reasons, the company decided that it was to its benefit to use the cars at least on main line runs. The railroad increasingly made conductors responsible for paperwork and other duties relating to the company's business enroute. The size of trains and crews increased, and the company willingly or unwillingly assumed greater responsibility for workers' welfare. A caboose not only housed a crew during the run, but often constituted its lodging at away-from-home terminals. During periods of labor shortage, experienced railroaders tended to gravitate to higher-paying railroads in the West. The B&O may have felt obliged to provide cabooses as

In a scene which could have been lifted from the Old Main Line or anywhere on the B&O in the Alleghenies, brakemen use human muscle to control the speed of a moving train weighing several thousand tons. Their place of work was the top of a car in motion, in all weather, sometimes for twenty hours at a stretch. The period between the Civil War and World War I saw the growth and intensification of railroading, rise of organized labor, and greatly increased concern for workers' safety. For men who had spent years literally out on the trains, the introduction of the caboose meant a material improvement in their comfort, safety, and potential longevity. (*The American Railway*, 1890)

an amenity to help retain experienced train crews as well as for reasons of operating necessity.

One of the most important reasons for the introduction of the caboose was to provide some measure of shelter and safety to the crew, even if brakemen could only occasionally return to the caboose for warmth and rest. To understand why such a seemingly common-sense measure took so long to adopt, one must consider the different physical conditions, expectations, and attitudes which prevailed in the mid-nineteenth century, for they stand in stark contrast to those of a hundred years later. For many people, outdoor work in all seasons was unavoidable. The weather generally was colder and winters more severe in the nineteenth and early twentieth centuries than today. Throughout the period, working conditions for both train and engine crews were severe, especially in inclement weather or during long periods on duty. Many locomotives had no cabs well into the 1850s. Yet, railroading was one of the few occupations offering year-around employment, and most railroaders were no doubt glad to have such good jobs at all.

A train crew might spend from ten to thirty hours at a stretch atop house cars or pot hoppers, exposed to wind, rain, snow, and cold. The need to quickly spring to duty tightening hand brakes on several cars when the engineer whistled for brakes exacerbated their lack of shelter and intense discomfort. The quality and effectiveness of clothing available to nineteenth-century railroad workers varied widely. Even the food available to workingmen was inferior to that of later periods. Most men had little access to hot drinks or carbohydrate-rich, balanced meals in their struggle against frostbite and hypothermia. Well into the twentieth century, memoirs and descriptions of railroad work mention the misery caused by adverse weather as a defining aspect of train service. In that kind of working environment, train crews would have done anything in their power to secure shelter of any type, such as an empty house car. Adding a few amenities (a stove, chairs, bunks) to an old house car dramatically improved its suitability as a refuge from the weather, and probably increased its effectiveness as a "command post" for the train. Without a doubt, train crews on the B&O of the 1850s and 1860s heard that northern railroads were adopting the caboose. It seems likely that they would have wanted them, too.

The B&O, like many companies of the period, had a strong paternalistic cast to its management. A significant factor in the adoption of cabooses may have been the conclusion, drawn by operating officials sympathetic to the plight of train crews, that some form of protection was necessary and humane. The nature of most freight movements meant that trains stood for varying periods of time on sidings waiting for superior trains to pass, so that even brakemen on the most distant parts of the train would have had an opportunity to seek shelter on the locomotive or caboose for part of the run. As trains grew longer and moved faster, and as night time operations increased, giving the men a place to rest and warm up surely equated to increased efficiency and fewer casualties.

In the same way as railroad-determined functions suggested the need for a caboose at the end of freight trains, crew-determined conditions would have made a caboose highly desirable as a convenient railroad bunkhouse. Railroaders were responsible for their own lodging and board at their away-from-home terminal. Before labor agreements limited the amount of time a man could be held at a remote terminal, train crews often faced difficulty and expense finding food and lodging at the far ends of their runs. By "laying over" in their caboose, even if it meant six or eight men sharing crude bunks in a converted boxcar, train crews could save the cost of a hotel room or boarding house bed. The crew could cook individual or communal meals on the caboose stove, and local traditions suggest that many crews carried firearms and fishing tackle aboard their cabooses so that they could hunt and fish as the opportunity presented itself. Brakemen were not highly paid throughout the late nineteenth century, so that the availability of a caboose as "away-from-home" lodging proved a substantial benefit. The company benefitted by keeping the men on railroad property and handy for call, while also keeping at least some of them away from saloons and other temptations.

Emerging and evolving notions of the rights of labor, collective action by railroad employees, and the B&O manage-

The photographer intended to record the B&O's Queen City Station in Cumberland, Maryland just after completion of the building in 1872. Unintentionally, he took what may be the earliest photograph yet found showing a B&O caboose in service. The car in the lower right corner has a smoke jack, indicating the presence of a stove. At least one window has been cut into the side of the car, and the end facing the camera shows a doorway. To the left of the door is a flag, which by rule and custom marked the end of a train. The car itself is built in the style of the 1850s and early 1860s, with a vertical brake wheel on the car's end. Because no markings are visible to make a positive identification, it could be an early express car. However, the stove, door, window, flag, and apparent position on the rear of a train (in this case, eastbound) fulfill the physical and functional criteria for a caboose. It differs from the express or baggage car coupled to the coach five tracks over. That car also resembles a boxcar with a smoke jack, but lacks a roof walk and has passenger car trucks. (The B&O Railroad Museum Collection)

ment's legal and ethical responsibilities also influenced the railroad's decisions regarding its caboose fleet. The modern era of collective bargaining and labor contracts did not begin on the B&O until the 1880s, but conductors had struck the company as early as 1857. Engineers on the B&O attempted to form a union in the 1850s. The rise of viable railroad brotherhoods and the increasing bureaucratization of railroad administration after the Civil War facilitated the practice of dealing with men as classes of employees rather then as individuals, and while no evidence has yet come to light, it is likely that after the war B&O train crews found themselves in a position to advocate the use of cabooses. Similarly, management proved receptive to the idea.

The B&O's decision to assign a caboose to each of its freight train crews took place over time as part of the ongoing, complex process of organizational and technological evolution which characterized nineteenth century railroading. In particular, the adoption of cabooses resulted from a combination of operating requirements, the crew's need for shelter and safety, and changing concepts of labor relations and the company's responsibilities towards its employees.

Almost without a doubt, the first cabooses were old boxcars appropriated by enterprising crews or conductors and modified to suit their immediate needs. Anecdotal evidence recounts the use of empty boxcars by freight train crews. It seems reasonable to conclude that crews in the 1860s fitted cars with seats and a stove and coupled them to regular trains with the acquiescence of local railroad operating management. These kinds of innovations were exceedingly common. The practice of assigning engine crews to a particular locomotive and requiring them to perform routine maintenance formed an obvious precedent. Work gangs living in camp cars might have been cited as another precedent by crews "claiming" a car to use as a caboose. Their use apparently spread across the system quickly, and by 1872 they became a distinct class of rolling stock formally listed in the Annual Report. Within a decade of its introduction to the B&O, the caboose attained a form and pattern of use which persisted for a century.

The Form of the Caboose

Like most railroad structures and equipment, the essential form of the caboose developed in the middle-to-late nineteenth century according to specific needs and uses. From the very first B&O caboose through the present cars in service on CSXT, the size, arrangement, equipment, use, and even appearance of the cars evolved through a complex process of conscious design, trial and error, and negotiation. Each class of caboose, sometimes virtually each car, resulted from a series of individual and collective decisions influenced by car building practice, state and federal law, railroad policy, safety concerns, labor aspects, and cost. Available records do not explain why the caboose in general or those of the B&O in particular assumed the shape and attributes which they did. We must resort to educated speculation and advance preliminary conclusions.

As the primary purpose of the caboose was to provide shelter for the crew and a platform for inspecting the train, the car's most essential features included windows, steps, ladders, and grab irons. Interior furnishings, special fittings such as flag holders and lantern brackets, and access to the hand brake while the car was in motion were important, but probably of secondary importance on the early cars. Certain functional aspects of train service, such as the need to mount and dismount the car or the ability to see clearly forward and backward, strongly affected the shape and configuration of the caboose. Physical attributes such as stoves, windows, bunks, and car construction followed whatever the B&O regarded as common practice. Within this fairly narrow range of options, the B&O created hundreds of caboose cars which reveal at least some of the thinking which went into them.

The first purpose-built B&O cabooses, as opposed to cars converted from other types, were eight-wheel vehicles following the standard practice for freight equipment. At some point, perhaps with the realization that the weight of an eight-wheel caboose had a material effect on a train's tonnage and efficiency, the railroad adopted the smaller and lighter 4-wheel caboose as standard. In the operating environment of the period, the short wheelbase and light weight of the Class K-1 cars probably did not make them unsafe or necessarily uncomfortable. If equipped with continuous drawbars (rods of wrought iron connecting the coupler pockets), the cars were as strong as most freight cars then in service. Freight train speeds averaged less than twenty miles per hour, and rarely exceeded thirty until late in the century. Tonnage trains (including the coal trains which made up so much of the railroad's traffic) moved even more slowly, so that even on the B&O's often rough track, a four-wheel caboose was satisfactory for main line use.

Although they were tiny by comparison to later cars, the four-wheel cars may have served as lodging for four or five men. A large number of railroaders in the nineteenth and early twentieth centuries lived in boarding houses, bunk houses, or single rooms. Men with families might have a house or even a farm. Society in general had different, less demanding conceptions of personal space, privacy, and physical comfort. For some railroaders, the crowded confines of a fully-occupied caboose were preferable to spending money for a second lodging at the away-from-home terminal or sleeping in the roundhouse or sand house. Very likely the railroad's position was to provide a caboose costing the absolute minimum to build, furnish, and maintain, consistent with service requirements. As the trainmen's labor organizations were not yet in a position to negotiate issues such as caboose size, the cars remained small and inexpensive for as long as the B&O could manage.

The cupola—the distinguishing feature of most cabooses—was a determinant form and quickly appeared on new cabooses, and possibly some of the converted cars. Especially after the gradual introduction of the air brake in the 1870s, both the railroad and the conductor found it advantageous to create an all-weather, unobstructed, bi-directional perch or platform from which to monitor the condition of the train. As trains became longer and operated at higher speeds, the importance of a clear view of the train would likewise have increased. That may have had some bearing on the creation of the high cupolas found on some Class K-1 and B&O Southwestern cars. Certainly the size, height, and position of the cupola varied with the opinions and requirements of individual railroads. For the most part, the B&O favored centered cupolas of average height, giving the crew the same viewpoint no matter which way the car was turned. As taller freight cars restricted the view forward, hind end crews were forced to rely on side views of the train as they looked for overheated journals, sticking brakes, and other defects.

By the late 1920s, as even ordinary boxcars began to tower over the tallest cupola, several railroads, including the

At least five Class K-1 cars under construction are visible in this mid-1890s photograph of the Freight Car Roundhouse at Mt. Clare. Raw materials lie on the floor in the foreground, and the standard tools of any wood car shop litter the floor. Compared with later classes, the K-1 cars were simple and inexpensive to build using freight car techniques. The B&O cut and milled its own lumber at Mt. Clare, drawing on its army of carpenters and carmen to finish cars on a gang basis. Later cabooses were built at other shops as Mt. Clare increasingly specialized in passenger car and locomotive work. The form a B&O caboose might take depended greatly on current car building techniques, materials, their cost, and the traditional array of company customs and idiosyncracies. (The B&O Railroad Museum Collection)

Left: The interior of just-completed I-5 C-1900 contrasts somewhat with the exterior as shown on page 53. The car's interior of rough-cut lumber is functional, utilitarian, and rather crude in appearance, whereas the outside "public" face seems to have a higher level of finish. The car has a stove, kerosene lamps, horsehair cushions covered in plush coach seat fabric, and a simple water tank and sink. Later production I-5 cars had an ice chest and lockers, but none were built with toilet facilities. Crews added small features as time, money, and company officials allowed. Although somewhat larger, this interior would not have differed markedly from the earliest purpose-built cabooses. The lack of hand holds, cushioned draft gear, and the presence of so many sharp corners and hard surfaces made moving about inside during rough slack action difficult and potentially hazardous. Employees accepted it as part of the job. (The B&O Railroad Museum Collection)

Right: A bay window car, such as the Class I-12 wagon top caboose shown here, was a good deal more spacious than a cupola car of the same size. Like the I-5, the interior of painted wood with a sheet metal ceiling was functional, but spartan. The photo shows Pullman-style bench seats at the bay windows. The stove, water tank, and sink are to the left. Visible to the rear are two more bunks and the fusee holder on the door. The B&O was somewhat more safety conscious when it built the I-12s in the early 1940s than it had been twenty years earlier. Appliances such as the overhead handrail and a Duryea cushion underframe gave trainmen a better chance of surviving slack action. (The B&O Railroad Museum Collection)

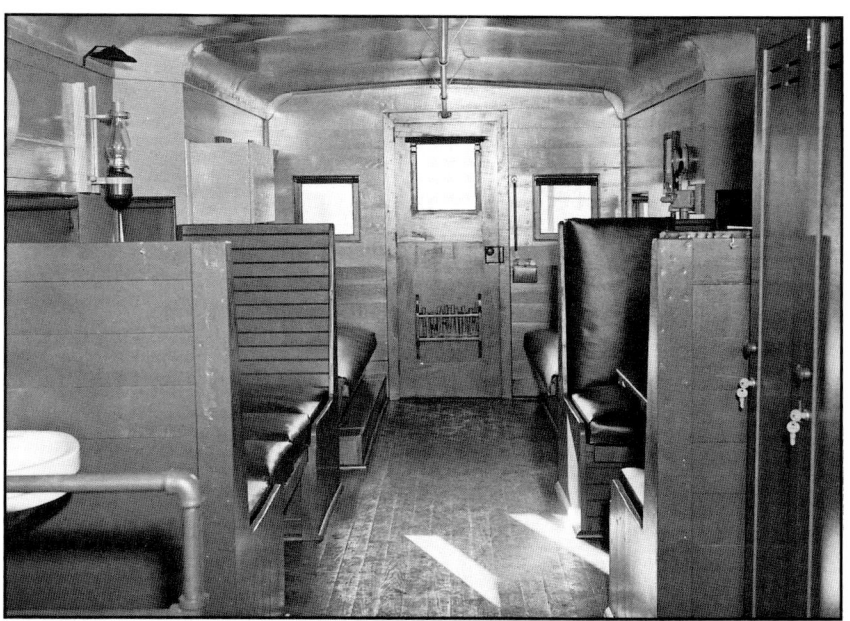

Left: The last of the B&O cabooses were utilitarian and functional, but they were well-equipped compared with the cars of a century before, and the level of comfort and finish was much higher. Each car had a powerful railroad radio, electric lights and built-in markers, a retention or Microphor toilet, lockers, an ice box, a mirror, and comfortable coach-style seats with high backs to protect against whiplash. The interior was of sheet steel, with rounded corners and a guard rail around the stove. When properly maintained, the modern Caban oil-fired caboose stove did not produce the sickening fumes common to earlier oil stoves. Better track and modern roller bearing caboose trucks combined with the full-cushion underframe to produce a ride smoother and safer than that of older cars. At the end, the B&O caboose was a fully-evolved vehicle expressly designed to preserve its human cargo in ways that earlier cars did not. (The B&O Railroad Museum Collection)

B&O and the Milwaukee Road, experimented with the bay window caboose. Conceptually, it was equivalent to the very first caboose cars converted from house cars. In those cars, the conductor might have leaned out the door for a clear view of one side of the train or the other. By returning to that older principle of inspecting the train from the side, the B&O gave up relatively little and gained a great deal of reliable visibility. On a railroad so generally curving as the B&O, there were many opportunities for the hind-end crew to observe most of the train as it passed from tangents to curves and through long curves with unobstructed views. Indeed, track crews routinely cut vegetation in certain locations precisely to ensure trainmen a clear view of their trains. The bay window innovation of John J. Tatum was less of a B&O idiosyncracy than the practical solution to a vexing operational problem.

The period between the early 1890s and the 1930s remains one of the most pivotal, interesting, and controversial eras in railroad history. The pace of change was rapid and unrelenting, and included the almost complete substitution of steel for wrought iron and wood; adoption of the air brake, automatic coupler, and modern steam locomotive; vastly higher train speeds and longer trains; the maturity of the labor organizations representing the operating crafts; and the almost complete regulation of all aspects of interstate commerce by federal, state, and local governments. There were many additional and substantive changes on the B&O, resulting in the modernization of the property and a revolution in operating and business practices. Each of these changes had profound and permanent consequences for the form and operation of the caboose, although many of those effects are subtle.

The Interstate Commerce Act of 1887 began the era of federal regulation of the railroads. Subsequent legislation further strengthened the government's powers to regulate interstate commerce, culminating in temporary federal control of the railroads at the end of World War I. Partly to bring some order to what had become an industry in chaos, and partly to satisfy an American public outraged over the numbers of casualties among railroad employees and alleged unethical operating practices, the government, through the Interstate Commerce Commission (ICC), enacted a series of statute and administrative laws that specified what equipment cars were to carry and how it was to be maintained. The Safety Appliance Act of March 2, 1893 was the first specific railroad safety regulation, requiring all cars and locomotives in interstate commerce to be equipped with automatic couplers and air brakes, with steps, grab irons, and ladders in specified locations. Most railroads, including the B&O, contested the government's right to legislate compliance, and resisted application of the equipment, claiming that it constituted an unacceptable financial burden. The ICC, together with Congress, granted several time extensions for completion of the work, and strengthened and supplemented the legislation with additional acts, amendments, rulings, court decisions, and administrative law proceedings.

These standards directly affected the timing and manner of the application of automatic couplers and air brakes to B&O cabooses. The laws also fixed the location, number, size, and function of hand brakes, grab irons, cut levers, and other appliances, and established maintenance requirements and penalties for non-compliance. Air brakes, for instance, had to be cleaned and tested at regular intervals, resulting in the air date stencils which so prominently decorated B&O cabooses. Many physical attributes of the B&O caboose (such as the grab irons at the corners of the cupola or the removal of roof running boards) resulted from the evolving federal standards and the changing operational environment created by compliance. John J. Tatum was free to produce a novel wagon top caboose carbody design only if it met minimum strength requirements and incorporated all of the mandated safety appliances for caboose cars with platforms. The last C-27A cars likewise conformed to an updated set of Federal Railroad Administration standards, which had a significant impact on the form and details of the cars.

Individual states also passed legislation having direct effects on the form or use of B&O cabooses. Ohio was one of

As an eastbound terminal transfer job clears Jackson's Bridge in Baltimore's Mt. Clare A Yard, a man swings aboard C-2602. It was a simple and essential task performed thousands of times daily across the B&O, but the consequences of a misstep could be injury or death. Railroads, labor organizations, the Interstate Commerce Commission, industry associations, and Congress devoted considerable time and energy to standardizing the size, location, and configuration of car safety appliances such as caboose grab irons. Caboose safety appliances evolved through a long process of trial and error. By 1970, roofwalks, cupola corner grab irons, and ladders were obsolete, but steps and their associated hand holds remained the primary point of contact between a caboose moving at 10 mph and a man trying to get aboard. (John P. Hankey)

the most densely populated states in the nation in the early twentieth century, and was criss-crossed by dozens of major and minor railroads. In 1913, with the urging of railroad labor organizations, the public, and state agencies concerned with work place safety, the Ohio legislature passed a bill mandating the use of eight-wheel caboose cars with 24-foot bodies (also known as 30-foot cars if measured over pulling faces) on trains operating in or through the state. Other provisions of the bill specified safety equipment and design standards. The object was two-fold: to force railroads (including the B&O) to adopt larger, presumably safer caboose cars while asserting the state's authority concerning the health and welfare of employees generally.

This one state law compelled many railroads to design a new standard caboose. The B&O's Class I-1 cars, introduced in 1913, fulfilled the law's requirements and became the standard system caboose. Basic attributes of the Ohio caboose were incorporated into designs created by the United States Railroad Administration during World War I. Class I-5 cars built by the B&O were updated Ohio caboose designs. In fact, the basic premise of the 1913 legislation carried through in modified form to the construction of the final B&O Class I-17 cabooses in 1965. Both the federal regulations and the 1913 Ohio caboose law illustrate how the form of a particular type of car may be determined, or at least affected, by government actions.

The B&O made additional modifications to cabooses for reasons of safety, efficiency, cost, or changing attitudes toward the crews who used them. As records become available and additional work is done interpreting the management and corporate culture of the B&O, it should become increasingly clear that a relatively few individuals made the majority of decisions as to how the B&O's cabooses were equipped, what they were made of, and how they were decorated. John J. Tatum may be the single most influential freight car man ever to work for the B&O. He had an immense impact on the form of every B&O caboose from 1900 until the 1950s. As yet, his role in designing cabooses, and the inner working of the B&O's Mechanical Department in general, remain poorly documented. While beyond the scope of this essay or book, detailed study of caboose designers, technology, and hardware will answer many questions as to why the B&O's cars appeared and changed as they did.

Finally, and perhaps most basically, railroad technology and the industry's own adopted standards had profound effects on the shape, construction, color, and life-cycle of the caboose. That held true for the B&O as well as every other railroad in the country. First the Master Car Builder's Association, and later the American Railway Association and its successor, the Association of American Railroads (AAR), promulgated standards for car sizes, construction, equipment, and maintenance. Whether a railroad built its cars of wood, steel, or a combination of materials, by the late nineteenth century there existed a substantial body of accepted practice and common (if not standard) designs. With the possible exception of the wagon top cars, the B&O built cabooses which were quite ordinary in form and materials, and they incorporated improvements in basic technology as they became available.

The AAR, for instance, determined after tests in the late 1920s that the AB air brake system was superior to the K systems then in service. After the AB brake became standard for new freight car construction in the early 1930s, subsequent B&O cabooses were so equipped, and most older cars eventually received the new brake systems. The same was true for trucks. After the adoption of the "AAR Double Truss Spring-Plankless Cast Steel Freight Car Truck" as standard in the 1920s (what most railroaders referred to as a "Bettendorf" truck, although that was a proprietary trade name like "Kleenex" or "Xerox"), the B&O first specified the new trucks for use under new revenue equipment, and gradually replaced the older, technically obsolete diamond arch bar trucks under cabooses and work equipment as money or trucks became available.

With few exceptions, the caboose cars built by the B&O were products of their time and place, reflecting the philosophy of the railroad at the time of their construction. Many variables, such as technology, precedent, law, specific operating requirements, and the organizational culture of the railroad combined to give the cars their distinctive appearance and almost endless variation. The form that each B&O caboose took, especially after decades of service, was thus a record of intent, use, and change in the same fashion as a work of architecture.

Life Aboard the B&O Caboose

In the course of their railroad careers, thousands of B&O Railroad men, and in later years a few women, spent a majority of their on-duty time on or working out of cabooses. During busy times, it was not unusual for a conductor or flagman to live on a caboose more than they did at home. Yet the *experience* of work on the railroad, as opposed to the organization of work or the technology workers made use of, is one of the least documented aspects of railroad history. Even the B&O, with a substantial historical literature and a sophisticated cadre of researchers and enthusiasts, lacks any kind of synthetic or in-depth treatment of the texture of the working lives of its employees. Cabooses offer one way to begin recovering the rich history of railroad experience.

The conductor had the authority to delegate tasks to anyone in the crew consistent with whatever labor contracts were in effect. In practice, the conductor directed only the work of the brakemen and flagman, and made consensus decisions with the engineer as to the overall conduct of the run. On the caboose, the conductor might assign one of the other men to occupy the cupola or bay window to monitor the condition of the train. In some cases, two men might continuously watch the train, one on either side. In other cases, one man might watch while another fixed dinner, assisted the conductor, rested, or performed some miscellaneous task. The conductor himself might perform any of these duties, and might have waybills to sort, wheel reports to make out, or a variety of paperwork to complete as part of the run.

In terms of life aboard B&O cabooses, 125 years of experience fundamentally reduce to two periods and two states, with the additional qualification of occupancy. The two periods represent the time of assigned cabooses, when men had some direct control over the use and condition of their cars, and the era of pooling, when men simply occupied an assigned car for the duration of the run. The two fundamental states which characterize cabooses are in motion, and at rest. For the hind end crews, work took place either aboard the caboose (which could denote relative comfort) or outside (which could mean extreme cold, rain, or physical discomfort). Merely being aware of the ramifications of these conditions helps broaden our interpretation of the physical reality of working aboard a B&O caboose.

From very early in the caboose era until the mid-1960s, most cabooses were assigned to specific crews, particular runs, or otherwise routinely used in the same fashion by the same people. Of course, even in the days of individual caboose assignments, certain runs were given cabooses on an ad hoc basis. Regularly assigned cabooses were also switched, substituted, and taken out of service for various reasons. After the C&O/B&O railroads began implementation of a pooling program in 1966, terminals or the dispatcher at the caboose desk in Baltimore assigned whatever suitable car was available to whichever crew required the use of one. In the pool era some cabooses operated in captive or restricted service. Depending on the pool arrangements, individual cars might still be exclusively assigned to certain crews. Nevertheless, pooling cabooses effectively ended the practice of some crews decorating, improving, or boarding in "their" cabooses.

The two periods thus comprise the interval before pooling, when most train crews could expect to use the same caboose day after day, and the period after system wide pooling, when a crew generally had little idea which caboose it would have from one trip to the next. One essential distinction between the two periods may be described by expectations and a form of "ownership." If a crew had an assigned caboose, the men had the reasonable expectation that they would use the same car each trip. They never forgot that the car was the property of the B&O Railroad. They knew that operating management, the car department, and a variety of entities within the company could reassign cabooses, claim "their" car, or otherwise exercise some sort of control. But in reality, crews routinely using a particular car could become quite territorial and defensive about the caboose. The caboose often became a form of "defended territory" in classic sociological terms, in the same way that people create social boundaries in their neighborhood, home, or place of work.

Well into the post-World War II era, crews continued to use an assigned caboose as their places of lodging away from their home terminals. They were also responsible for cleaning and maintaining their cabooses, and for arranging with the mechanical department for necessary repairs. Some crews "improved" or customized their cars, adding such amenities as they wished and engaging in a form of informal, ongoing negotiation with the railroad as to the cost and extent of "unofficial" modifications. William Knapke cited an example of a conductor's alterations to what seems to be a World War II era B&O class I-13 or I-16 caboose.

Like candid pictures of period homes, images of real life aboard B&O cars are difficult to find. However, even one photograph can provide a wealth of information. This photo shows George Pratt and the interior of his assigned caboose in West Virginia. This car obviously has fancy cushions, art decorating the walls, and what appears to be a careful paint job, illustrating the kinds of "improvements" a conductor and crew might make (or induce shopmen to make) to their assigned car. Steve Davidson related that Pratt "was an old head conductor on the `Parkersburg Branch'. He is standing in the doorway, his face obscured by outside light—and his flagman obscures one of the `turn of the century pin-up girls'. . . (Pratt's caboose) was later destroyed in a rear end collision, George barely making it off the front platform and up the bank. Watching it burn, he said, `Well, I guess 41 years on the Branch is long enough!' and retired." (S.P. Davidson)

"Rebuilt from the stripped-down framework of an old 36-foot Baltimore & Ohio car, it had bay windows and a custom-built icebox, the latter by courtesy of a friendly car foreman. My regular brakeman and I further equipped it into what was truly—for the era we were railroading in—a rolling home on wheels.

"Kerosene lights were not good enough for us then. We managed to wire the car for electricity with a long extension cord that enabled us to plug into the nearest 110-volt circuit at each caboose track. . . . this gave us an electric fan for cooling purposes and electric hot-plates for cooking, and radios, and other little luxury items. We also managed to have on board a small gasoline stove (even though it was not strictly according to regulations) so that between terminals we could prepare coffee and even full meals. . .[1]

Because crews or individuals felt that they had a right to control or use their cabooses as they saw fit, and because the cars did, after all, belong to the B&O for use in routine service, there was an ongoing process of negotiation between the company, the train crew to whom cabooses were assigned, and anyone else who wanted or needed to be on that particular caboose. Obviously, men who worked hard to keep their car clean and perhaps even decorated would resist seeing that effort undone by careless co-workers. Often a crew would keep clothes, food, and personal belongings on their caboose, and would regard it as an extension of their home or assigned lockers at terminals.

The work itself determined who had rights on the caboose. For example, after the nearly universal use of air brakes, a typical mainline hind end crew would have comprised the conductor, perhaps a hind end brakeman, and a flagman. The head end brakeman was located on the locomotive, but, as part of the train crew, he had valid reasons to be on or about the caboose. Each member of a regular crew using a caboose had a repertory of occupational tasks, routines, and duties which required them to use tools, equipment, facilities, and space aboard the car.

Generally, only the men who actually worked aboard the caboose had a claim on a bunk, part of the stove top for cooking, a locker, or the privilege of living aboard. In many cases, especially during emergencies, inclement weather, or other extreme conditions, the engine crew or other railroaders were welcomed aboard the caboose and accommodated in a variety of ways. A particularly close knit crew might even have shared meals, sleeping space, and other social aspects of the caboose between the train crew and the enginemen. However, under ordinary circumstances, only the train crew called the caboose "home." Engine crews, carmen, laborers, station agents, and other railroad employees may have been tolerated as visitors, but would not have been permitted to hang around too long. Wise bosses also knew when to appear, and when to depart.

While standing still on the caboose track or at the end of a train in a siding, the caboose could be a sanctuary, a cozy resting place, or at least a boring place to wait for something to happen. In motion, a caboose could either ride like a Pullman if the speed was moderate and the engineer considerate, or the car could move like an amusement park ride. One of the main sources of contention between engine crews and train crews was the quality of the ride aboard the caboose. An unskilled or unthinking engineer could make life hell for the men on the hind end, and in some situations, even a skilled engineer diligently trying to run a smooth train could not eliminate the hard "raps" felt on the caboose. Slack was the culprit.

One of the reasons B&O cabooses received both steel underframes and draft gear cushioning devices was the toll that harsh slack action took on both men and the cars themselves. Much of the B&O comprises tough, challenging operating territory necessitating helpers and generating heavy in-train forces. The B&O's longstanding penchant for operating long, heavy trains and mixed consists (blocks of relatively heavy and relatively light cars interspersed, resulting in peculiar train dynamics) exacerbated the problem of dangerous slack at the caboose. Much of the problem lay in the very nature of American railroad practice.

Unlike the railways of Europe and other systems throughout the world, North American couplers and draft gear include certain amount of "free slack," or looseness of fit between individual parts and mated couplers. The existence of free slack allows the engineer to start the train one car at a time, with the momentum of the portion of the train already in motion used to accelerate the portion of the train standing still. The free slack of a train may total several feet or as much as a car length. That slack will constantly "run in" and "run out" as the train is in motion, depending on whether it is accelerating, coasting, or braking. The presence of summits, curves, "hogbacks" (short, sharp hills) and dips may also cause violent slack action as one part of the train responds to gravity and impacts another part. Slack "run in" means that the rear of the train is pushing against the front, and that the slack is being "bunched." The train is compressed together. Slack "run out" means that forces are acting to stretch the train out, placing the train in a condition of "draft." The length of a typical B&O train of the railroad's final three decades could total 6000 feet long when bunched, and 50 feet longer in draft.

The ramifications of in-train forces and track-train dynamics for cabooses (and the men in them) had to do with acceleration. Most freight, if it is properly secured, will not be harmed no matter what the rate of acceleration, although it can be damaged by severe shocks. Train crews are not freight, and they may be killed, injured, or at least greatly annoyed by too much rough handling. That is one reason why trained railroaders are always aware of the condition of the slack in their trains, and why they instinctively listen for and respond to the machine-gun-like sound of slack running in or out.

To give a concrete example of the action of slack on the caboose, for many years at the division point of Brunswick, Maryland (where the West End of the Baltimore Division met the East End of the Cumberland Division), westbound trains of empty hoppers would stop to change crews, and often power. In the last days of caboose use, operating department rules required the engineer to rely on the dynamic brake for the majority of the train's retarding force, supplemented by an automatic air brake application as the train neared a stop. Because the braking power was concentrated at the locomotives rather than being distributed throughout the train, the cars would bunch and the train would stop "solid," with couplers and draft gear in "buff."

Above: By the early twentieth century, railroading was a well-paid, stable, and respectable, albeit dangerous, line of work. Zanesville shop markings on the caboose place the photographer and crew somewhere in or near Ohio, probably in 1904 or 1905. The men's names are unknown, but they display rather solemn pride in their work and their equipment. They pose with their tools: the engineer with an oil can, fireman with a shovel, and brakemen with their flags. The man to the far left may be the head-end brakeman. The dapper gent on the caboose platform is almost certainly the conductor, standing in the symbolically superior position as befits his responsibilities. The engine crew might have regarded the 563 as an almost sentient creature capable of performance and mischief. To the train crew, the 100656 was more like home, providing shelter, personal space, and status. Promotion to conductor and assignment to a regular run and caboose meant that a brakeman had survived the most hazardous period of his railroad career and that the company wished to reward his service. (John P. Hankey Collection)

Below: On a Summer's day in 1949, two 7100s shove hard on the rear of 54 cars of coal at Austen, West Virginia. The train appears to be travelling at less than 10 mph, and in this situation there is almost no chance of heavy slack action at the caboose. There was little danger of helper locomotives telescoping the caboose, but on the B&O's curving main lines, cars with short truck center-to-center distances, relatively light weight, and too much side-to-side coupler play could be lifted from the rail, turned sideways, and crushed. The boys sandwiched between 8000 horsepower and 4500 tons of coal on a 2.2% upgrade probably appreciated the fact that while the C-2426 could be an oven in July, the all-steel I-12 had been designed specifically for use in heavy pusher territory. (E.L. "Tommy" Thompson, The B&O Railroad Historical Society Collection)

When the train got underway again, the locomotives would pull the first car, which would attain speed and momentum by the time the free slack ran out and it yanked the second car into motion. That sequential bang would propagate back through the train until it reached the caboose. Even though the free slack amounted to only two inches per car, by the time all 140 cars were moving the head end might be travelling at 6 or 8 miles per hour. When the hind coupler on the last coal car started moving, it almost instantaneously accelerated the caboose from a standstill to 8 miles per hour. A man standing at the front of the caboose when that occurred would be slammed against the back wall (or thrown out the door) with enough force to kill him. That, in fact, has happened.

Even during ordinary runs, the slack running in and out as

Above: Not all caboose cars wheeled down the main line at the end of 80 cars of fast freight giving the hind-end crew the ride of their lives. By law and union contract, after the turn of the century, almost all freight and work trains operating outside yard limits had a caboose. On the Landenburg Branch, the daily local paused to take water at Ashland, Delaware, in October, 1947. On non-main line runs, the caboose could be in any part of the train or could lead in backing movements. In those cases, the engineer took signals from a trainman on the platform, who also had the emergency valve and back-up whistle if needed. On a job like this one, the crew did not worry too much about slack action, hind end protection, or walking long trains in hip-deep snow to replace a broken knuckle. The caboose was as much a rolling lunch room as the train's command post. (Charles A. Brown, The B&O Railroad Historical Society Collection)

Left: As train length and reporting requirements grew, conductors often had considerable paperwork to accomplish over the course of a run. Filling out wheel reports, checking waybills, and reading the newspaper could be tiresome working by the light of an Aladdin caboose lamp fueled by kerosene. No matter how homey or comfortable a crew made a caboose, spending hours and hours aboard a small car—sometimes at night, frequently just waiting—was a tedious and often unpleasant routine. To the conductor's left is the duplex air brake gauge, showing trainline pressure and the pressure developed by the brake cylinder under the caboose. The conductor's valve was nearby, allowing a man on the hind end to make a controlled or emergency brake application. (The B&O Railroad Museum Collection)

the train progressed could easily generate similar forces. Experienced crews knew which combinations of train make-up, track characteristics, and train handling caused severe slack and where the best they could do was sit down, brace themselves, and hope the car held together. In other situations, slack action would be mild or non-existent. Ascending heavy grades at low speed, where the caboose was either at the end of a stretched out train or bunched between helpers and the hind cars, was a good time to cook food, adjust the stove, inspect the track behind, or do whatever chores required the crew to move about the car. A caboose in motion represented a working environment vastly different from, and considerably more hazardous than, a caboose standing still.

Over the course of a run the men on the caboose experienced periods of concentration and intense activity alternating with intervals of relative quiet and inactivity. For instance, with a long train operating through difficult territory, the hind end crew had to watch the train carefully and continuously. The more difficult the operating environment, the more the likelihood that some unintended event in the train would require some action by the crew. Peering intently at a long train as it snakes around curves or grinds upgrade was a tiring chore, especially at night or in inclement weather.

Above all, when the train was in motion the main task of the hind end crew was to inspect the train ahead for hotboxes, shifted loads, and any other obvious defects, while also watching the track behind the train for signs of derailed wheels, dragging equipment, leaking loads, or fires caused by the locomotive. The entire crew (but especially the conductor) kept an eye on the train's speed, noted its location, watched for signals from the head end, stations, and people on the ground, and made sure that speed restrictions, train orders, special instructions, and other operating directives were properly complied with. If anyone on the hind end took exception to the engineer's train handling, saw a serious defect in the train, or received any kind of signal which indicated danger, they would "turn on the spigot" or "put the air on" the engineer. By using the conductor's valve in the caboose, a crewman could make either a controlled or an emergency brake pipe reduction and bring the train to a stop. Upon noticing a brake pipe reduction, the engineer would close the throttle, place his automatic air brake handle in the lap position, and ride the application to a stop.

With a few exceptions, trains stopped on the main line had to protect themselves. That meant someone on the caboose walking back from the train a sufficient distance with flagging equipment prepared to halt any train which might be approaching on the same track. Again, railroad folklore and the anecdotal literature is thick with descriptions of wrecks caused by "short flagging," (the flagman did not go back far enough to prevent a collision), flagmen left behind because they did not hear the whistle signals calling them in, flagmen's encounters with animals or odd situations, or the perils of flagging in extreme weather. One common consequence of short flagging was the destruction of the caboose on the stopped train, and often injury to the crew on board.

While waiting on a siding in territory equipped with automatic block signals, interlocking signals, or on tracks otherwise protected against following movements, the flagman, brakeman, or conductor could remain in the caboose. The hind end crew could relax somewhat, while remaining vigilant for the release of air brakes or slack run-out indicating imminent movement. In certain locations, a crew aboard a stopped caboose would also want to watch out for hoboes or vandals, kids, railroad management intent on "trapping" a crew, or ordinary railroad movements.

Unlike most other railroaders, whose work took place either largely inside or largely outside, men on cabooses might alternate working in and out for short or long periods. In summer, if it was hot outside, the caboose could be hotter, and there was little difference in the level of discomfort. But in winter, especially in the Allegheny Mountains or on those parts of the B&O with heavy snow and high winds (as on the Buffalo Division), moving between the warmth of the caboose and conditions outside could take a physical toll. In the middle of the night, especially if a man was drowsy, it took fortitude to put on your coat, pick up a lantern, caps, fusees, and flags, and head out into a blinding snowstorm knowing that you may have to stand there for hours. Conversely, the sight of a warm caboose was a welcome sight to a man who has been outside flagging, switching, or fixing crippled cars for hours at a stretch. There were many good reasons for the affection railroad men held for their cabooses.

Conclusion

The caboose was a strategically located platform upon which to place railroad employees assigned to specific duties. The most important function of the caboose, from its introduction until the present, has been to permit the train crew to monitor the condition of the train as it progresses. Especially after the adoption of air brakes, the caboose provided a safe vantage point for the train crew to closely observe the train while in motion, at the same time positioning men where they were needed for signalling, switching, and back-up movements.

As on other railroads, the caboose on the B&O was but one part of a complex network of equipment, places, and structures housing observers who monitored the physical process of railroading. They included crossing watchmen's shanties and towers; stations, interlocking towers, and block stations; switchmen's shanties, telephone booths; the locomotives and cabooses of passing trains; and any other place or structure from which a person was in a position to observe the passing of a train. All of these were analogues to the caboose.

From the mid-nineteenth century to the present, railroad rules required a variety of employees to visually inspect each passing train. They watched for hot journals, sticking brakes, dragging equipment, shifted loads, flat or broken wheels, and so forth. Persons on the ground or in towers could indicate trouble with the train to men on the caboose through a series of hand signals, enabling the hind end crew to take appropriate action. The men watching the train from the rear end (and receiving signals from railroaders on the ground) were part of a much larger system of train inspection and human surveillance. Such close scrutiny was vital with steam locomotives and older car and track technology, and most effective when a train was rarely more than ten or twenty miles from an occupied station.

By the 1980s, a combination of technologies both obviated the necessity for frequent visual inspections and provided substitutes for human senses. First, the almost total use of roller bearings and the shift to closed, specialized cars greatly lessened the potential for hotboxes and shifting loads. Similarly, improvements in air brakes lessened the incidence of sticking brakes. With high horsepower multiple unit diesel locomotives making possible train lengths of a mile and a half and more, hind end crews could not visually monitor more than a fraction of the train. Strategically placed wayside equipment defect detectors notified crews via radio of certain types of defects. Finally, improved metallurgy and metal fabrication techniques drastically reduced the incidence of wheel and axle failures, coupler failures, and car failures.

In the meantime, crossing watchmen and switchmen virtually disappeared, as had stations manned by agents. The continuing consolidation of interlocking and control functions first to dispatchers' offices, and then to the CSXT Control Center in West Jacksonville, rendered most towers and block stations obsolete and unmanned. Within the space of two decades, the entire system based on visual inspection changed to one of automatic sensing and remote control. Close observance of all passing trains is still required of all operating employees, and the head end crew must look back frequently over the train to monitor its condition. But taken together, changes in how the modern railroad operates substantially lessened the roles of hind end crews, and consequently the need for cabooses. When lamenting their loss, mourn also for the demise of the tower, shanty, and station: all were part of the same process, and all have been superseded by new hardware and techniques.

The widespread adoption of the Flashing Rear End Device (FRED), End-Of-Train Device (EOT), or "electronic flagman" represents much more than a straightforward case of the substitution of capital for labor, modernization, or technological innovation. It is characteristic of a profound shift in operating practice and the continuing process of automation within railroad transportation. The EOT is also part of a larger system of technology, including remotely controlled switches, radio communications, sensing devices, and other "smart" technologies which merely recast and relocate the work traditionally accomplished by train crews on the hind end.

The caboose, in its traditional form and use, had a lifecycle. Railroaders brought it into being to fulfill certain needs, revised it (albeit slowly) into a final form, and then adopted different tools as both operating requirements and the means to satisfy them changed. The historical outline and interpretations which follow can only begin to place the B&O Railroad's 125 years of experience with cabooses in some sort of context. As the data, photographs, and engineering history demonstrate, the physical history of this one car type is a surprisingly complex subject. Cabooses offer yet another window through which to view the richly textured, resolutely idiosyncratic history of the Baltimore and Ohio Railroad itself.

[1] William F. Knapke, with Freeman Hubbard, *The Railroad Caboose: Its 100 Year History, Legend, and Lore* (San Marino, Ca.: Golden West Books, 1968), 13-14.

Above: In this 1970 view, the man leaning out from C-3754 will snatch the conductor's set of train orders from the hoop stand. On the ground, the operator of ND Tower at Viaduct Junction in Cumberland, Maryland has just given the Chicago-bound Trailer Jet the required "roll-by" inspection, and is signalling the man on the left side of the car that everything looked good. This was a transitional time for the C&O/B&O Railroads as they prepared to reorganize as The Chessie System, invest heavily in new technologies, and challenge allegedly outmoded work rules and operating practices. On this day, despite the intermodal cargo and modern steel cabooses, traditional railroading prevailed. Besides an armstrong interlocking plant and wood stairs, ND tower retained its railroad Morse line up the hill to Sand Patch. Today, ND Tower controls this busy junction on borrowed time. (John P. Hankey)

Upper Right: The B&O adopted train radios for system-wide use relatively late, but experimented in the 1950s with radio-telephones on the Fairmont, Morgantown, and Pittsburgh Subdivision. Prior to radio, the hind end could communicate with the head end by manipulating the air brake trainline pressure and sometimes by lantern or hand signals. The engineer could use whistle and hand signals, and communicate a pre-arranged signal by applying or releasing the brakes. More complex discussions required the conductor to walk to the head end. The C-2481 shows part of the view from the bay window and examples of the small additions made to assigned cabooses by their crews in later years. The union sticker reads "This Crew 100% Brotherhood of Railroad Trainmen"; the framed work of art visible to the right is a pin-up girl. (B&O Railroad, Ralph L. Barger Collection)

Middle Right: At almost every location where trains originated or terminated, yard crews and locomotives like L-2c 709 at Salamanca, New York in June, 1953 spent a great deal of company time and money attaching and removing cabooses. When the head end was down by the water plug, station, or crew shanty, the caboose could be a mile out in the country, requiring a double stop to change the caboose or crew. Sometimes a yard engine made a circuitous trip to the rear end to attach or remove the caboose, or the road power and crew handled the caboose for their train. Accommodating caboose moves in crowded, busy yards were challenges that operating officials tried to minimize or eliminate, first through pooling and then through the use of end-of-train devices. (R. L. Long, The B&O Railroad Historical Society Collection)

Lower Right: As a train of "coal cars" (the local name for a train of empty coal hoppers) passes Relay and swings into the Patapsco Valley just west of Baltimore, a hind-end man takes in the view. At no more than 30 mph with the train stretched on the slight upgrade, there would be little slack. Passing time on the rear platform could be pleasant, indeed. Some of the least documented, but most interesting, aspects of railroading were the intangible benefits of employment. At times it could be challenging, satisfying, and occasionally downright enjoyable. The next thirty miles through Patapsco State Park along the original route of the B&O offer some of the most historic and pleasant scenery to be found in the East. With a good engineer, a good train, and good weather, "coal cars" from Curtis Bay to Brunswick made an easy—and maybe fun—trip for a caboose crew. Sometimes, it even eased memories of the bad trips. (The B&O Railroad Museum Collection)

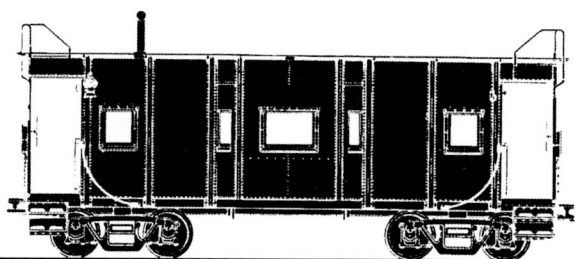

HISTORY & DESCRIPTION

Historical Overview

Although cabooses were in use on other railroads prior to the Civil War, the earliest documented reference to B&O caboose cars found thus far dates to 1868. This first specific evidence of a B&O caboose appears in the company's annual report for the year ending September 30, 1868. It mentions that four cabooses were transferred to the camp car category. Through the middle of the nineteenth century, annual reports included a roster listing the total quantities of various types of equipment in service. The report for the year ending September 30, 1872 indicated 143 cabooses on hand. This was the first time the roster included cabooses as a separate line item. The annual reports for preceding years do not include a caboose category in the roster, although a few make passing mention of caboose cars. This suggests that cabooses were carried under another category in rosters prior to 1872, perhaps as a type of "house" car (what we would call a boxcar today).

The number of cabooses steadily increased. From the 143 cars listed in September, 1872, the fleet grew in just four years to 234 cars listed in the annual report dated September 30, 1876. After that, the annual reports changed to a format which did not include an equipment roster. Between 1872 and 1876, the reports listed only eight-wheel cars. Later rosters indicated that the B&O operated four-wheel Class K-1 cars built as early as 1878. The number of four-wheel cabooses increased until they outnumbered eight-wheel cars by a large margin. The number of four-wheel caboose cars peaked at the beginning of 1911, when there were 1062 four-wheel cabooses on the roster, compared to about 120 eight-wheel cars.

By the turn of the century, the four-wheel K-1 was the B&O's standard caboose, although the Baltimore and Ohio Southwestern (which operated with some autonomy) favored eight-wheel cars. The K-1 might have remained the B&O's standard car longer had not outside influences hastened change. In 1913, the Ohio State Legislature passed Senate Bill 298 laying down criteria for the use of cabooses on any railroad operating within the state. Among other requirements, the law specified that railroads must use only eight-wheel cabooses of at least 24 feet in length excluding platforms in or through Ohio. Practical implementation of Senate Bill 298 took place gradually. Railroads had to increase the number of suitable cabooses on their lines in Ohio by at least 15% each year, until all were in compliance by 1919. Railroads were free to transfer cabooses from other locations, build new cars, or modify existing cabooses to fulfill the conditions of the law.

The B&O chose to acquire new cars, and the total number of caboose cars of all types peaked in 1919, when the B&O rostered 443 eight-wheel and 769 four-wheel cars, for a total of 1212 cabooses.

B&O correspondence of the period indicates that the Class I-1 was built in response to this legislation. The I-1 was an eight-wheel car 30 feet long with a 24-foot enclosed carbody—exactly what the law demanded, and nothing more. The B&O designed the I-1 with a steel underframe, wood body, and center cupola. The design became the railroad's standard caboose, and formed the basis for the Class I-1A and I-5 cars. From 1913 until 1929, the railroad built hundreds of similar composite (wood and steel) "30 foot caboose cars," some of which remained in service on the B&O into the 1980s. The number of four-wheel cabooses gradually decreased until the last one was retired in 1953.

The next major innovation occurred in 1931 with the construction of the Class I-7 caboose. It was built on the frame of a wrecked I-5 car, retaining the 24-foot carbody and general arrangement. The carbody, however, was built of steel with a bay window instead of a cupola. The design and material apparently served well, for although the I-7 was a one of a kind, from this time forward all new cabooses built by or for the B&O were of steel with bay windows. The only exceptions were cabooses converted from box and stock cars during World War II, and the peculiar Class C-28 transfer caboose turned out by DuBois Shops in 1976.

The B&O did not build new cabooses in quantity until 1941, when wartime traffic began to tax the railroad's existing fleet. At that time, the B&O favored the wagon top style of construction developed by John J. Tatum, who became Superintendent of Freight Car Equipment in 1907. While distinctive, the I-12 wagon top shared many basic dimensions with the I-5 and I-1 cars. The last I-12 rolled out of the B&O's shops in 1945. The B&O did not build cabooses again until the Class I-17 in 1952. By this time, the wagon top design had fallen out of favor. The I-17 had a conventional riveted freight car design with the same basic dimensions as the I-12, which were derived from the 1913 Class I-1. The railroad built the almost duplicate I-17A cars until 1965, so that for nearly thirty-five years (from the experimental I-7 through the last I-17A), the standard B&O caboose design was a 30-foot long steel bay window car. Moreover, the B&O stayed with a 24-foot car body from the I-1 of 1913 through the I-17A, for a total of 52 years.

In late 1965, after the Chesapeake and Ohio Railway acquired stock control of the B&O, the railroad acquired its first Class I-18 cars. The B&O needed to quickly acquire a large number of quality cars to implement a caboose pooling plan and chose an outside car builder. These cars were constructed using a longer 30-foot carbody. Their design and equipment set the standard for all subsequent caboose purchases through the Class C-27A of 1980—the last ones acquired by the B&O. All of these cars were built to the most modern designs and equipped with almost every available device for crew safety and comfort. Just a few years after the Chessie System purchased the new C-27A cars, major railroads and the United Transportation Union negotiated an agreement permitting railroads across the country to eliminate most caboose cars, especially in mainline operations. Chessie System and its successor, CSX Transportation, moved quickly to substitute electronic monitoring devices at the end of the train, rendering hundreds of almost-new cabooses obsolete after a relatively few years use. While a limited quantity remain in specialized service of various kinds, the mainline caboose era effectively ended for the B&O in the late 1980s. In 1994, CSX Transportation had only a little over 400 cabooses in service throughout its vast system, a far cry from the thousands that once served its many predecessor lines, including the B&O, just a few decades ago. For example, the B&O alone rostered a total of 673 cabooses in March 1968.

B&O Caboose Numbering Systems

Unfortunately, the early rosters found in B&O annual reports do not list the numbers carried by the various types of equipment. The earliest available numerical list of equipment dates to June 1885 and lists B&O cabooses as having the number series 1500 through 1899. Also, Pittsburg & Connellsville (P&C) cabooses, occupying the series 1900 through 1999, were later relettered to B&O retaining the 1900 series numbers. The railroad mixed both four and eight-wheel cabooses indiscriminately within this series.

Given the hazardous nature of railroading in those days, the life-span of any given car could be quite short. The B&O built "replacements" for destroyed cars, reusing the original number. However, the cars were not necessarily identical to the originals, being instead a later, more current revision of that type. That practice leads to great confusion when studying early rosters. For example, the number 1500 could have been carried by several different cabooses. Furthermore, while the first 1500 may have been an eight-wheel car, a later 1500 could have been a four-wheel car. As mentioned, the earliest known numbers for B&O cabooses were in the series 1500-1999. Originally these were mostly eight-wheel cars which were gradually replaced with four-wheel cabooses of the same number, until the majority (but not all), of the series were of the four-wheel type.

As the B&O expanded to the West and South, it required more cabooses. The railroad assigned these cars the 1400 series numbers previously used for express boxcars. Most, and possibly all, of the cabooses in the 1400 series were of the four-wheel type. Thus, by the turn of the century, both four and eight-wheel cars occupied the number series 1400 through 1999. Subsidiary railroads, such as the Baltimore & Ohio Southwestern, Ohio River Railroad, and Columbus & Cincinnati Midland had their own number series separate from the B&O's caboose numbering scheme.

In mid-1900, the B&O began a general renumbering of all freight equipment, including cabooses. The railroad attempted to integrate the equipment of subsidiary railroads into the B&O number series, and, for the first time, four and eight-wheel cabooses were given separate number series. Cabooses with eight wheels were assigned the number series 100000 through 100199, while four-wheel cabooses were assigned the number series 100200 through 100999. Continuing construction of standard four-wheel cabooses required that number series to be expanded to 100200 through 101134. One exception to this numbering is known: in 1901 and 1902, eighty-one boxcars were converted to eight-wheel cabooses and numbered in the series 100350 through 100430. This was temporary, and they were replaced in late 1902 by four-wheel cabooses. Also, during this era the B&O continued the practice of building replacement cars. For example, there were several different eight-wheel cabooses which carried the number 100000.

The 100000 series numbers were relatively short lived. About the middle of 1907, the B&O began another renumbering of caboose equipment whereby the eight-wheel series were renumbered to the C-1 through C-134 series while the four-wheel were assigned the C-200 through C-1299 series. Cabooses belonging to newly acquired subsidiaries such as the Cleveland Terminal & Valley and the Cleveland Lorain & Wheeling were also included in the renumbering.

The B&O produced the four-wheel caboose in quantity until 1913, causing an expansion of its number series to C-200 through C-1399. At the same time, new construction expanded the Class I series from C-1 through C-141. In 1913, production of the I-1 caboose began. Since this was an eight-wheel caboose, the first I-1s were numbered to fill gaps in the series C-1 through C-141. Subsequent production of the Class I-1 filled the series C-142 through C-199. Soon the railroad required more numbers, and between 1914 and 1918 renumbered the four-wheel cabooses remaining in series C-200 through C-499 to fill gaps in the C-500 through C-1399 series. The vacated numbers above C-200 were then assigned to new Class I-1 cabooses. Progressively higher "C" numbers were assigned new B&O classes as they were acquired or constructed, with some exceptions. The "C" numbers are probably the best known to B&O fans since this series of caboose numbers expanded and continued to be used for 75 years.

The last major renumbering of B&O cabooses began in 1982 as Chessie System (by then an operating unit of the CSX Corporation) strove to rationalize and coordinate equipment numbering. Non-revenue equipment and cabooses received numbers in the 900000 through 920000 series without any letter designation or hyphen. B&O cabooses, which by this time occupied the number series C-2400 through C-3986, were renumbered by dropping the "C" prefix and replacing it with the digits "90". For example, B&O caboose C-2882 became 902882. The last cabooses ever built for the B&O, Class C27A, were delivered with numbers in the series 904000 through 904093.

The B&O used the numbering systems described above for caboose cars in revenue operations. Before 1900, the railroad had "service" cabooses used in work train service and numbered in the 19000 series shared by all non-revenue or service equipment. In the 1900 general renumbering, the B&O renumbered service equipment into series with the prefix "X" and assigned the series X-3000 through X-3099 to its service cabooses. Between 1905 and 1913, several boxcars were rebuilt to service cabooses and added to the series; they were the last of that type created. Retirements gradually diminished the series, until the B&O in 1925 renumbered the last remaining X-3000 cabooses into the C-1800s. After this time cabooses were occasionally converted to work equipment and given an "X" number, but these were intended to be various types of maintenance of way cars and not cabooses.

B&O Caboose Classification System

It is not yet clear when the B&O began to use a formal car classification system. The "official" list of equipment published by the B&O's Car Record Office in 1888 does not show car classes, whereas B&O correspondence dated as early as January 29, 1894 refers to certain freight cars by class, indicating that the alpha-numeric system was in place at least by that time and probably earlier. Under the B&O's system, each type of car was assigned a letter of the alphabet followed by a number for each new type of the same kind of car. Variations within the same class of car were indicated by letters following the number. The desired result was to indicate "families" of cars with similar basic attributes while allowing for sub-classes created by rebuilding, modification, and the acquisition of additional cars. The railroad attempted to assign classes in chronological sequence of construction or acquisition.

In the B&O's system, the class letter "I" was to be used for eight-wheel cabooses and the class letter "K" for four-wheel cabooses. The Class I comprised a collection of wooden eight-wheel cabooses of varied appearance and origin. The railroad assigned the next group of eight-wheel cars Class I-1, and assigned succeeding groups of eight-wheel cabooses Class I-2, I-3, etc. The B&O's standard four-wheel cabooses were known as Class K-1. A few references have been found to Class K cabooses but what, if any, cabooses were assigned Class K is unknown at present. At times the B&O deviated from this system. For example, four-wheel cabooses acquired with the Buffalo, Rochester & Pittsburgh (BR&P) and the Buffalo & Susquehanna (B&S) theoretically belonging in the B&O class "K" series were instead assigned Class I-8, I-11 and I-12 (1st), even though they were not eight-wheel cars.

As noted above, the B&O classification system was in use by 1894, if not earlier, and continued to be used until the mid-1960s when the combined C&O/B&O Railroads adopted a new equipment classification system unifying what had been separate B&O, C&O and WM classes. This system assigned the class letter "C", followed by a number, to caboose cars. The B&O reclassified its existing cabooses, and assigned "C" classes to cars subsequently built or acquired. The translation from the B&O class to this new C&O\B&O system is given in Table 1. Since the subject of this book is B&O caboose cars, it uses the B&O caboose classification system in describing them whenever possible, and refers to caboose types by the C&O\B&O system only when a caboose is too new to have been assigned a B&O class.

B&O cabooses included in this latter category are the C-26s through C-27As, the C-28 and a variety of secondhand C&O cars.

TABLE 1
Cross Reference of
B&O Class With C&O/B&O Class

B&O Class	C&O/B&O Class
I-1	C-1
I-3	C-2
I-10	C-3
I-1A	C-4
I-5	C-6
I-5D	C-6A
I-5C	C-6B
I-7	C-11
I-5B	C-12
I-5BA	C-12A
I-13	C-17
I-12	C-18
I-16	C-19
I-17	C-22
I-17A	C-23
I-18	C-24

Class Descriptions

The following presentation of descriptions and analysis of each B&O caboose class, together with representative photographs and clearance diagrams, when available, provides a close look at the evolution of the B&O caboose roster. It should be noted that each class is presented roughly in order of its appearance on the B&O, which was, for various reasons, not strictly in numeric order of class designation.

Above: Behind SW900 9428 is one of the Class M-26 box cars converted to an unclassed caboose-like rider car for transfer service. The XM-3023 was photographed in Dayton, Ohio on September 15, 1965. (Louis A. Marre)

ROSTER OF B&O CABOOSES

NUMBERS	CLASS	DATE BUILT	NOTES
C-1 to C-141 (1st)	I	1872-4/10	Renumbered from B&O 100000-100199
C-5 to C-137 (2nd)	I-1	8/13-11/15	Not all numbers used
C-142 to C-199	I-1	12/13-12/15	
C-200 to C-399 (1st)	K-1	1888-8/05	Renumbered from B&O 100200-100399
C-200 to C-399 (2nd)	I-1	8/14-4/18	
C-400 to C-499 (1st)	K-1	1887-11/05	Renumbered from B&O 100400-100499
C-400 to C-499 (2nd)	I-1A	3/22-9/23	
C-500 to C-1399	K-1	1878-2/13	Renumbered from B&O 100500-101134
C-1401 to C-1434	I-1A	10/23-12/23	
C-1500 to C-1529	I-2	1887-1905	Renumbered from CH&D 1-65
C-1530	I-2	1892	Number assigned to CH&D 69
C-1531 to C-1533	I-2	1892-1905	Renumbered from CH&D 70, 71, 76
C-1534	I-2	1892	Number assigned to CH&D 79
C-1535 to C-1560	I-2	1892-1911	Renumbered from CH&D 80-143
C-1561 to C-1570	I-2	2/17	Renumbered from B&O X-4800 through X-4809
C-1571	I-2	Unknown	Renumbered from M&K 101
C-1594 to C-1599 (1st)	I-9 (1st)	7/87-12/90	Numbers assigned to BR&P 6, 9, 32, 36, 46, 49
C-1594 (2nd)	I-9 (2nd)	1889	Renumbered from BR&P (R&FC) 1
C-1599 (2nd)	I	Unknown	Renumbered from B&O C-1824 (1st)
C-1600 to C-1614	I-3	11/15-6/16	Renumbered from CH&D 150-164
C-1615	I-3	10/92	Renumbered from B&O T-207
C-1616	I-3	Unknown	Renumbered from D&U 2
C-1650 (1st)	I-4	8/98	Renumbered from B&O C-2000 (1st)
C-1650 (2nd)	I-14	9/97	Rebuilt from B&O SF-19
C-1650 (3rd)	I-14A	2/10	Rebuilt from B&O X-6198
C-1651 to C-1661	I-14	11/83-2/00	Rebuilt from B&O SF-42, SF-43, SF-13, SF-44, SF-10, SF-11, SF-12, SF-45, SF-41, X-2235, X-2628
C-1676 to C-1696	I-6	1916-1921	Renumbered from CI&W 1-21
C-1697	I-6	1921	Number assigned to CI&W 22
C-1698 to C-1699	I-6	1923	Renumbered from CI&W 23-24
C-1700 to C-1711	C&C	1909-1913	Renumbered from C&C 100-111
C-1712 to C-1716	M&K	6/06-8/09	Renumbered from M&K 102-106
C-1750 to C-1764	I-8	2/98-12/15	Numbers assigned to BR&P 2, 12, 14, 18, 20, 27, 43, 44, 48, 55, 63, 68, 81, 101, 105
C-1765	I-8	8/05	Renumbered from BR&P 107
C-1766 to C-1772	I-8	8/05-8/07	Numbers assigned to BR&P 108, 109, 112, 115, 117, 118, 119
C-1773 to C-1781	I-11	Unknown	Renumbered from B&S 1-9
C-1782 to C-1799	I-12(1st)	Unknown	Numbers assigned to B&S 70-98
C-1800 to C-1835 (1st)	I	1872-3/01	Renumbered from B&O C-1 through C-141
C-1800 to C-1835 (2nd)	I-13	4/41-8/41	Rebuilt from B&O 13000-13048
C-1836 to C-1875	I	1877-4/10	Renumbered from B&O C-1 through C-141
C-1876 to C-1881	None	4/98-9/98	Rebuilt from B&O 96993, 97959, 99046, 96040, 97076, 87677
C-1882 to C-1884	None	1883-10/87	Renumbered from B&O X-978, X-2904, X-3857
C-1900	I-5	1/24	Rebuilt to Class I-5D
C-1901 to C-1999	I-5	11/25-2/26	Some rebuilt to Class I-5C & I-5D
C-2000 (1st)	I-4	8/98	Rebuilt from B&O 87110
C-2000 (2nd)	I-5	2/26	Rebuilt to Class I-5D
C-2001 to C-2099	I-5	7/26-9/26	Some rebuilt to Class I-5C & I-5D
C-2100 (1st)	I-5	9/26	
C-2100 (2nd)	I-5	4/27	Rebuilt to Class I-5C
C-2101 to C-2299	I-5	4/27-11/29	Some rebuilt to Class I-5C & I-5D
C-2300 to C-2374	I-16	11/42	Rebuilt from Class M-13, M-13A and M-13B boxcars
C-2400 to C-2499	I-12(2nd)	12/41-1/42	Renumbered to B&O 902400-902499
C-2500	I-7	1/31	Rebuilt from B&O C-1911
C-2501	I-5A	2/36	Rebuilt from B&O C-419
C-2502 to C-2507	I-5B	6/36-10/40	Rebuilt from Class I-1A & I-5 Cabooses
C-2600 to C-2610	I-10	1/14-5/18	Renumbered from BR&P 150, 250-259
C-2611 to C-2612	I-10	5/18	Numbers assigned to BR&P 260-261
C-2613 to C-2621	I-10	5/18-10/23	Renumbered from BR&P 262-270
C-2622	I-10	10/23	Number assigned to BR&P 271
C-2623 to C-2647	I-10	10/23-11/23	Renumbered from BR&P 272-296
C-2648	I-10	11/23	Number assigned to BR&P 297
C-2649 to C-2665	I-10	11/23-12/23	Renumbered from BR&P 298-314
C-2700 to C-2799	I-16	7/43	Rebuilt from Class M-13, M-13A and M-13B boxcars
C-2800 to C-2824	I-12(2nd)	8/45-10/45	Renumbered to B&O 902800-902824
C-2850 to C-2861	I-17	12/52-1/53	Renumbered to B&O 902850-902861

ROSTER OF B&O CABOOSES

NUMBERS	CLASS	DATE BUILT	NOTES
C-2862 to C-2909	I-17A	2/54-6/58	Renumbered to B&O 902862-902909
C-2925 to C-2960	I-17A	4/59-11/65	Renumbered to B&O 902925-902960
C-3000 to C-3045	I-18	1/66	Renumbered to B&O 903000-903045
C-3050	C-15B	4/41	Renumbered from C&O 90099
C-3051	C-28	7/76	Rebuilt from B&O 285084
C-3700 to C-3827	C-26	3/71-12/71	Renumbered to B&O 903700-903827
C-3828 to C-3924	C-26A	1/75-6/75	Renumbered to B&O 903828-903924
C-3925 to C-3986	C-27	2/78-5/78	Renumbered to B&O 903925-903986
90363 to 90370	C-5	4/18-11/23	Renumbered from B&O C-2604, C-2613, C-2635, C-2617, C-2636, C-2601, C-2609, C-2642
90619, 90631	C-9	4/26	Relettered from C&O, same numbers
90689, 90697, 90743, 90746 to 90748, 90764, 90771, 90800, 90831, 90837, 90846, 90848, 90850, 90855, 90860, 90877, 90915, 90922, 90966, 90969, 90998	C-8	11/24-11/29	Relettered from C&O, same numbers
100000 to 100199	I	1872-4/10	Renumbered to B&O C-1 through C-141
100200 to 101133	K-1	1878-8/06	Renumbered to B&O C-200 through C-1399
904000 to 904093	C-27A	7/80-10/80	

ROSTER OF B&OCT CABOOSES

NUMBERS	CLASS	DATE BUILT	NOTES
C-195, C-198	none	unknown	Renumbered from CTT series
C-1716 to C-1746	K-1	1878 - 1910	Renumbered from B&O C-500 through C-1399 series
C-1777 to C-1781	I-11	1903 - 1907	Renumbered from B&O C-1777 through C-1781
C-1782	C&C	1909	Renumbered from B&O C-1701
C-1883 to C-1886	I-1	6/14 - 2/18	Renumbered from B&O C-81, C-179, C-297, C-380
C-1887 (1st)	none	unknown	Renumbered from B&OCT X-3078 to X-3099 series
C-1887 (2nd)	I-1	2/18	Renumbered from B&O C-384
C-1888	none	unknown	Renumbered from B&OCT X-3078 to X-3099 series
C-1889 to C-1899(1st)	none	unknown	Renumbered from B&OCT X-3078 to X-3099 series
C-1899 to C-1890 (2nd)	I-1	7/17, 2/18	Renumbered from B&O C-246, C-371
C-1891 to C-1896(2nd)	(ex-M-43)	1909 - 1910	Renumbered from B&O 189004, 189070, 189072, 189096, 189268, 189289
C-1896 (3rd)	I-1A	2/23	Renumbered from B&O C-478
C-1897 (2nd)	I-3	unknown	Renumbered from B&O C-1616
C-1898 (2nd)	I-1	1913 - 1918	Renumbered from B&O C-5 through C-399 series
C-1899 (2nd)	I-1	11/13	Renumbered from B&O C-82
C-1900	I-1	2/16	Renumbered from B&O C-233
C-1901 to C-1903	I-1A	4/22 - 11/23	Renumbered from B&O C-414, C-1407, C-1420
C-1904	I-1	7/17	Renumbered from B&O C-334
C-1905 to C-1906	I-1A	10/23, 11/23	Renumbered from B&O C-1410, C-1415
X-3078 to X-3099	none	1895	Renumbered from CTT 106-206 series
74308 to 74377	none	1895	Renumbered from CTT 106-206 series

RAILROAD NAME INDEX

B&O	Baltimore & Ohio
B&OCT	Baltimore & Ohio Chicago Terminal
CI&W	Cincinnati Indianapolis & Western
B&S	Buffalo & Susquehanna
CTT	Chicago Terminal Transfer
BR&P	Buffalo, Rochester & Pittsburgh
D&U	Dayton & Union
C&C	Coal & Coke
M&K	Morgantown & Kingwood
C&O	Chesapeake & Ohio
RF&C	Reynoldsville & Falls Creek
CH&D	Cincinnati, Hamilton & Dayton

Class I Cabooses

First Number Series	1500 to 1999
Second Number Series	100000 to 100199
Third Number Series	C-1 to C-141
Fourth Number Series	C-1800 to C-1884
Fifth Number Series	C-1599

Evidence strongly suggests that the earliest B&O cabooses were eight-wheel cars of varying design and origin. By the mid-1880s, the railroad settled on a standard four-wheel design and a majority of the B&O's cabooses of the time were of the four-wheel variety. The railroad's early fleet of eight-wheel cabooses consisted of cars built by the B&O as cabooses, cars converted from boxcars, and cabooses acquired from railroads absorbed by the B&O. Before 1900, the B&O's eight-wheel cabooses occupied numbers in the series 1500 to 1999, while the subsidiary lines retained their own number series. Beginning in 1900, the eight-wheel cabooses on the B&O and subsidiary lines were consolidated into series 100000 through 100199. When the B&O began to classify equipment, it assigned Class I to eight-wheel cabooses and converted boxcars irrespective of their ancestry or appearance. Several different types of Class I cabooses are known to have existed. For example, notice the photograph of B&O Class I caboose 1871 on page 30. This is a center cupola car believed to have been a converted boxcar. B&O Cabooses C-1856 and C-1599 on page 30 offer a quite different appearance. These end cupola cars are of B&O Southwestern ancestry, but all three are included in Class I.

In the renumbering of 1907, Class I cabooses were assigned numbers in the series C-1 through C-134. Later, the series was expanded to include numbers C-1 through C-141. In 1925, the railroad renumbered the surviving Class I cars to the series C-1800 through C-1875. That same year the rebuilding of six Class M-8B boxcars into cabooses necessitated a further expansion, adding C-1876 to C-1881. In August 1926, the B&O again expanded the series when it converted service box cars X-978, X-2904, and X-3857 to cabooses C-1882 through C-1884. One Class I car (C-1824) survived until April 1941, when the railroad renumbered it C-1599 to clear the series for I-13 cabooses then being converted. Figure 1 is an early B&O clearance diagram for Class I cabooses. Note that the dimensions describe an off-center cupola caboose, which does not match the end cupola C-1856 or C-1599, nor the center cupola 1871 presented in this book. Figure 4 on page 36 is a much later clearance diagram purported to describe both Class I-1 and I cabooses, including the C-1599. This diagram actually describes the I-1 cars and clearly does not match the photograph of the C-1599.

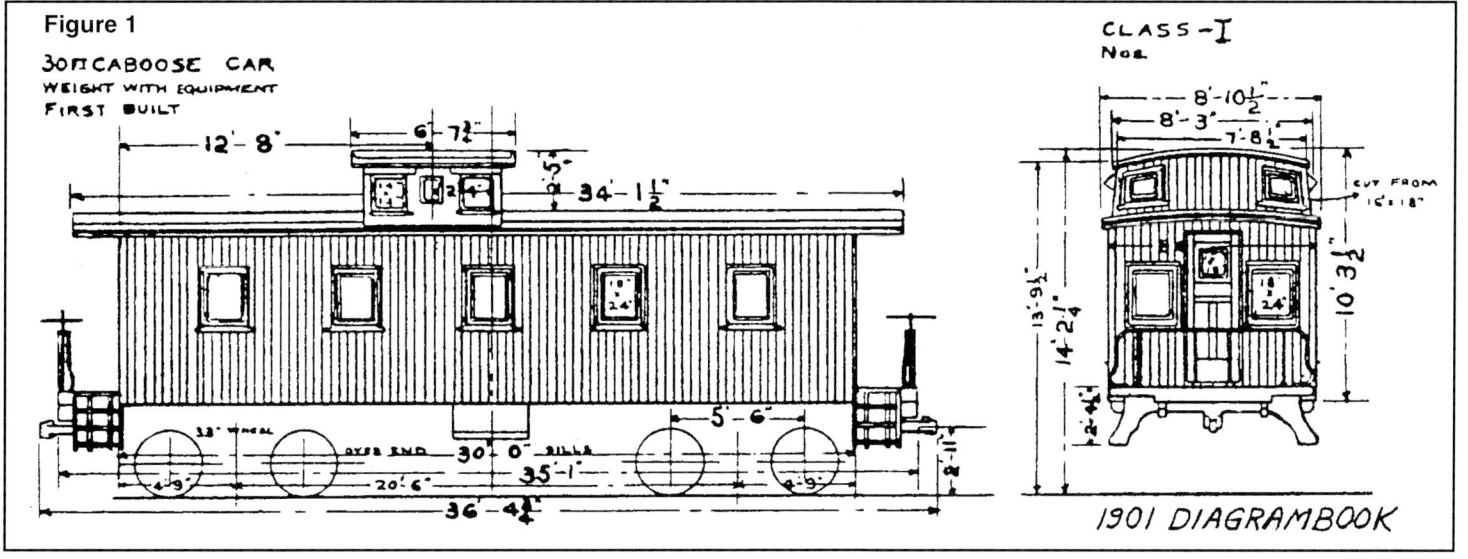

Figure 1

Why this train paused on the Fink truss bridge near Clarksburg, West Virginia sometime in the 1870s is now lost. The number of the caboose is not visible, but its eight wheels would place it in Class I when the B&O's car classification system is implemented. Note how large the caboose is, nearly dwarfing the locomotive and almost as large as the baggage car. If most eight-wheel cars were this big, it seems little wonder that the B&O soon adopted the four-wheel car as standard. The car has truss rods, link-and-pin couplers, and trucks which closely resemble passenger car trucks. From this angle the car resembles B&O cabooses in service a hundred years later. The experience of riding and living aboard this car would not change appreciably until the 1930s. (DeGolyer Library, Southern Methodist University, Dallas, Texas)

Upper Left: B&O Class I caboose 1871, photographed at Brunswick, Maryland on February 17, 1899, was probably converted from an older box car. Note that the railroad name and car number are painted in white panels on the side, a common practice on freight cars of this era. The car remains equiped with link and pin couplers. A combination of what seem like the vestiges of queen posts for truss rods and the wide truck spacing make a good case for previous use as a boxcar. Note that the car has no roof walk or ladders. (John Malone Collection)

Middle Left: By the mid-1930s, the C-1856 was tired, probably stripped, and ready to be burned to recover the scrap metal. The tilting spring plank on the left-hand truck suggests broken springs; the absence of a smoke jack usually meant that the stove had been removed. The dead giveaway is the distinctive "Unfit for Service" stencil to the right of the lettering. This former B&O Southwestern all-wood car has an uncommon queen-post and truss rod underframe. Especially as slack action became more severe with the longer trains and higher speeds of the twentieth century, wood cars such as this "worked" in the same way that a wood chair becomes weak at the joints. One solution was to brace the tall cupola with steel rods. Another was to install sway bracing, the angled steel rods extending from the tops of the doors to the lower corners near the bolsters. (S. P. Davidson)

Lower Left: This view of the C-1599 shows the last of the Class I cabooses just months before retirement in 1957. As a class, they were a long-lived group of varied cars having only eight wheels, and usually a cupola, in common. An ex-B&O Southwestern car with a distinctive high braced cupola, C-1599 appears to have received a steel underframe at some point. This was a common betterment for all-wood cars in otherwise good condition, and it may have accounted for this one's long life. Note also the B&O "family resemblance," enhanced by standard grab irons, coach-style steps, window visors (which doubled as rain gutters), and many other small details. (Bob Chapman)

Class K-1 Cabooses

First Number Series   1400 to 1999
Second Number Series   100200 to 101134
Third Number Series   C-200 to C-1399

The standard caboose for the B&O before and shortly after the turn of the century was a four-wheel, twenty-foot, center cupola, all wood car. The railroad built hundreds of them at a number of different shops between 1878 and 1913. When the B&O instituted its classification system, these cars were designated as K-1. This classification was also used to describe four-wheel cabooses acquired from subsidiary lines even though their appearance was quite different from the B&O equipment. Originally, the B&O numbered its four-wheel cabooses in the series 1400 through 1999, while subsidiary lines had their own number series. Beginning in 1900, the four-wheel cabooses of the B&O and the subsidiary lines began to be consolidated into the number series 100200 through 100999. New Class K-1 cars, built after this renumbering, necessitated an expansion through the number 101134. This number series was relatively short lived, for beginning in 1907, the K-1 and four-wheel cabooses from lines acquired since the previous renumbering were assigned numbers in the series C-200 through C-1299. Cars built and acquired after the renumbering created an expansion of the series through C-1399. From 1913 to 1918 the series was reduced to C-500 through C-1399, to make room for the new eight-wheel, steel underframe cabooses then under construction.

The first K-1 cabooses were equipped with link and pin couplers and had no air brakes. Later, the surviving cars, as well as the last K-1 cars to be built, were equipped with both automatic couplers and air brakes. Figure 2 shows a B&O clearance diagram for the Class K-1 caboose in the C-500 series as equipped with automatic couplers. Many of the cars had their cupolas removed in later years. The B&O sold or transferred some Class K-1 cabooses to subsidiary lines such as the B&O Chicago Terminal and the Staten Island Rapid Transit for use in yard and transfer service.

B&O Records describe Class K-1 cars as "all wood." As yet, no reference has been found indicating that any K-1 cars were built with steel underframes. Photographs show at least a few cars with steel underframes, possibly betterments added to extend the useful life of an obsolete, but otherwise sound, caboose or the result of wreck repairs to a damaged caboose. On a car as small as a K-1 caboose, the addition of a simple steel center sill with steel floor beams and side sills was a straightforward project well within the capability and authority of many shops and repair facilities. See the photograph of B&O caboose C-845 below for an example of a K-1 with a replacement steel underframe. Class K-1 cabooses continued to be used in yard and secondary service for many years, until the B&O retired the last one in 1953.

Above: B&O Class K-1 caboose C-845 was photographed on May 23, 1948 at St. George Yard, New York on the Staten Island Rapid Transit. It was one of the last K-1 cabooses in service on the B&O or any of its subsidiaries, and was not retired until 1953. The car's steel underframe is clearly visible, curious since the Class K-1 cars were of all-wood construction and no references have been found that indicate cars built or modified with steel underframes. This was probably a local repair made to extend the useful life of an obsolete, but otherwise useful, car. Despite the company's best efforts, the condition or attributes of a car often varied from what the "official" records showed. (Wilson Jones, Dave Oroszi Collection)

Upper Left: In the nineteenth and early twentieth centuries, many itinerant photographers made their living by travelling to different railroad facilities to photograph train and engine crews with their equipment, selling prints to the railroaders thus nobly portrayed. Class K-1 100714 was the background, not the subject, for this ca. 1905 image. As the car was last refurbished in Keyser, the location is almost certainly somewhere on the Cumberland Division West End. The caboose is in a transitional form, with automatic couplers, a "straight air" brake pipe but no air brake equipment, and no ladders or roof walks. The crew, however, is obviously quite proud of "their" caboose. Almost certainly the man standing jauntily with the tie, derby, and flag—one symbol of conductorial authority—was the boss. (John Malone Collection)

Middle Left: Resting outside the roundhouse with variously customized cousins, the C-1741 looks to be fresh out of the paint shop in 1947. The B&OCT refurbished it in the East Chicago shops, which were actually in western Indiana. Myriad little details differentiate B&OCT equipment from "Baltimore's": the period at the end of the road name, a different class designation (D-3 as opposed to K-1), and the location of the stove in the center of the car. Unlike the C-1725 (which was painted in 1944), the C-1741 has yellow handrails and steps. It retained its original side grab irons and had round, rather than flat, hand grabs for the roof ladder. These kinds of minor variations are common, and are significant only in illustrating the B&O's somewhat casual adherence to standards and its corporate culture of tinkering. (Paul Dunn)

Lower Left: In the late 1940s, the Baltimore and Ohio Chicago Terminal Railroad used a number of former B&O K-1 cabooses for transfer and switching runs around Chicago. The B&OCT had a reputation for being somewhat independent-minded, spelling out the "and" along with adding "Co." The car shows a variation on the usual sway bracing, possibly because the Chicago Terminal handled long cuts of cars in territory where the slack could be severe. Bracing like this helped the carbody resist the "rocking" motion which was so hard on the sides. The man in the summer-white cap seems to be enjoying his respite. No doubt he is reading the B&OCT rule book, as reading anything but company material was forbidden. (Paul Dunn)

Upper Right: The photographer of this crew at Glencoe, Ohio around 1906 apparently was so pleased with the image that he turned it into a post card. The low-angle light and leafless trees suggest winter or early spring. In a classic pose, the conductor wears his gloves, holds the flag, and rests his right hand on the car as if to say "this may belong to the B&O Railroad, but it is *our* car." Note the split knuckle in the coupler, necessary for coupling to the cars which still had link and pin couplers at this late date. A dragging cable with links is draped over the tool box, and neither hand brake nor air brake are visible on this end. The diagonal sheathing on the end is a nineteenth century practice, and the men on the platform vividly show the reason for the bars over the windows. Without them, anyone standing on the platform when the slack ran in or out would end up at least partway through the window. (The B&O Railroad Historical Society Collection)

Middle Right: In 1934, the C-1145 was serviced by the carmen at Lorain, Ohio. Two years later and looking the worse for wear, it sits in Parkersburg, West Virginia, awaiting condemnation. The signs are everywhere: running and peeling paint, rotting car siding, and a cupola that looks like it has worked loose from too many hard raps on the hind end of coal drags. Clearly visible on the left is the curved extension added to the top of the original end railings. As built, the cars had low railings with an open center section to permit trainmen to pass from the caboose to an adjacent car. The low railing was hazardous, as harsh slack action could pitch a man right over the railing and onto the track. As cars received standard handrails, ladders, and roofwalks, they also got these flat steel railings extending all the way across the platform starting in September 1913. Note also the coil spring in place of the leaf (or elliptical) spring above the left journal box. Trainmen preferred leaf over coil springs because the former dampened much of the bounce, resulting in a much smoother ride. (S. P. Davidson)

Lower Right: As if to mirror the increasingly gloomy circumstances in which it operated, the C-1180 looks a little tired in this ca. 1929 view at the east end of Locust Point Yard in Baltimore. Wood cars such as this might be re-sided several times in their useful lives, and sometimes the shop or rip track doing the work might be somewhat indifferent to what it applied. This car has at least two different kinds of car siding: the common 3-inch tongue and groove car siding above and below the windows, and 5-inch "two-for" car siding similar to ordinary wainscot over the rest of the side. The 5-inch siding was milled as tongue and groove work also, but it had a "false" groove in the center resulting in the appearance of 2 1/2-inch wide T&G siding. (George F. Nixon, The B&O Railroad Historical Society Collection)

Left: Unlike locomotives, B&O cabooses carried notations of their "home places." In this fine photograph from the late Leonard Rice's collection, the C-754 has few secrets. This is a Locust Point car, most likely assigned to a terminal crew doing switching and terminal transfer work around the Baltimore Terminal. The service and repack dates of 2-26, combined with the fresh paint job, suggest the photograph was taken in 1926. The stencilled words "United States Safety Appliances" indicate to ICC inspectors and union men alike that the car complied with the various safety appliance laws, and that the crew could expect brakes and grab irons to be in appropriate places. The photo clearly shows the sway bracing on the end commonly applied to cars in need of a little stiffness. In the nineteenth century, cabooses required a tool box with a generous assortment of crude tools and spare parts because cars required more frequent repairs and there were dozens of coupler knuckle types in interchange service. In 1931, the railroad ordered the boxes removed and placed the needed tools and supplies inside the car in a locker beneath one of the bunks. (L. W. Rice, The Baltimore & Ohio Railroad Historical Society Collection)

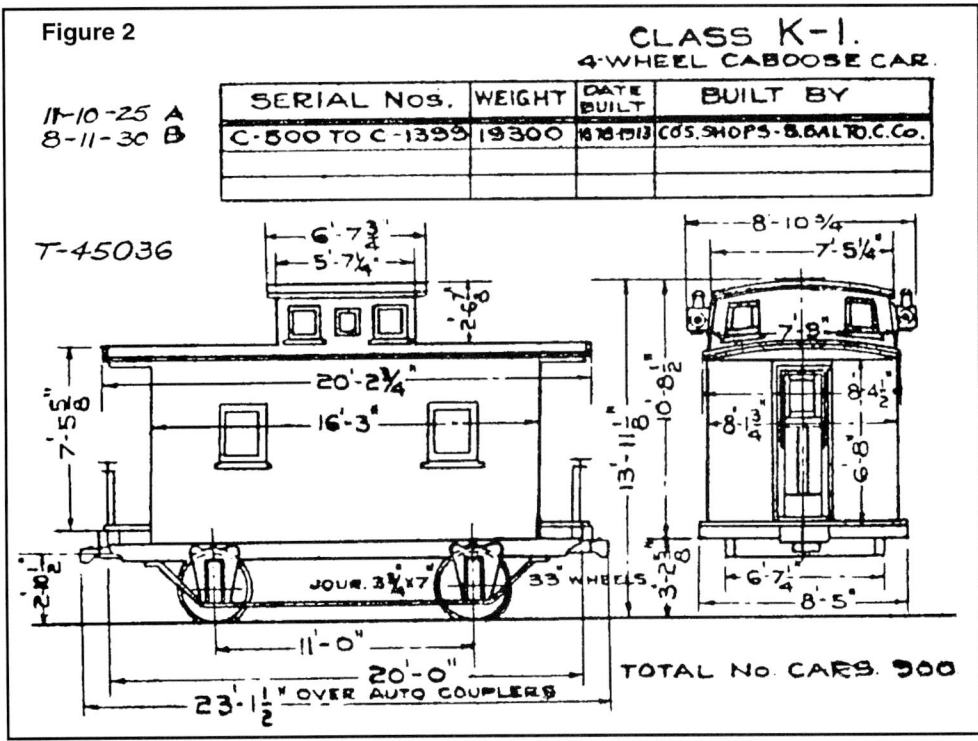

Lower Left: Shorn of its cupola and relegated to the far reaches of the railroad for service on the Staten Island Rapid Transit, the C-721 gamely soldiered on well after World War II. By then it had been considerably modernized, and remained adequate for terminal or branch line service. When used as transfer or local cabooses, the need to inspect the train in motion was less rigorous, hence the removal of the cupola. That alteration greatly increased the useable room inside the tiny car, which for all intents was a mobile office, lunch room, and passenger vehicle for terminal crews. Like the fast express engine demoted to work train service in its last years, cabooses were given less demanding assignments as they aged. (C. W. Abbott Collection)

Class I-1 Cabooses

Number Series   C-5 to C-399

In August 1913, the B&O shops released the first example of the new standard eight-wheel caboose, Class I-1. The car had a steel underframe, type K air brakes, and diamond arch bar trucks. To meet the requirements of the 1913 Ohio Caboose Law, the B&O designed a 30-foot car with a 24-foot, center cupola, wood body. The narrow end platforms had coach-type steps. The railroad built additional I-1 cars between August 1913 and April 1918. A good likeness of the Class I-1 as they appeared when new is the C-356 on page 38. Figure 3 shows the original clearance diagram for the Class I-1 caboose while Figure 4 is a later version of this diagram. Plans for the interior arrangements of the I-1 cabooses are shown in Figures 5 and 6.

With the exception of the steel underframe, the I-1s were constructed according to standard wood car practice of the day. Over the years, the railroad replaced the trucks under individual cars with newer types as they became available. The diamond arch bar truck was adequate for light duty such as a 35,000 lb. caboose, but each truck was fabricated of dozens of bars, bolts, castings, and parts which continually loosened and required maintenance. By substituting more durable AAR double truss trucks (derived from the three-part truck designed by William P. Bettendorf early in the twentieth century), the railroad reduced maintenance and the chance that a truck part would fail and cause injury or accident. The railroad also updated the safety appliances, air brake systems and couplers on the cars in response to the changing standards promulgated by the Association of American Railroads and the Interstate Commerce Commission. Usually, the railroad applied replacement trucks, exchanged the type D couplers for type E, and upgraded the air brake system from type K to AB in piecemeal fashion. As individual cars went in for refurbishing or wreck repair, or if a particular shop had the time and materials, cabooses received whatever modifications were needed or appropriate. The B&O removed the cupolas from some cars used in switching or terminal service. Others had their end platforms widened and the steps replaced with the vertical caboose steps used on the later Class I-5 cars. An example of such a modified caboose is the C-307 on page 39.

The first I-1 cars built received numbers between C-5 and C-137 filling gaps in the Class I number series. As the production of I-1 cabooses continued, the B&O assigned numbers in the C-142 through C-399 series, intended to be an extension of the Class I number series. The B&O sold several cars to subsidiary lines such as the B&O Chicago Terminal and the Alton Railroad.

Between about 1930 and 1960, individual Class I-1 cars showed wide variations in equipment according to what upgrades they had received at each major shopping. Especially on the B&O, the modernization of a class or fleet proceeded unevenly, according to resources available, local custom, opportunity, and the judgement of the mechanical department officer in charge. This view of the C-374 shows an altogether unremarkable I-1 of the late 1940s-early 1950s. After more than thirty years in service, the car retains a mix of old features (grab irons, narrow platform and wood steps, K brakes) and betterments (AAR double-truss trucks, E couplers, and possibly an oil stove). (Paul Dunn)

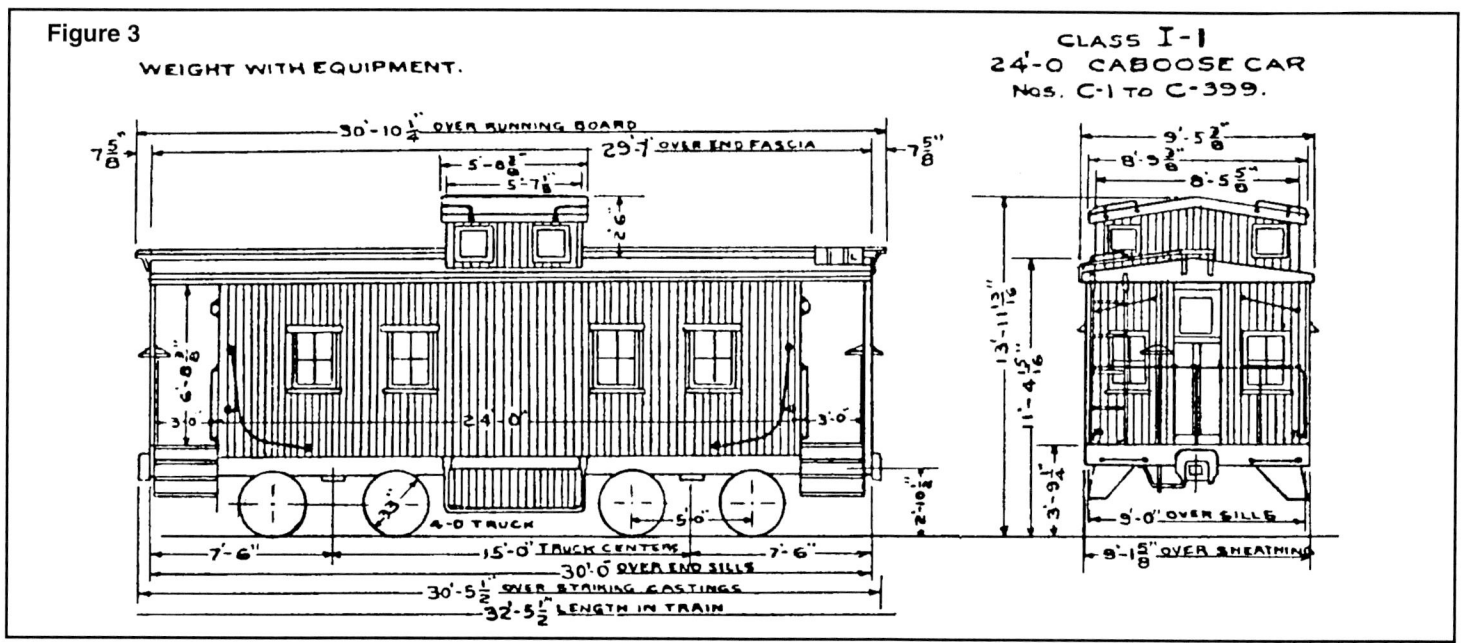

Figure 3

Figure 4

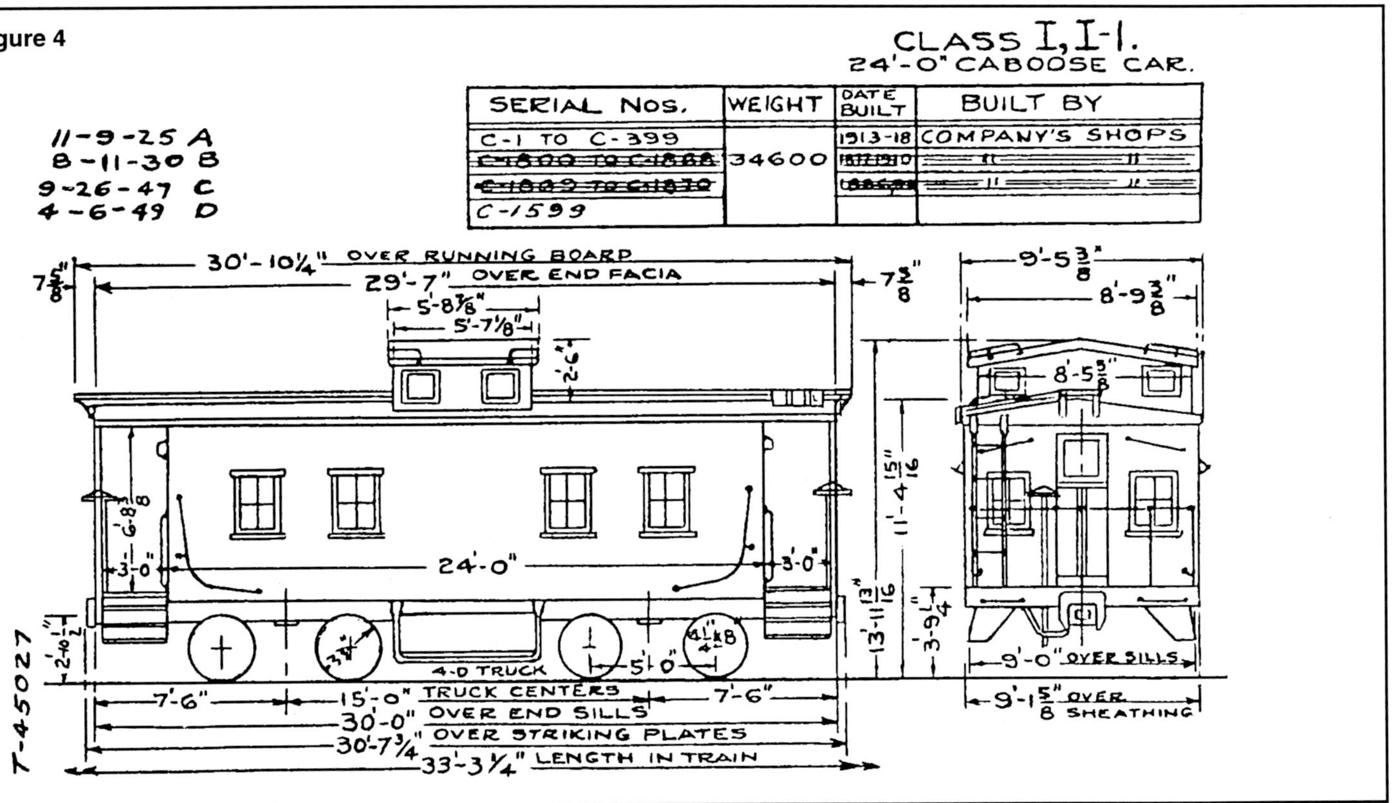

CLASS I, I-1.
24'-0" CABOOSE CAR.

SERIAL NOS.	WEIGHT	DATE BUILT	BUILT BY
C-1 TO C-399	34600	1913-18	COMPANY'S SHOPS
~~C-1800 TO C-1888~~		~~1977-1910~~	"
~~C-1889 TO C-1870~~		~~1886~~	"
C-1599			

11-9-25 A
8-11-30 B
9-26-47 C
4-6-49 D

T-45027

Upper Right: In their last years on the road, I-1s came to look very much like I-5s as they had platforms widened, new steps applied, and standard grab irons added. Partly, this improvement derived from an increasing awareness of "human engineering," or the principles of industrial engineering which apply to how workers actually use tools and move about the workplace. Having two nearly identical types of car with very different kinds of platforms could, and no doubt did, lead to accidents and injuries. One of the most tricky conditions for a working railroader to adjust to is the need to mount or dismount differing kinds of steps. Throughout the 1950s, the B&O tried to rationalize and standardize appliances such as caboose steps so that train crews would have an easier—and safer—time of it. The Andrews trucks beneath the C-372 are obsolete but functional, and ironically used parts from even older arch-bar trucks. (Julian W. Barnard, The B&O Railroad Historical Society Collection)

Figure 5

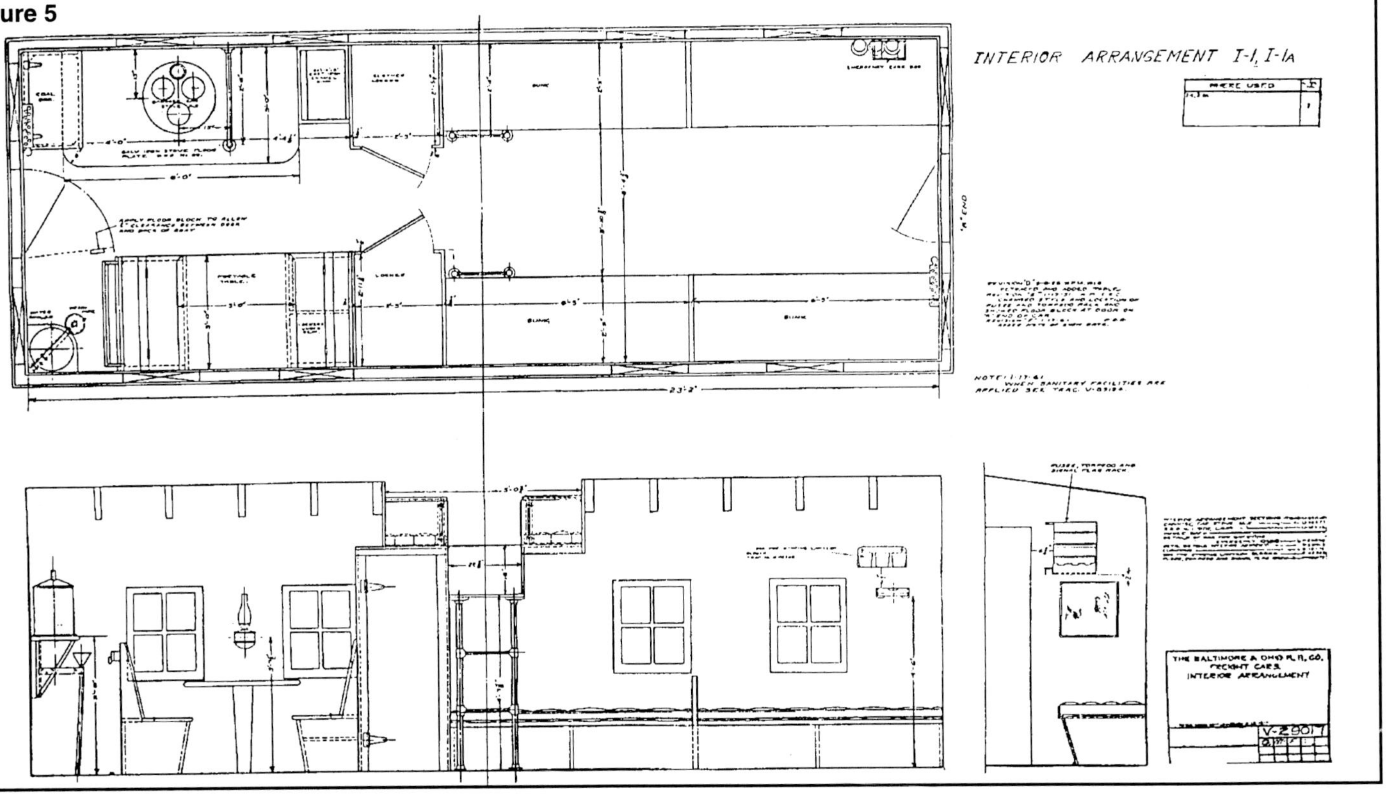

INTERIOR ARRANGEMENT I-1, I-1a

Middle Left: Although the basic design was sound, the B&O made the usual modifications and improvements to the I-1s. This September, 1954 view of C-189 at Cincinnati shows the more modern quarter-circle grab irons on the sides, an updated AB air brake system replacing the earlier K system, and replacement double-truss trucks probably salvaged from a freight car. Curiously, the car retains its "Air Brake" lettering in the lower right hand corner. Stencilling cars with air brakes was important in 1900, less so in 1916, and rarely needed after World War II. Note also that the car has been "distressed," probably by being derailed or hit hard in switching. The consequences are most visible in the gaps showing above the herald. Even though it had a substantial steel center sill, the car itself was framed and sheathed of wood. Even such composite cars flexed and "worked" when treated roughly. (Paul Dunn)

Figure 6

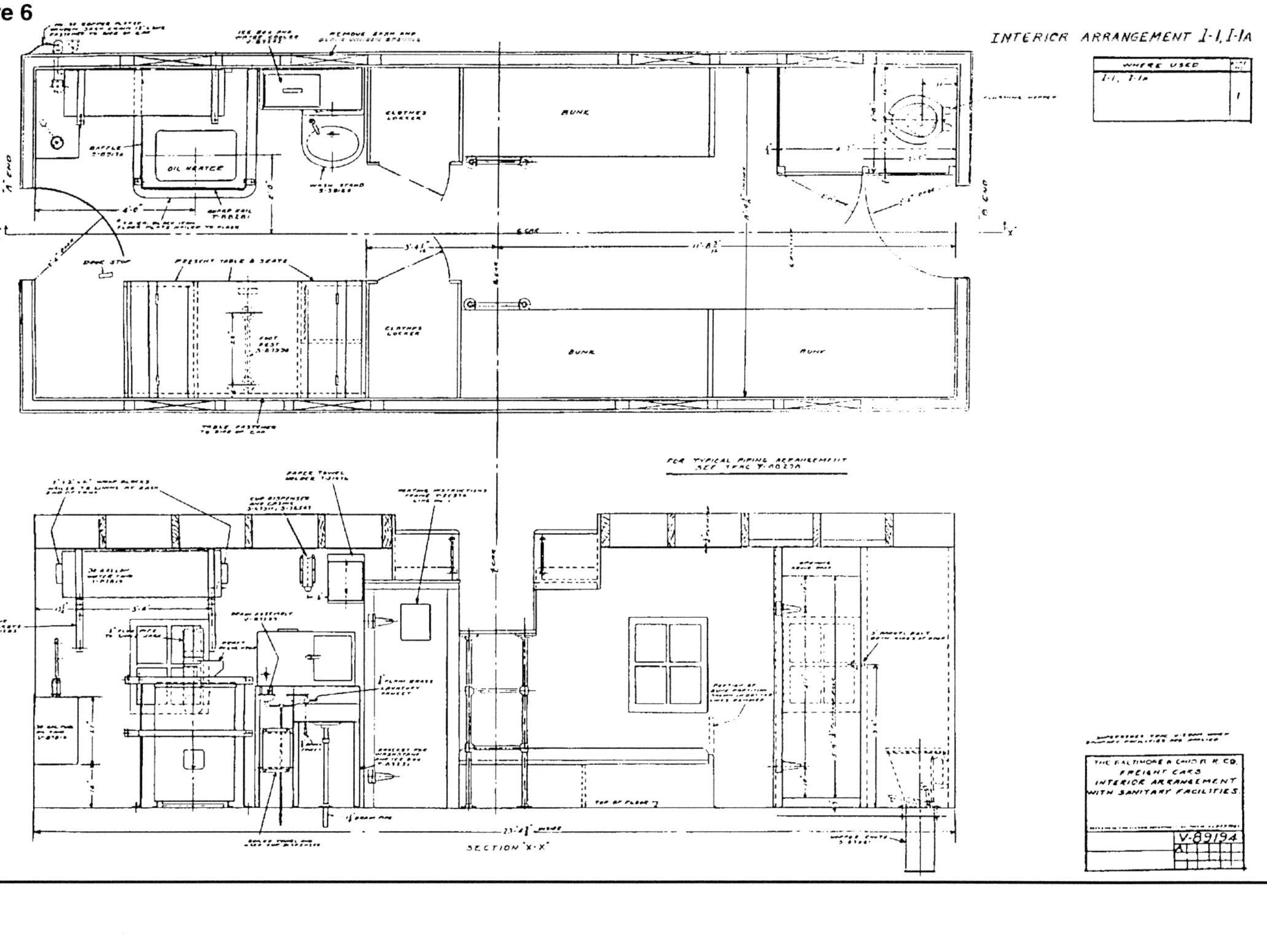

Left: An "Ohio Caboose Law" car rests at Hamilton, Ohio in August, 1921. The car exists substantially as-built, with fancy patent metal roof, arch-bar trucks, an early version of standard handrails and safety appliances (note the ladder to the roof), and 5-inch "two-for" car siding. The normal "working" of the wood structure on the C-356 has slightly opened the true tongue and groove seams, while the appearance of the false seams in the middle of the 5-inch boards remained unchanged. That resulted in the alternating pattern of wide seam-narrow seam visible in cars sided with that particular material. The arch-bar trucks were used primarily because cabooses were light, and the second-hand freight car trucks that the B&O most likely used were more than adequate for the service. The car was nonetheless modern for its day, as in the design of the wide, coach-style steps, steel underframe, and interior layout. (Dan Finfrock Collection)

Lower Left: Sideswipes are some of the most costly, common, and easily avoided accidents in railroading. Usually, no one gets seriously hurt, but the damage can be extensive. The C-220 at Dayton in November, 1957, shows the effects of a common terminal accident. One may speculate that the car was struck by a movement in the opposite direction on a converging track. Sometimes, the engineer would stop his train in a yard thinking or hoping that the rear of the train cleared the necessary switches. The conductor or hind end man had to eyeball the situation and judge. In this case, it would appear that the car simply did not make it into the clear in a leading-point movement, so that when something came through the same switch in a trailing point movement, it contacted the caboose lightly in the middle and with increasing contact and force as it reached the end of the car. Of course, the caboose could have been pulled past a fouling car, too, but the effect would have been the same. The little white sign on the end says "Handle With Care." (Dick Fullerton, Robert Hubler Collection)

Upper Left: The I-1 set the standard, at least on the B&O, for how a proper caboose should look. They were well-proportioned, aesthetically pleasing, and roomy, especially as compared with the K-1 or many of the mishmash Class I cabooses. C-275 is almost two decades old in this ca. 1935 shot. The folks who maintained it at Lorain, Ohio cared for the looks of their classic cabooses. Functionally, the pattern set by the I-1 was duplicated in slightly different form through the Class I-17 cars. In general outline, the I-5 was similar, differing in framing material (steel), construction details, and minor improvements in steps, windows, and so forth. In this shot, the I-5 coupled to the C-275 clearly shows its newer style of steps, arranged to maximize the available platform area, making mounting the car safer for the crew. (C. W. Abbott Collection)

Top Right: Like their four-wheel predecessors, I-1s occasionally lost their cupolas. The B&O removed cupolas for a number of reasons, but generally only on cabooses used in transfer, switching, or some other restricted service. A car without a cupola or bay window is nearly blind to the train ahead, requiring the crew to step out onto the platform for a good look. Nevertheless, at many locations the caboose functioned more as a local office, bunkhouse, passenger vehicle, and platform for backing movements than as a lookout for a long freight train. The C-242 is in service on the Monongah Division just after the end of World War II. With its original arch-bar trucks and truncated top, it looks more like a product of the nineteenth century than 1916. (Paul Dunn)

Middle Right: The durability of B&O cabooses may be inferred from this July, 1973 photograph of C-307 at Benwood, West Virginia. Relegated to work train service, equipped with a gas bottle for fuel, and neglected for twenty years, this car represents the bitter end for a successful class of equipment. We could dwell on the ignominy of a mainline caboose losing its cupola, being allowed to weather and peel, and finally wearing out and being burned for scrap. Instead, this car demonstrates the sound original engineering, and adequate construction and maintenance, all of which contributed to its long years of service. The I-1s were a useful, durable, versatile class of car, and the B&O got its money's worth. (Robert Hubler)

Lower Right: In 1940, the Baltimore & Ohio Chicago Terminal Railroad acquired six M-43 boxcars from the B&O and converted them into cabooses. One was the C-1895, shown at Whiting, Indiana on November 6, 1965. It was converted from M-43 boxcar 189268 (originally BR&P boxcar 4783). Some B&O Summaries of Equipment labeled these six cabooses as Class I-1s, but the car in this photograph clearly bears no resemblance to Class I-1 cars. (Eileen Wolford Barnard, The B&O Railroad Historical Society Collection)

A Mystery and Speculation

How Many Class I-1 cabooses did the B&O build?

Before the I-1 cabooses were built, the Class I occupied the number series C-1 to C-141. The first I-1 cabooses filled gaps in this series. Additional I-1 cabooses were assigned the numbers above C-141, eventually reaching C-399. The following numbers below C-141 were known to have been filled by I-1 cabooses: C-5, C-7, C-9, C-10, C-13, C-15, C-16, C-17, C-20, C-22, C-25, C-26, C-27, C-43, C-46, C-48, C-50, C-51, C-52, C-54, C-55, C-58, C-64, C-66, C-69, C-79, C-81, C-82, C-84, C-86, C-93, C-95, C-96, C-99, C-105, C-107, C-109, C-117, C-120, C-123, C-124, C-128, C-135, and C-137. This is a total of 44 cars. Note that there may have been other I-1 cabooses numbered below C-141 as well, but the numbers listed above are the only confirmed I-1 cars. If the numbers between C-142 and C-399 were completely filled, the B&O would have had an additional 258 cars, for a total of 302 Class I-1 cabooses.

AFE (Authorization For Expenditure) records found in the minutes of the B&O's Board of Directors' meetings do not answer the question. At their meeting on July 9, 1914, the Board approved the construction of 100 eight-wheel, steel underframe cabooses. On May 13, 1915, the Board approved the construction of an additional 100 eight-wheel, steel underframe cabooses. At their meeting on October 26, 1916, the Board approved the construction of 50 more eight-wheel, steel underframe cabooses, followed by a final 50 cars authorized by the board at their meeting on January 31, 1917. These four items would seem to indicate that only 300 Class I-1 cabooses were built by the B&O. If, in fact, only 300 Class I-1s were built and 44 of these were known to have been numbered below C-141, then there could have been only 256 Class I-1s numbered between C-142 and C-399. Since there are 258 numbers between C-142 and C-399, this meant that 2 numbers were left vacant. All this poses the somewhat esoteric question: which two numbers between C-142 and C-399 were unused, and why?

To further muddy the waters, B&O correspondence from the period indicates that 300 I-1s were built and charged to Capital Expenditures, while two replacement cars were built and charged to Operations. This brings the total back to 302 cars. However, during this era, replacement cars (which were new cars built specifically to replace cars destroyed in wrecks) were assigned the same numbers as the former cars they replaced. This would mean that, although 302 I-1 cabooses may have been built, only 300 numbers would have been applied to these cabooses. Thus our mystery could be stated as: How many Class I-1 cabooses were there and what numbers did they carry?

Class I-2 Cabooses

Number Series, First Group	C-1500 to C-1560
Number Series, Second Group	C-1561 to C-1570
Number Series, Third Group	C-1571

The B&O assigned the I-2 classification to three distinct groups of cabooses. The first and largest was a series of cars acquired with the Cincinnati Hamilton & Dayton Railway (CH&D). In 1917, the 61 cabooses remaining in CH&D series 1 through 143 were assigned to Class I-2 and given B&O numbers C-1500 through C-1560. CH&D 69 and 79 were retired before being renumbered to B&O C-1530 and C-1534, leaving at most 59 of these cars to have actually received their B&O numbers.

The second group of I-2 cabooses began as ten "poultry attendant cars" built by the B&O in February 1917. These were numbered X-4800 through X-4809 and were identical to the I-1 cabooses being built at that time. In 1920 these ten cars were reclassified as I-2 cabooses and renumbered to C-1561 through C-1570.

The third distinct type of Class I-2 caboose was former Morgantown & Kingwood (M&K) caboose 101. When the B&O absorbed the M&K, it assigned Class I-2 to this caboose and numbered it C-1571.

Figure 7 is the B&O clearance diagram for the Class I-2 equipment. The dimensions shown represent an end cupola caboose and, as such, probably match some of the CH&D cars which were assigned to the I-2 class. The second group of Class I-2 was identical to the Class I-1 cabooses and are described by that diagram. No record of the dimensions or equipment of the M&K caboose has been found. Like Classes K-1 and I, Class I-2 and I-3 appeared to be convenient designations for otherwise dissimilar or unclassified cars. With the application of subsequent class designations, the B&O became much more specific in the assignment of classes to specify the variations between cars.

Figure 7

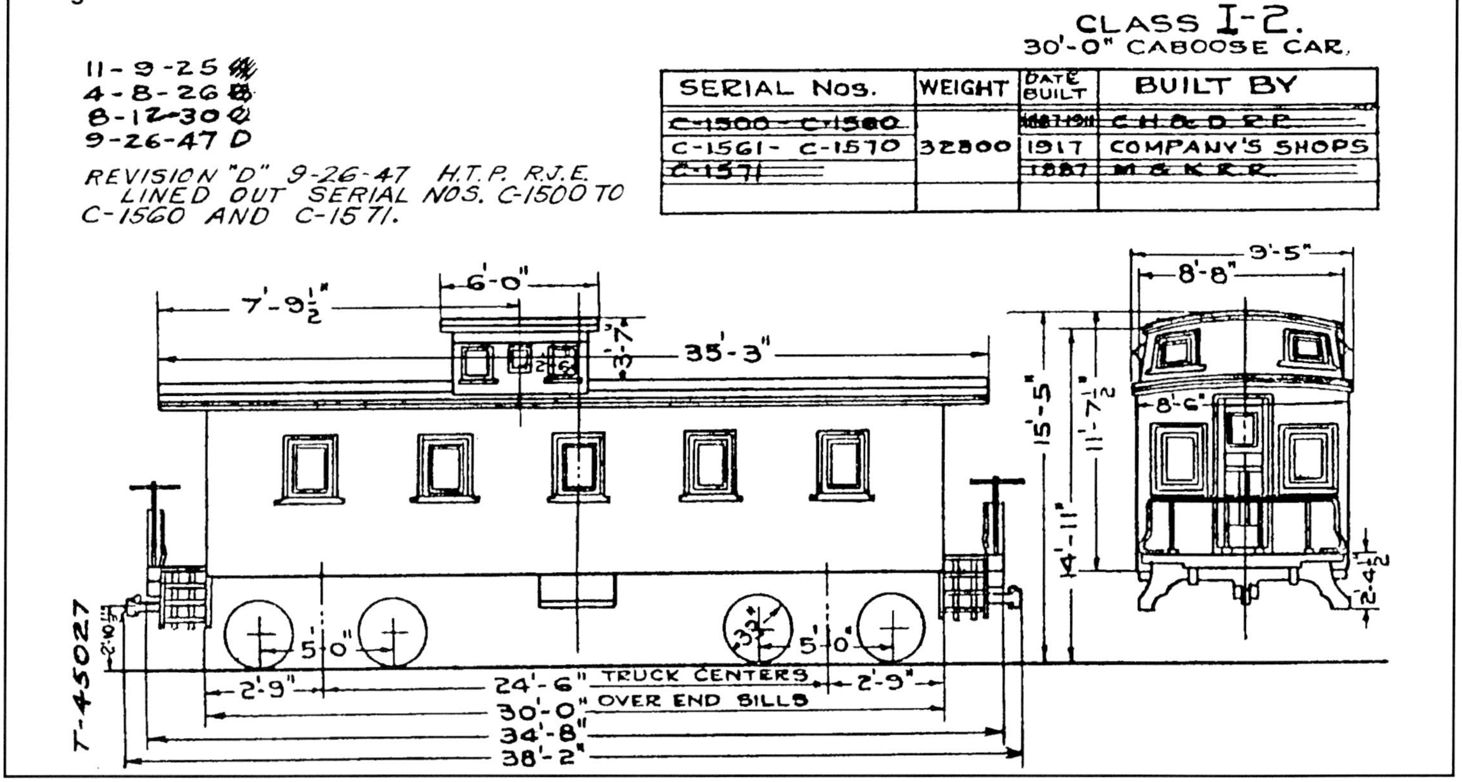

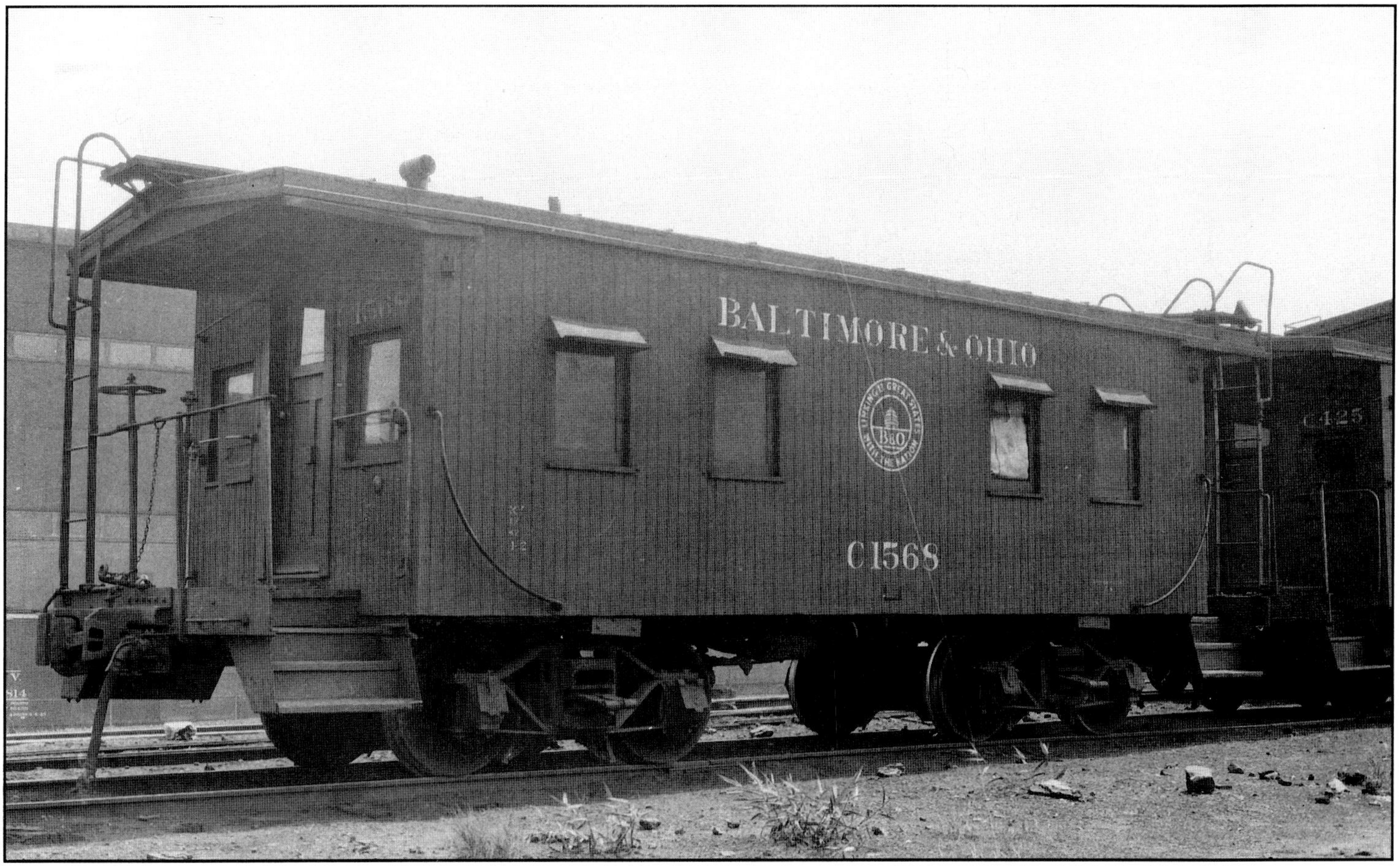

```
11-9-25
4-8-26
8-12-30
9-26-47 D
REVISION "D" 9-26-47 H.T.P. R.J.E.
   LINED OUT SERIAL NOS. C-1500 TO
   C-1560 AND C-1571.
```

CLASS I-2.
30'-0" CABOOSE CAR.

SERIAL NOS.	WEIGHT	DATE BUILT	BUILT BY
C-1500 – C-1560		1887-1911	C.H.&D. R.R.
C-1561 – C-1570	32800	1917	COMPANY'S SHOPS
C-1571		1887	M.&K. R.R.

T-45027

Above: B&O C-1568 was one of the second group of Class I-2s, renumbered from "poultry attendant cars." The appearance of the C-1568 suggests that these cars were identical to Class I-1 cabooses built at about the same time. All available photographs of this group show them without cupolas, but it is not known if they were built that way or if the cupolas were removed at a later date, as was the case with a number of I-1s. (Paul Dunn)

Above: This photo, taken from an old glass plate negative, shows Cincinnati Hamilton & Dayton caboose 92 just out of their shops at Dayton, Ohio, in March, 1911. It was renumbered to B&O I-2, C-1544. The side door, narrow end platforms, wide truck spacing, and end framing suggest that it was a conversion from an old boxcar. The car is also a nice illustration of how a few characteristic caboose features can be combined differently to produce a wide variety of cars, with strikingly different appearances. (Robert Hubler Collection)

Below: This very old photograph shows Cincinnati Hamilton & Dayton caboose 30 at an unrecorded location on July 18, 1905. It was renumbered to B&O C-1514 after the B&O acquired the CH&D, and represents the first and largest group of cabooses assigned the Class I-2. The majority of these CH&D cabooses were eight-wheel, all wood, end cupola cars. Apparently this particular car was built as a caboose rather than converted from an old boxcar, as were a number of other CH&D cabooses. (Dan Finfrock Collection).

Class I-3 Cabooses

Number Series, First Group   C-1600 to C-1614
Number Series, Second Group C-1615
Number Series, Third Group   C-1616

The railroad applied Class I-3 to three distinct groups of cars. The first group included cabooses acquired with the Cincinnati Hamilton & Dayton Railway (CH&D). In 1915 and 1916, the B&O built a total of 15 cabooses for the CH&D, then under B&O control. The railroad constructed the cars at its Washington, Indiana shops based on the B&O's Class I-1 cabooses also being built at this time. On the CH&D, they carried the numbers 150 to 164. Like the I-1, Class I-3 cars rode on arch bar trucks and had a narrow end platform with coach-type steps. When the B&O absorbed the CH&D in 1917, it assigned Class I-3 to the CH&D cars and numbered them C-1600 through C-1614. A good likeness of this group of cars as they appeared when they were new can be seen in the photograph of Class I-3 caboose C-1603 on page 44. Like the I-1, the I-3 cabooses had their arch bar trucks replaced with newer types over the years and many cars had their end platforms widened and the steps replaced with vertical type steps. An example of such a modified I-3 caboose is the C-1611 on page 44.

The second type of Class I-3 was B&O tool box car T-207 (ex-B&O Class V boxcar 76193, originally West Virginia & Pittsburgh boxcar 1382) renumbered to B&O C-1615 in March 1926. The third type of I-3 was former Dayton & Union (D&U) caboose 2. When the B&O absorbed the D&U, it assigned Class I-3 and number C-1616 to the car.

Figure 8 is a B&O clearance diagram for Class I-3 cabooses. The dimensions listed in the diagram do not match those of the first group of I-3 cabooses since these were identical to the dimensions of the I-1 cars. Perhaps, the diagram represents the dimensions of the C-1615 or the C-1616.

Right: This photograph of the C-1602, taken late in its career, illustrates the modifications which were made to the Class I-3 cars during their years of service on the B&O. The original arch bar trucks were replaced with AAR double truss trucks, the end platforms widened, and the vertical style steps added. Along with the application of more modern AB brakes and grab irons, the caboose had plywood sheets applied over the tongue and groove siding, suggesting what the cars might have looked like had the B&O built them of steel. (C. W. Abbott)

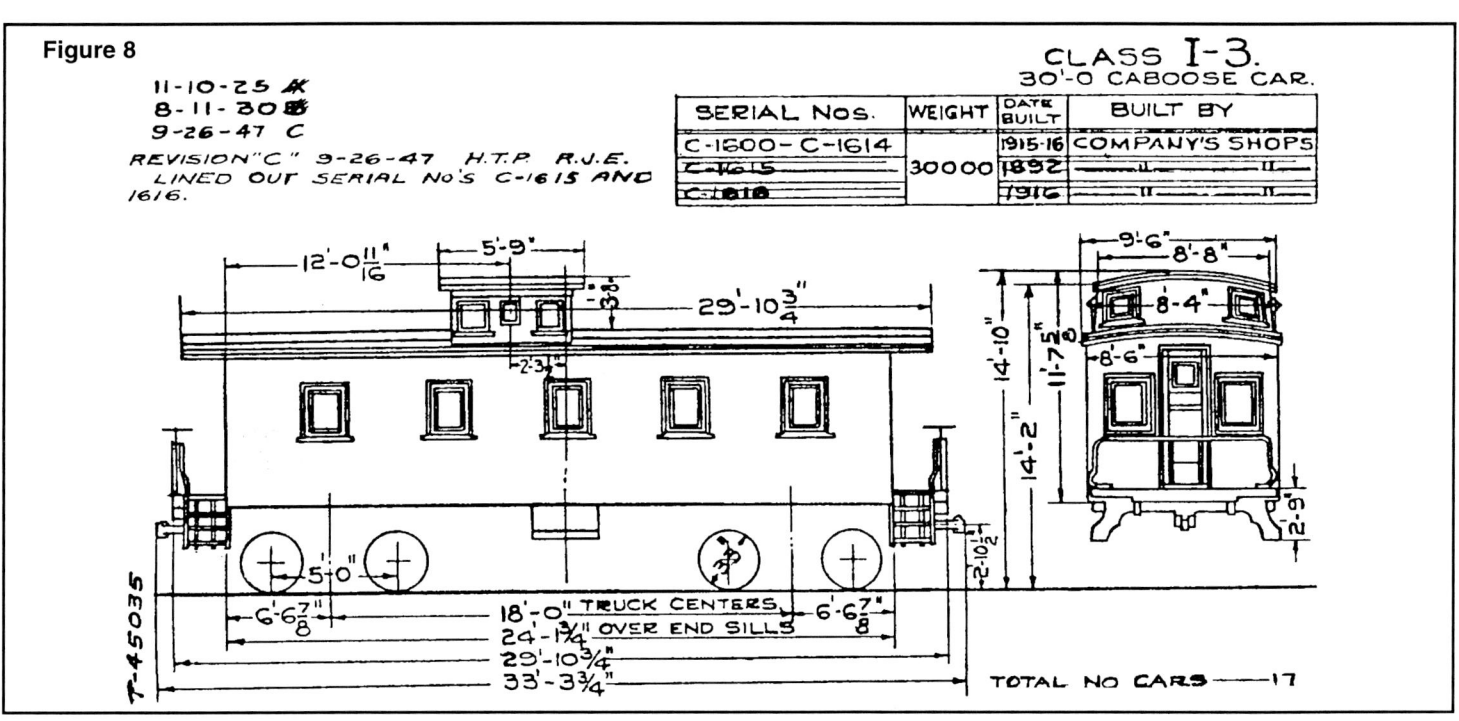

Figure 8

Above: Class I-3 caboose C-1611, at Newark, Ohio in 1959, was built as CH&D caboose 161 by the B&O at its Washington, Indiana Shops. This group of former CH&D cabooses was identical to the Class I-1 cars, and over the years received many of the same modifications. In the case of the C-1611, these included replacing the original arch bar trucks, widening the end platforms and applying the I-5 style vertical steps. In addition, the grab irons were updated and the K type air brakes replaced with AB air brakes. (Paul Dunn, Robert Hubler Collection)

Below: B&O C-1603 (formerly CH&D 153) was one of the largest group of cabooses assigned Class I-3. The cars were built by the B&O at the same time as the Class I-1 cabooses, and appear to have been identical with the I-1s. This photograph illustrates several of the cars' original characteristics, most prominently arch bar trucks and narrow end platforms with coach-type steps. The C-1603 was photographed at Youngstown, Ohio on April 28, 1946. (J. M. Gruber, The B&O Railroad Historical Society Collection)

Class C&C Cabooses

Number Series   C-1700 to C-1711

In 1918, the B&O took over the Coal & Coke (C&C) Railroad and acquired 12 cabooses numbered C&C 100 to 111. They were all wood, four-wheel, center cupola cars. The B&O renumbered them to C-1700 through C-1711, but did not assign a class under the B&O system, simply referring to them as C&C cabooses. Visually, Class C&C cars closely resembled Pennsylvania Railroad Class ND cabooses. The Coal & Coke purchased second hand locomotives and passenger cars from the PRR, but C&C historian Allen Clark's research for a forthcoming book indicates the C&C built its cabooses at its Gassaway, West Virginia shops. The characteristics of the C&C cabooses invite speculation that they were built from PRR plans, or that their design was influenced by PRR practice. This kind of technological diffusion was common in the railroad industry, and the distinct PRR "look" of the C&C cars could have resulted because the man in charge of the railroad's freight cars may have learned his craft on the Pennsylvania Railroad. The last Class C&C caboose was retired in 1954. No drawing of a C&C caboose has yet become available.

Left: Although the photograph is partially obscured, it still provides a good image of B&O caboose C-1703, the former Coal & Coke 103. The C&C cars were longer than the B&O's Class K-1 cabooses. Note that the C-1703 had interesting braces for the cupola and possibly retained the original Coal & Coke style ladders. Note also the long tie rods connecting the bottoms of the pedestals on each side. The four-wheel configuration generally required the maintenance of some semblance of alignment between the axles and the carbody. The car was photographed at Norton, West Virginia on December 8, 1940. (Lars Byrne Collection)

Below: B&O caboose C-1709 (former Coal & Coke caboose 109) lost its cupola over the years. Note also that the roof appears to have been peaked, rather than the arched-style of other C&C cabooses presented in this book. This photograph is undated but may be from the late 1940s or early 1950s, since the C-1709 carries the large "13-states" herald. (Paul Dunn, Robert Hubler Collection)

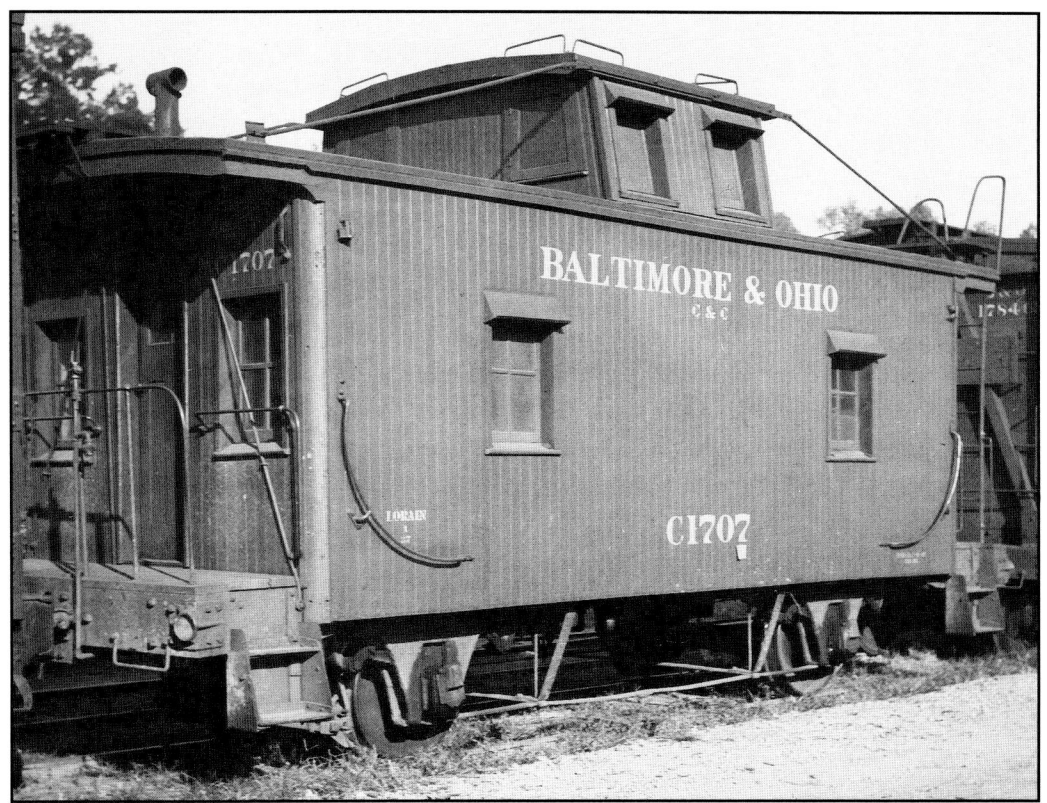

Left: This photograph provides an excellent view of B&O caboose C-1707 (former Coal & Coke 107). This well-lighted shot shows the end detail, as well as the wheel arrangement. Note the braces for the cupola. Students of cabooses will note that the Coal & Coke cars bore a strong resemblance to Pennsylvania Railroad Class ND cabooses. We know that the C&C purchased second hand locomotives and passenger cars from the Pennsylvania Railroad. However, the C&C cabooses were built at the Gassaway Shops. The C-1707 was photographed at Spencer, West Virginia on September 9, 1937. (S. P. Davidson)

Class M&K Cabooses

Number Series   C-1712 to C-1716

The B&O took over the Morgantown & Kingwood (M&K) Railroad in 1919 and acquired a group of five cabooses numbered M&K 102-106. They were all wood, four-wheel cabooses and were renumbered B&O C-1712 through C-1716. They were not assigned a class under the B&O system, but simply referred to as Class M&K cabooses. The last M&K caboose was retired in 1929. No diagram is known to exist. An overall photograph of the M&K's Sabraton, West Virginia shop complex shows the only image available of an M&K caboose.

Above: In 1916, the B&O company photographer recorded this view of the Morgantown and Kingwood Railroad's shops at Sabraton, West Virginia. Three years later, the B&O absorbed the M&K, and with it five ordinary wood four-wheel cabooses. They lasted ten years in B&O service but disappeared almost without a trace. This photograph shows what almost certainly was one of the five cars parked beside the engine house. It demonstrates both the fact that the caboose was common and regarded as "part of the landscape," and also the difficulties in finding data on cars which provided unremarkable service on small, obscure railroads a half-century previous. (Gary Schlerf Collection)

Class I-4 Caboose

First Number Series	C-2000
Second Number Series	C-1650

On July 24, 1920, the B&O's Mt. Clare shops released the one-of-a-kind I-4 caboose. This caboose was originally B&O Class M-8 boxcar 57110, built by the Michigan Peninsular Car Company of Detroit and placed in service on August 30, 1898. The railroad renumbered it to 87110 at Keyser, West Virginia on November 1, 1904. Mt. Clare rebuilt it into Class I-4 caboose C-2000 using a secondhand steel underframe. The car had end platforms, but no cupola or bay window. In 1925, the B&O renumbered it C-1650 to clear the series for increasing numbers of Class I-5 cabooses. The car suffered severe fire damage at Brunswick, Maryland on April 10, 1933, and as a result, the B&O scrapped it there in July 1933. Figure 9 is the clearance diagram for the Class I-4 caboose.

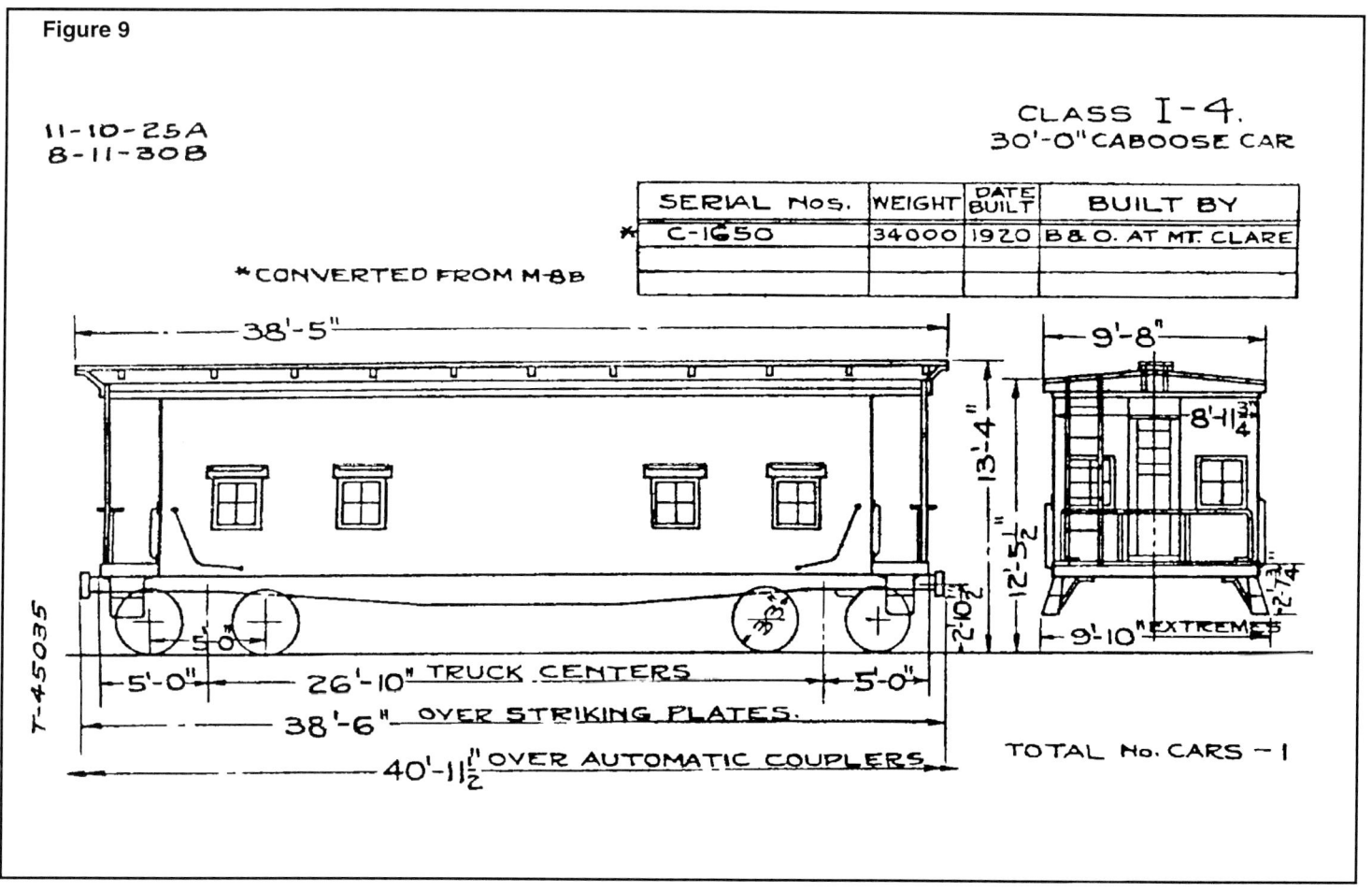

Class I-1A Cabooses

Number Series   C-400 to C-499 & C-1401 to C-1434

Between March 1922 and December 1923, the B&O built 134 additional eight-wheel steel underframe wooden cabooses in its shops. Numbered C-400 through C-499 and C-1401 through C-1434, the cars had carbodies externally identical to the earlier I-1 cabooses. Based on its experience with the Class I-1 cars and rapidly increasing in-train forces generated by larger locomotives, heavier cars, and longer trains, the B&O redesigned the center sills and assigned Class I-1A to this group of cars. By increasing the dimensions of the steel structural shapes used to form the center sill, the railroad produced a car better able to resist the buff forces created when helpers shoved on the rear of a train. Making the center sill as strong as the typical freight car of the day also lessened the chance of damage to the caboose if the car was placed between the locomotive and the rest of the train, as often occurred in switching moves.

Like their immediate predecessors, the I-1As were equipped with arch bar trucks and had a narrow end platform with stair type steps. The photograph of I-1A C-1425 on page 50 is an example of a car in nearly original condition. The B&O gradually modified cars in this class in the same fashion as I-1 cars, replacing trucks, couplers, platforms, safety appliances, and body elements as necessary. Despite the fact that the carbody was framed and sheathed in wood, many I-1 and I-1A cabooses remained in service for four or five decades—a remarkable performance in a time of increasingly rigorous service requirements and operating conditions. The railroad sold or transferred Class I-1A cabooses to subsidiary lines such as the B&O Chicago Terminal and the Alton Railroad. Figure 10 is the B&O's clearance diagram for the Class I-1A cabooses.

Figure 10

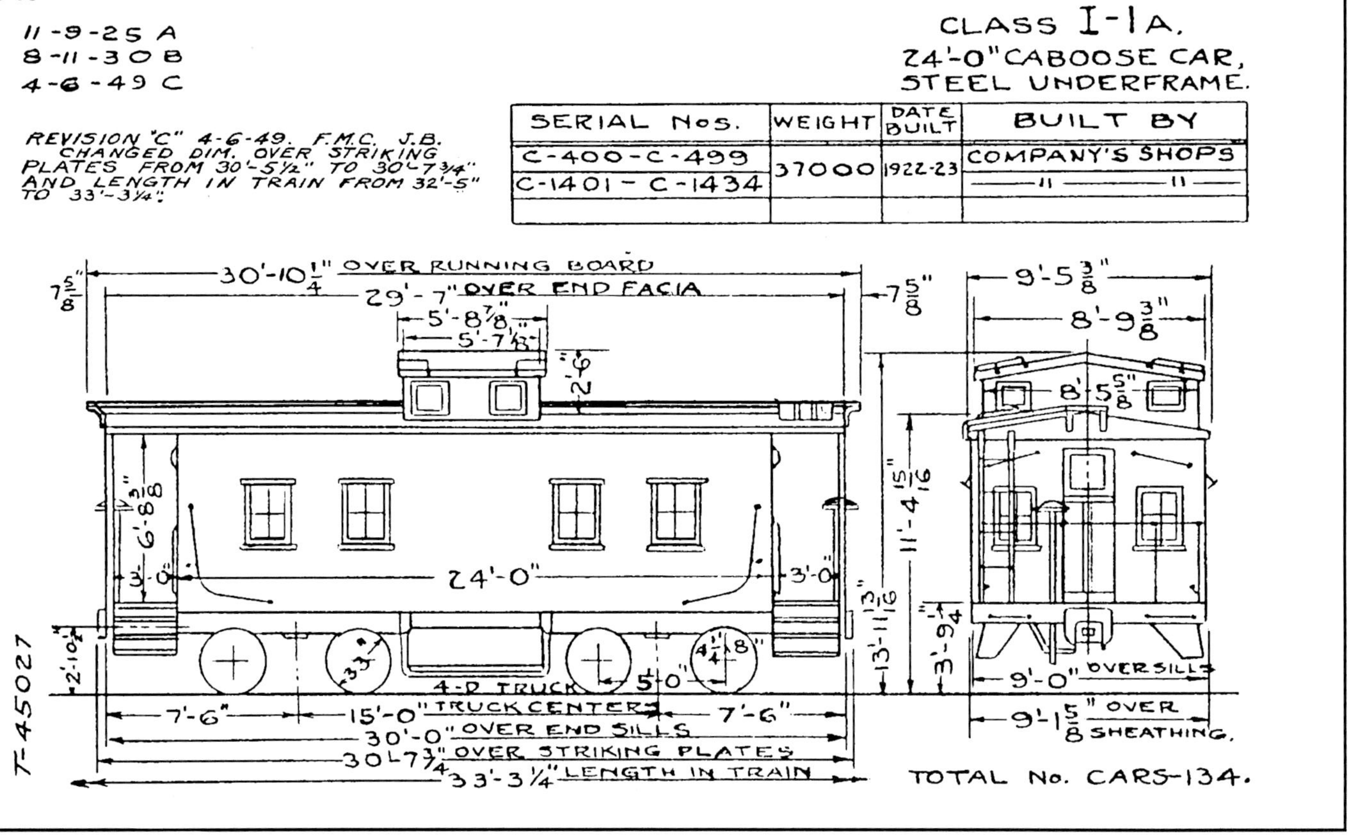

[Drawing: Class I-1A, 24'-0" Caboose Car, Steel Underframe. Drawing T-45027]

SERIAL NOS.	WEIGHT	DATE BUILT	BUILT BY
C-400 — C-499	37000	1922-23	COMPANY'S SHOPS
C-1401 — C-1434			" "

TOTAL NO. CARS — 134.

A Mystery and Speculation

What ever happened to B&O caboose C-1400?

Available records indicate that the B&O built 134 Class I-1A cabooses. They were numbered C-400 to C-499 and C-1401 to C-1434. The fact that the second group is numbered from C-1401 to C-1434 is unusual for two reasons. First, while some railroads routinely numbered blocks of equipment beginning with the number "1", this was not the usual B&O practice. The B&O generally numbered blocks of equipment beginning with the number "0". Second, it was unusual during this era to build a group of 34 cabooses (recall that the I-1 was apparently built in groups of 50 and 100 cars). It would have been much more typical if the second group consisted of 35 cars. To build only 34 was decidedly unusual.

The AFE (Authorization For Expenditure) information found in the minutes of the B&O's Board of Directors meetings indicated that at their meeting on December 14, 1920, the Board approved AFE C18103 covering the construction of 100 eight wheel, steel underframe cabooses. Then, at their meeting on May 29, 1923, the Board approved AFE C21628 covering the construction of **35** eight-wheel, steel underframe cabooses.

As a possible explanation, the author offers the following, unconfirmed speculation. The last I-1A (C-1434) was placed in service in December 1923, and the prototype I-5 (C-1900) was placed in service in January 1924. While the latter was a design based on the I-1A cars, surely it could not have been conceived and built in only one month's time. The I-5 must at least have been on the drawing boards while the last of the I-1A cabooses were being built. Also, the AFE for the prototype I-5 has not been found. This prompts the speculation that one caboose of the last order of I-1As was instead built as the prototype I-5. Perhaps the B&O intended to number the prototype I-5 C-1400, but changed it to C-1900 before the car was placed in service. We would welcome any additional information anyone can provide on the mystery of the missing C-1400.

Above: In later years, if the tongue and groove siding and side frames were sound but beginning to peel, rot, or come loose, the railroad would sheath the sides with plywood as an expedient. Although much more commonly done to Class I-5 cars, I-1A C-474, at Youngstown, Ohio on August 1, 1964 was thus modified. The car retains its original end platforms and steps. Note the two different types of trucks under the car; one end features the normal leaf spring truck while the other rides on a truck equipped with coil springs. (Eileen Wolford Barnard, The B&O Railroad Historical Society Collection)

Below: Class I-1A caboose C-490 has reached the end of its career on the B&O. This weary old caboose is seen sitting at Mt. Clare on June 12, 1965 in rather deteriorated condition. The narrow end platform and the coach type steps show up nicely in this view. While the caboose is lettered with the large "B&O" and the "13-states" herald, older lettering schemes are beginning to reappear through the well-worn paint. (Julian W. Barnard, The B&O Railroad Historical Society Collection)

Left: This beautiful shot of I-1A caboose C-1425, taken at Fostoria, Ohio, on August 30, 1945, shows many of the original features of this class, such as the steps, trucks and grab irons. The 1941 lettering scheme was the first to incorporate the capital dome emblem. (C. E. Helms, C. W. Abbott Collection)

Middle Left: This photograph of B&O Chicago Terminal I-1A caboose C-1906 illustrates the typical appearance of the I-1 and I-1A classes on the B&OCT. The C-1906 (formerly B&O I-1A C-1415) had its cupola removed, but retained the original end platform and step arrangement. The trucks and side grab irons were replacements, and the vertical post running from the end sill to the roof on the right side of each end was a modification found only on B&OCT cabooses. It was photographed at Whiting, Indiana on November 6, 1965. (Eileen Wolford Barnard, The B&O Railroad Historical Society Collection)

Lower Left: In July, 1966, Class I-1A C-1402 was found in Zanesville, Ohio. The caboose is typical of the I-1A cars which survived until this time. Its appearance is representative of the final configuration of this class. Specifically, the B&O replaced the original arch bar trucks with a more modern AAR double truss type, widened the end platforms, and applied vertical steps. The tool box had long since been removed, the brake system upgraded, and the original grab irons replaced with more current types. (Paul Dunn, Robert Hubler Collection)

Class I-5 Cabooses

Number Series　　　　　　　C-1900 to C-2299

In 1924, having revised the Class I-1 design, the B&O produced the first Class I-5. Internally, the carbody had steel framing as opposed to the wooden framing of the earlier Class I-1. Externally, the ends of the car were steel instead of wood and the cupola sides were slanted instead of straight. This book's endpapers present B&O diagrams of the framing and dimensions of the body and the original interior arrangement for the I-5. The basic carbody dimensions were the same as the earlier Class I-1, although the cupola was bigger. The I-5 cabooses were built with full-width end platforms and vertical steps, an arrangement later applied to a number of Class I-1, I-1A and I-3 cabooses. C-1900, the prototype I-5 caboose, was outshopped from Mt. Clare in January 1924. The Washington, Indiana car shops built the remaining cars in four groups of 100 cars each between 1925 and 1929. The Class I-5 was the second largest group of B&O cabooses; only the K-1 was built in larger numbers.

When new, the I-5 had a large tool box under the car between the trucks. All B&O cabooses were equipped with tool boxes until 1930 when they were ordered removed as the equipment went through the shops. Figure 11 is the clearance diagram for the Class I-5.

The I-1 and I-5 classes together represent the transition between traditional all-wood carbuilding and the modern steel car era on the B&O. The I-5 was a true composite car, combining essential elements of steel and wood car building techniques. It derived its structure from a sturdy riveted box-section center sill and heavy angle-section steel body truss. The steel ends provided stiffness and a greater measure of collision resistance than earlier cars. Partly to lessen first cost, partly from established practice, and partly because wood bodies were easy to repair and provided good insulation in summer and winter, the B&O completed the steel body truss with wood framing and sheathing. Thus the cars possessed both the advantages and disadvantages of the two types of construction, but they were durable, functional, long-lasting cars modified in dozens of ways over their five decades of use. In 1994, the B&O Railroad Museum acquired Class I-5 cars C-2024 and C-2204 for its collection.

Right: By the 1920s, the caboose had been in common use on the B&O for at least sixty years, and had evolved into a somewhat determinant form, with little or no room for improvement in the basic arrangement and type of parts. The government had prescribed safety features on cabooses since 1893, and these cars incorporated the latest standards. Some features may seem archaic—arch-bar trucks, kerosene lamps, the coal stove, the wood tool box—and may indeed represent a kind of technological inertia or tradition. On the other hand, they were current practice in the 1920s, and comprise the features most likely to be upgraded as those technologies advanced. Note especially the details of the caboose as a tool to be used by railroaders. A combination of long experience, federal standards, advice from trainmen and their unions, and an increased concern with worker safety resulted in many subtle features which made it much easier and safer to work aboard an I-5 caboose. The steps are wide, low to the ground, and faced with wood for surer footing; the slots permit snow and ice to blow or be kicked through the back as a man mounts the car. Full-width platforms provide a larger, safer area to stand. The grab irons are where the men need them to be, and the photograph clearly shows little details like the reverse curve to give a gloved hand more clearance at the bottom of the grab iron on the carbody end. End railings are high, the end windows high up and small, and the stem brake, cut lever chain, back-up whistle, and emergency valve are located where a trainman may efficiently and safely reach them. Even in the twentieth century, train service was a hazardous occupation, and well-designed equipment made a trainman's job easier and increased the chances of his remaining in one piece. (The B&O Railroad Museum Collection)

Figure 11

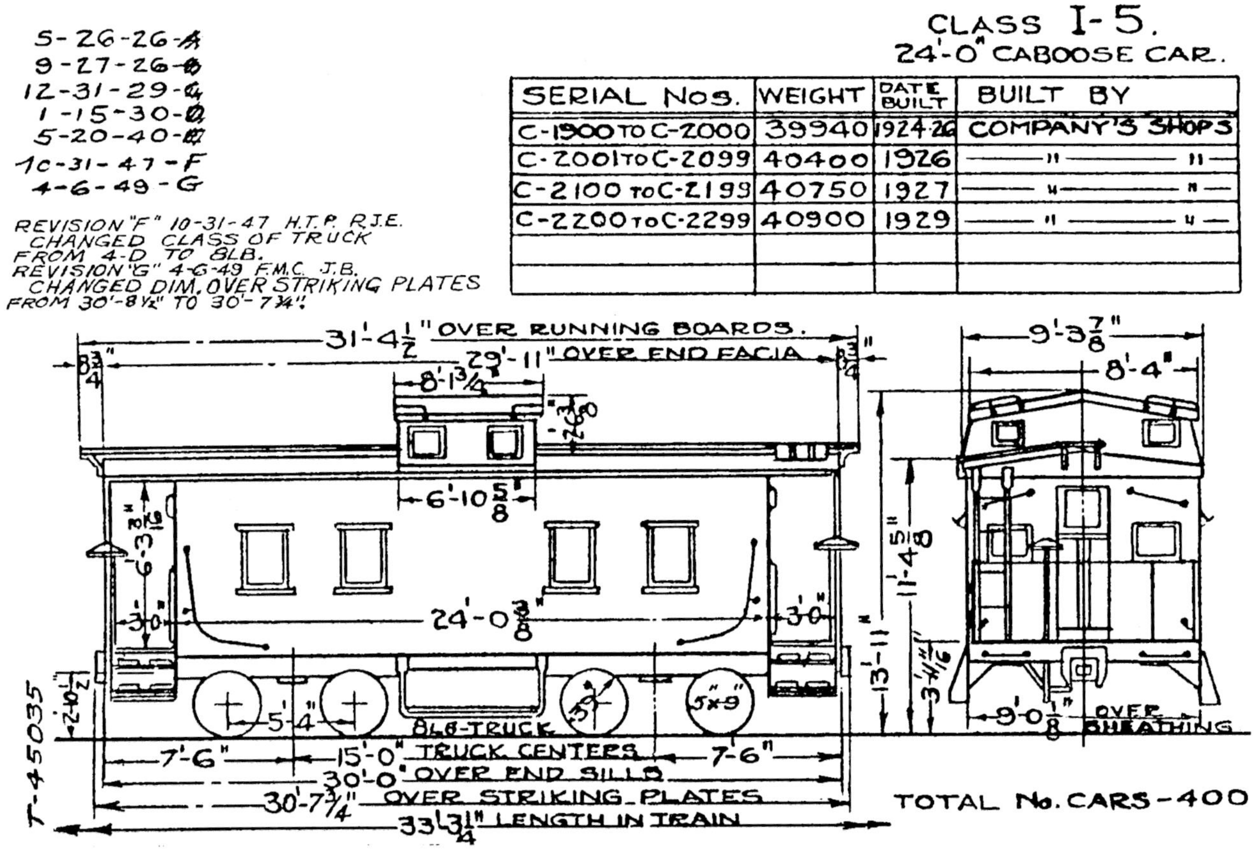

SERIAL Nos.	WEIGHT	DATE BUILT	BUILT BY
C-1900 TO C-2000	39940	1924-26	COMPANY'S SHOPS
C-2001 TO C-2099	40400	1926	" "
C-2100 TO C-2199	40750	1927	" "
C-2200 TO C-2299	40900	1929	" "

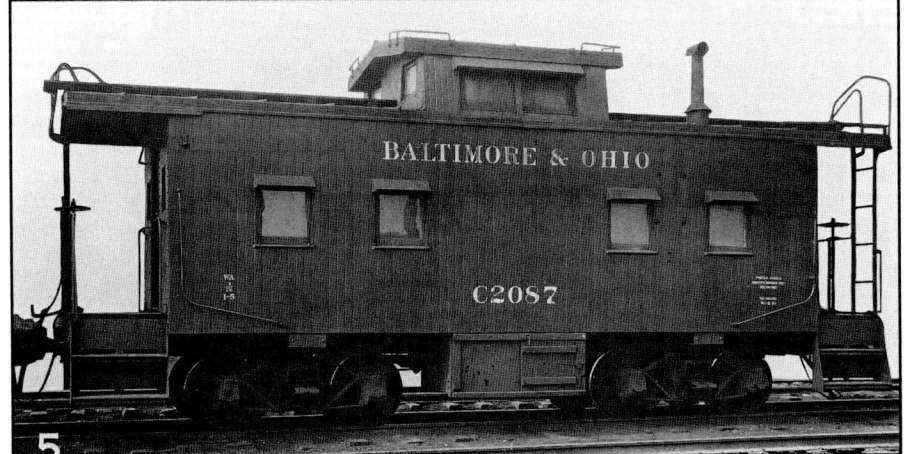

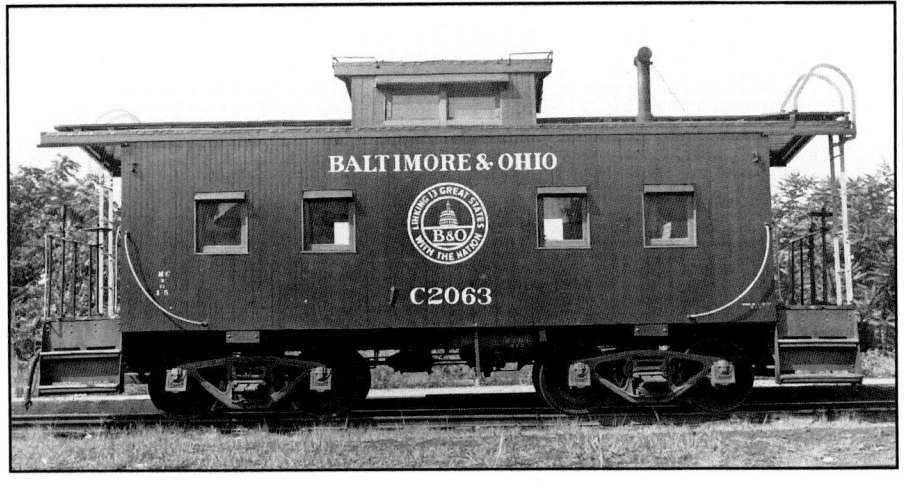

Middle Left: Like many freight cars of the period, the I-5s were composite cars with a sturdy riveted steel box-section center sill, body trusses of heavy angle sections, and rigid plate steel ends, making a relatively light weight but stiff carbody. The metal skeleton was augmented with oak ribs, purlines, auxiliary framing, and standard car siding and trim of poplar, pine, or other easily worked wood. The B&O built them at the very end of the wood car era, when the railroad still had an immense capital and labor investment in wood technology and tens of thousands of cars with a substantial wood content. This construction had the advantages of being cheap, easy to repair with common materials, and reasonably durable, while still proving to be strong and rigid enough for the most rigorous main line service. Wood also made sense because it was a good insulator. Early experience with metal cars suggested that steel cabooses were much hotter in summer and colder in winter than similar wood cars. The C-2087 is almost new in this photograph, and exhibits typical features of the first groups of production cars. (The B&O Railroad Historical Society Collection)

Above: The company photographer recorded the prototype I-5 as it sat outside the Passenger Car Shop at Mt. Clare on January 28, 1924. The Erecting Shop in the background occupied part of the site of the nineteenth century Freight Car Roundhouse in which so many K-1 cabooses were built. Anticipating a substantial production run, the B&O used and tested this car for over a year before commencing mass-production of the class at Washington, Indiana. As it was a near copy of the Class I-1, few modifications were found necessary. Production cars had their side windows slightly lower, slotted step backs to reduce the build-up of ice and snow, slightly different fascia and other body details, and minor mechanical variations (see the photograph of C-2087 on page 52 for comparsion). Most importantly, the steel frame, wide platform, and full complement of safety appliances proved to be a durable, successful design. (The B&O Railroad Museum Collection)

Lower Right After four decades of service, the C-2282 exhibited the common complaints of elderly wood cars. Even though its structure may have been perfectly sound, years of sun and rain weathered and rotted at least some of the siding and trim, making the car shabby in appearance and a high-maintenance piece of equipment. In cases like these, the car foreman might decide to re-side the car in kind, or he might sheath the car with plywood as an expedient measure. By now, the car was drafty and probably drab and dirty on the inside, and a crew would not have been overjoyed to be assigned to this particular caboose. Nevertheless, to the man approaching the car as it stands at Willard, Ohio on this cold, snowy day in March, 1965, the main question would have revolved around heat. Even a worn caboose with a good stove and a low fire is a cozy place to be, while a damp, frigid caboose can feel like one of the coldest and most forsaken places on earth. (Julian W. Barnard, The B&O Railroad Historical Society Collection)

Lower Left: After a quarter century of hard service, C-2063 represents the classic I-5 configuration most familiar to modelers, post-World War II railroaders, and the public expecting a "little red caboose." Leaf-spring Bettendorf caboose trucks have replaced the original arch-bar sets, and the K type air brake has given way to the newer AB brake with improved features. The quarter-circle grab irons on the outside corners become even more distinctive when painted yellow. They are a typical caboose modification, although the B&O tolerated all kinds of minor variations so long as they met the ICC safety standards. In bright red with white lettering, yellow safety appliances, and green trim, the car epitomizes traditional B&O railroading in its last period of prosperity before C&O affiliation in 1962. Photographed at Frederick, Maryland on July 8, 1951. (L. W. Rice, John R. King, Jr. Collection)

Below: The 1960s were a kind of "Indian Summer" for the B&O, a final expression of traditional corporate culture and independence before its 1973 assimilation into the Chessie System. The C-2204, at Dayton in 1960, typified the B&O of steam locomotives and first generation road units. The car carried coal for fuel, oil for light, Devil's Red paint, and operated in an environment of whistle signals from the head end and towers twenty miles apart on the main line. As the rest of the world underwent tumultuous change in the next ten years, the B&O changed, too. By the early 1970s, the Mechanical Department had moved to Huntington, West Virginia; pooled cabooses were being painted yellow and blue; the B&O had built its last main line cabooses, and purchased a wholly new type from an outside car builder; new technologies were revolutionizing railroad operations; and the end was clearly near for any remaining wood cars. However, the C-2204 was not to suffer the fate of most of its kind., It survived its retirement from the B&O in private hands and was donated to the B&O Railroad Museum in August 1994. (Dick Fullerton, Robert Hubler Collection)

Middle Left: This nearly broadside view of the Class I-5 C-1952 illustrates one of the most prominent features of the Class I-5 cabooses; the relatively short 15-foot distance between the truck centers, and the resulting overhang at each end of the caboose. Comparing this photograph with that of Class I-5C C-1949 on page 61 illustrates the increased distance between the trucks, which was one of the major distinguishing features of the I-5C and I-5D cabooses. (Robert Hubler)

Lower Left: The C-2064 was one of the last wood cabooses in service on the B&O when this photograph was taken in Baltimore on September 2, 1979. The "R" behind the number indicates that the car is in restricted service, in this case as a terminal transfer caboose. Usually the "R" was followed by the words "age," "coupler," "yoke," and "trucks," indicating the reasons for the restriction. The dark rectangle of the "consolidation stencil" lists required pertinent data on the car—weight, air brake dates, clearances, and so forth. In spite of the seemingly few modifications, the car may have only a fraction of its original fabric, having received new trucks, brakes, siding, roof parts, and possibly interior wood throughout its 53 years in service. In their last years, they were disliked by the crews, no longer regarded as rolling billboards for the company, and especially prone to vandalism and fires. Many of the last wood cars ended up in Brunswick, Maryland at what had been the last system wood car shop. They were burned and scrapped by the same men who had rebuilt them many times. Ten years after this photograph, even the Brunswick car shop had been erased from the earth. (Robert Hubler)

Above: At some point, the B&O blanked the window behind the stove of C-2245, creating a relatively rare 7-window Class I-5. The only other known examples of unmodified I-5s with 7 windows are C-2204 and C-2293. This is just another example of the railroad's penchant for modification. The C-2245's unique combination of red paint, Chessie-style sans-serif "B&O," and 1960s herald exemplify a time when most wood B&O cabooses had their own unique attributes. Most of its sister cars had been converted to I-5C or I-5D cabooses, with widely varying combinations of lettering and paint, window arrangements, sheathing variations, radios, oil stoves, and furnishings. While it looked good here at Chillicothe, Ohio on Independence Day, 1974, the C-2245 appears doomed. Perhaps it had to do with the recent arrival of the new Class C-26 cabooses, or maybe it had thin wheels, worn draft gear, or no use as a terminal or branch line caboose in that particular region. Whatever the proximate cause, it carried the grammatically incorrect but dreaded stencil "Hold for Dismantle," along with the car foreman's initials and the date of condemnation. The stencil noted that the appropriate form has been made, and sternly admonished "Do Not Load," for once a car was marked for disposal, it was no longer part of the fleet. However, this caboose was saved and is privately owned in Tobosco, Ohio. (Robert Hubler)

A Mystery and Speculation

How many Class I-5 cabooses did the B&O build?

ANSWER: They built 401, but used only 400 numbers for them. The prototype I-5 (C-1900) was released from Mt. Clare in January 1924. Then, from 1925 to 1929, the B&O built four groups of I-5 cabooses at Washington, Indiana. Each group consisted of 100 cars, thus making a total of 401 Class I-5 cabooses. The first group, built under AFE C24559, was placed in service between November, 1925 and February, 1926 carrying the numbers C-1901 to C-2000. The second group was built under AFE C26932 and went into service between July, 1926 and September, 1926 with the numbers C-2001 to C-2100. The third group, built under AFE C28528, was placed in service between April, 1927 and June, 1927 and supposedly carried the numbers C-2100 to C-2199. The fourth and last group, built under AFE C32664, came into service between August and November, 1929, and carried the numbers C-2200 to C-2299. Note the obvious conflict in that both the second and third groups supposedly included a caboose numbered C-2100.

Now, digging a little deeper into this, it seems that the first I-5 caboose to be retired was the C-2094. Company records show that the C-2094 was destroyed in a wreck at Swan Creek, Maryland on October 4, 1926, less than one month after it was completed and placed in service. In spite of this, a caboose numbered C-2094 continued to appear in B&O records up through the 1960s, and photographs of the C-2094 have been found dated as late as 1967. This suggests the obvious conclusion that the third order of I-5 cabooses was really numbered C-2094 (2nd) and C-2101 to C-2199. Perhaps this was one last instance of the B&O following the ancient practice of building "replacement" cars for equipment destroyed in wrecks. Of course, one other explanation is possible (but far less likely because it is so much more complicated). Perhaps the C-2100 (1st) was renumbered to C-2094 (2nd) and the third order of I-5s really was numbered C-2100 (2nd) and C-2101 to C-2199.

Class I-5A Caboose

Number Series   C-2501

The I-5A was the first wagon top caboose, built as an experimental car in early 1936. Like the C-2500 of five years earlier, the railroad used parts from a damaged cupola caboose. Class I-1A C-419 was heavily damaged by fire at Willard, Ohio on July 8, 1933, and eventually moved to Mt. Clare. Its body was scrapped, but the center sill and other hardware was used as the basis for a radically different form of caboose designed by the B&O's Superintendent of the Car Department, John J. Tatum. When Mt. Clare released C-2501, the car was unlike anything else in the B&O caboose fleet or any other railroad's fleet. (See J. J. Tatum Sidebar on page 59)

Photographs show that the B&O modified C-2501 later in its career by increasing the distance between the truck centers from 15 to 19 feet and making minor alterations to the body and interior. When the railroad changed truck centers on I-5 and I-5B cabooses, it reclassified them. That was not done for the modified C-2501, probably because it was the only car in its class. No doubt the B&O had good reasons, but available evidence does not reveal why the railroad created one new steel caboose from the frame of an I-5 and assigned a new class (I-7), then created another new steel caboose on the frame of an I-1A and designated the resulting car as an I-5 sub-class (I-5A). Figure 12 is the clearance diagram for the Class I-5A caboose showing it with 15-foot truck centers. The C-2501 was dismantled at DuBois, Pennsylvania in June 1968.

Above: In the depths of the Great Depression, President Roosevelt labored mightily to "get America working again." John J. Tatum, a longtime veteran of the B&O's Mechanical Department and head of freight car design, took the admonition seriously and created a series of novel designs for an entire fleet of equipment. The company had an ancient, but effective, steel rolling mill at Cumberland as part of the Cumberland Bolt and Forge Shop; it had scrap steel lying all over the railroad; it needed new cars of all types, especially if prosperity returned; and thousands of B&O men and women had been furloughed. The C-2501 was one solution to all of those problems. It was the prototype "Wagon Top" caboose, built at Mt. Clare on the steel underframe of an I-1A caboose. "Bolt and Forge" rolled the ribs and structural shapes, and possibly the sheets. Except for proprietary items such as trucks, couplers, air brakes, and small parts, the entire car was homemade of essentially found materials, demonstrating that the company could keep the work "in house" and recycle material on hand. Posed for its official portrait in November, 1935 just west of Carey Street at Mt. Clare, the C-2501's distinguishing features are its 15-foot truck centers (a legacy of the I-1A frame), outward facing brake wheels, and the angled side sill at the bottom. (The B&O Railroad Museum Collection)

Figure 12

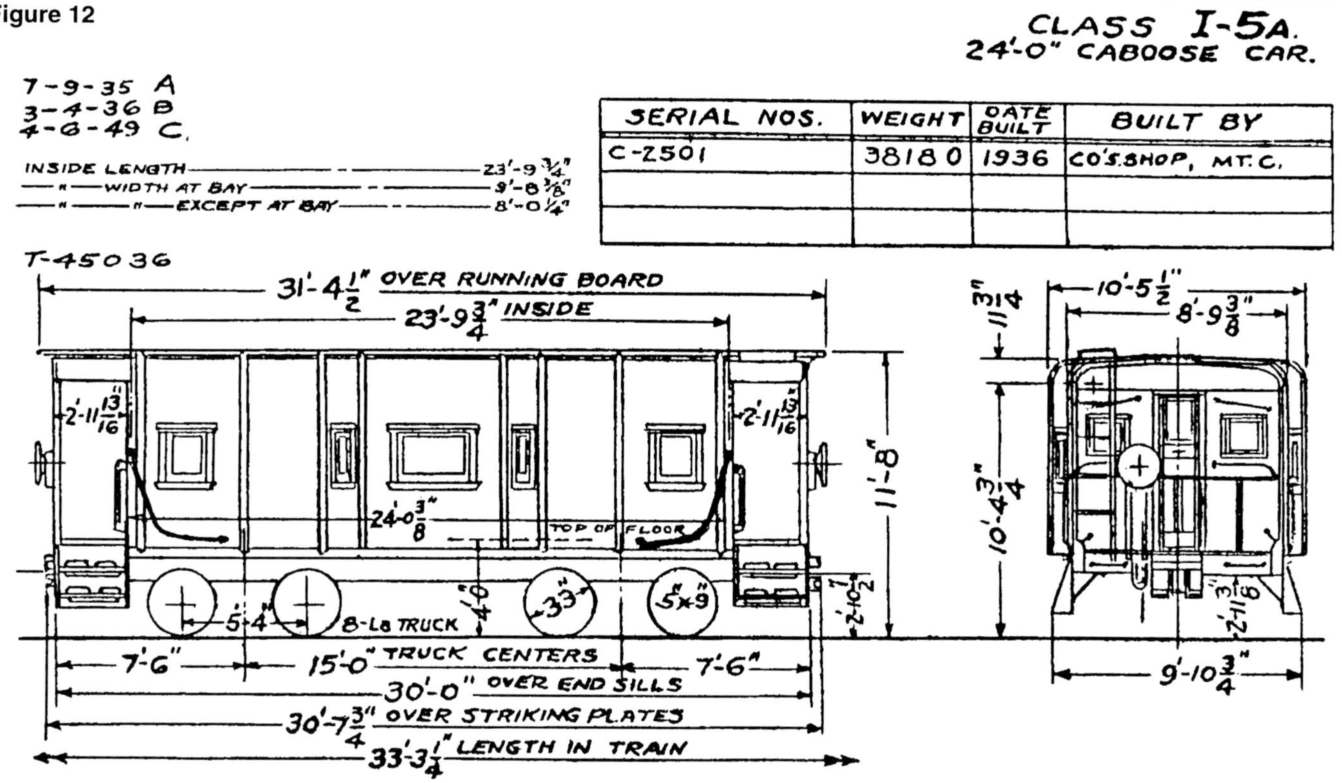

CLASS I-5A.
24'-0" CABOOSE CAR.
7-9-35 A
3-4-36 B
4-6-49 C.
INSIDE LENGTH 23'-9 3/4"
WIDTH AT BAY 9'-8 3/8"
EXCEPT AT BAY 8'-0 1/4"
SERIAL NOS. | WEIGHT | DATE BUILT | BUILT BY
C-2501 | 38180 | 1936 | CO'S.SHOP, MT.C.
T-45036
31'-4 1/2" OVER RUNNING BOARD
23'-9 3/4" INSIDE
TOP OF FLOOR
8-LB TRUCK
TRUCK CENTERS
30'-0" OVER END SILLS
30'-7 3/4" OVER STRIKING PLATES
33'-3 1/4" LENGTH IN TRAIN

BALTIMORE
& OHIO
C2501

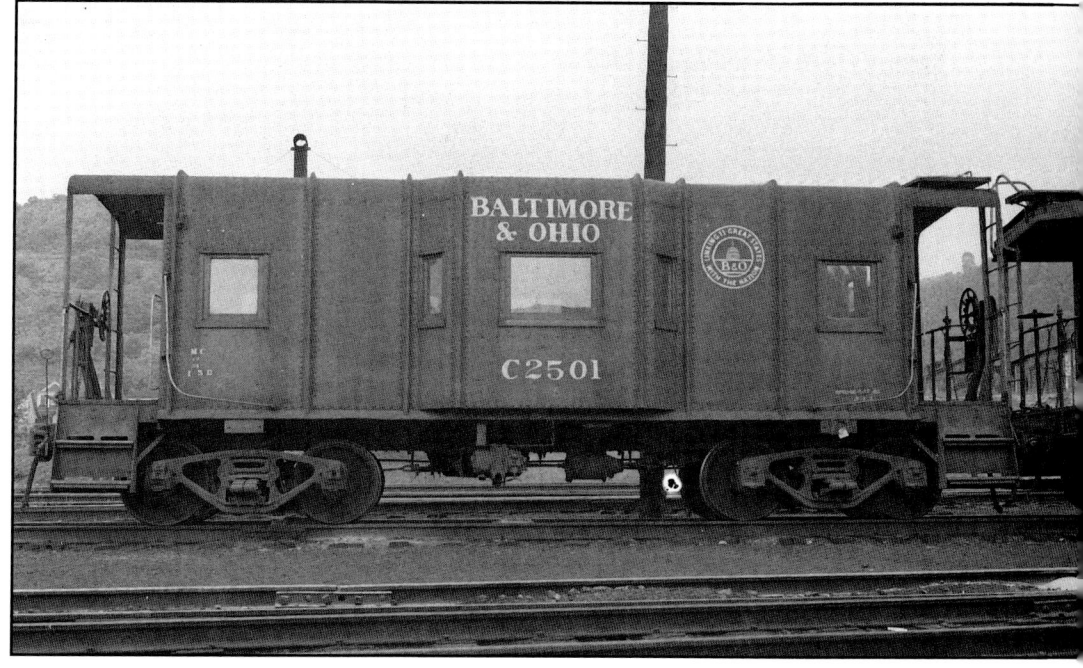

Right: Almost twenty years later at Benwood, West Virginia., the C-2501 has become just another wagon top caboose. Placing the brake wheel so that it faced away from the ends required the trainmen either to reach awkwardly from the platform or hang dangerously from the ladder to apply and release the brake. At some point, the railroad reversed them on this car, facing them inward on all subsequent cars. The B&O moved the truck centers out to 19 feet (but without changing the car's class, probably because it was a one-of-a-kind). It seems not to have received end ladder extensions, and like all long-lasting cars, the C-2501 had its share of unique, idiosyncratic, custom modifications. (Paul Dunn)

Class I-5B Cabooses

Number Series C-2502 to C-2507

Shortly after producing the I-5A, Mt. Clare shops built a second experimental wagon top, using the frame of I-1A C-400 heavily damaged by fire at Cambridge, Ohio on February 21, 1935. The C-2502 was released from the Mt. Clare shops in June 1936 and was the last wagon top caboose to be built there. The B&O assigned Class I-5B to the car. Beginning in 1939, the shops at Cumberland, Maryland, built five more I-5B cars using frames salvaged from destroyed I-5 cabooses. The railroad numbered them C-2503 through C-2507. The porthole-style windows were a distinguishing feature of the Class I-5B, as they were the only B&O cabooses built with this visually distinctive type of window. While the cars were the prototypes for the I-12 cars of 1941 and 1945 and appeared to be similar if not identical, many questions remain as to the cars' structural and mechanical details, and why the B&O classified the cars as it did. The clearance diagram for Class I-5B cabooses is shown in Figure 13. The interior arrangement for I-5B cabooses is shown in Figure 14.

Figure 13

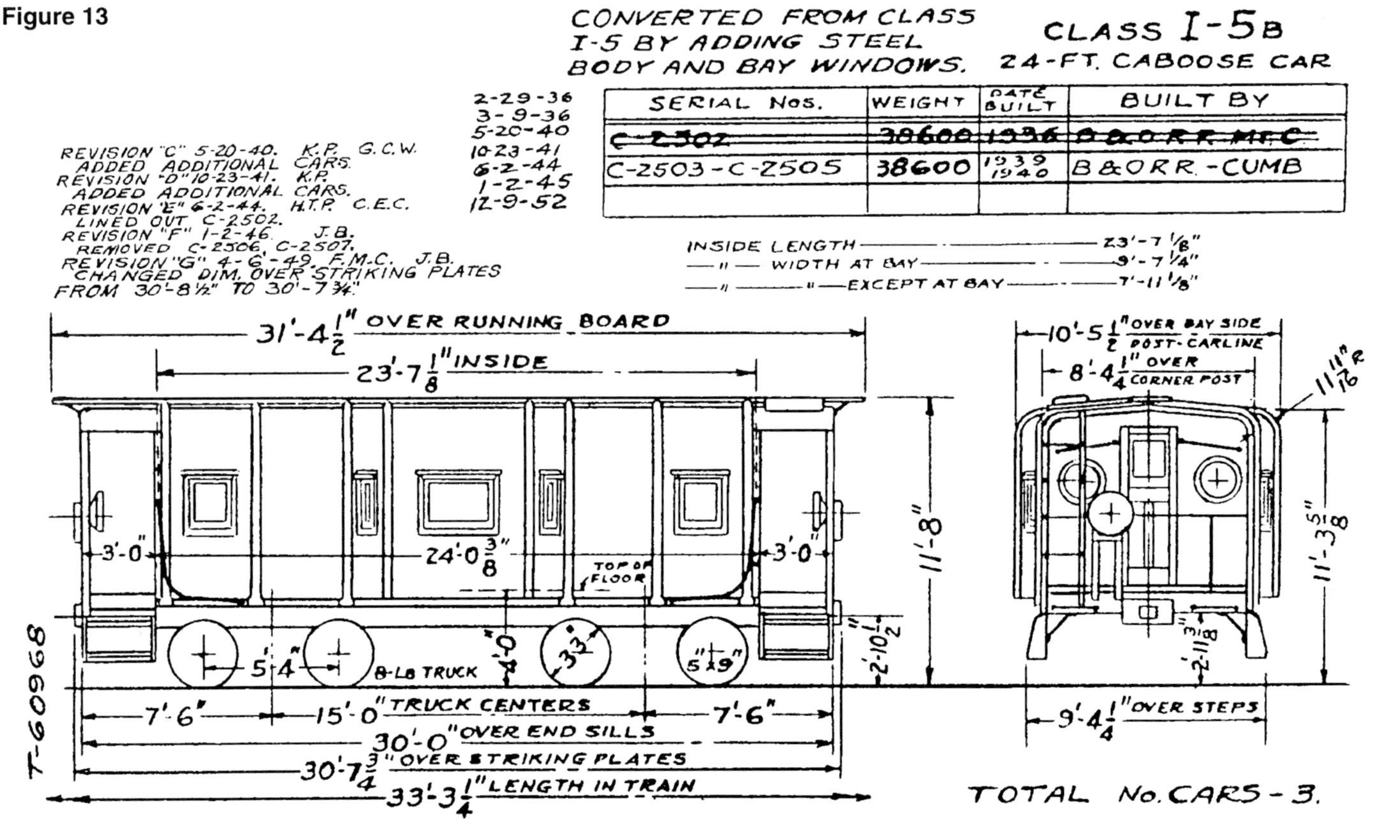

Right: This overhead view of I-5BA C-2504 provides a rare look at the roof arrangement of these wagon top cars. Some features to note are the spacing of the ribs in the area of the bay window, the fact that the ribs do not deform as they curve around the roof of the caboose, and how the roof sheet over the end platforms curve downward at the outer end to allow for rain water to run off. The C-2504 was photographed at Grafton, West Virginia on August 9, 1978. (Robert Hubler)

Figure 14

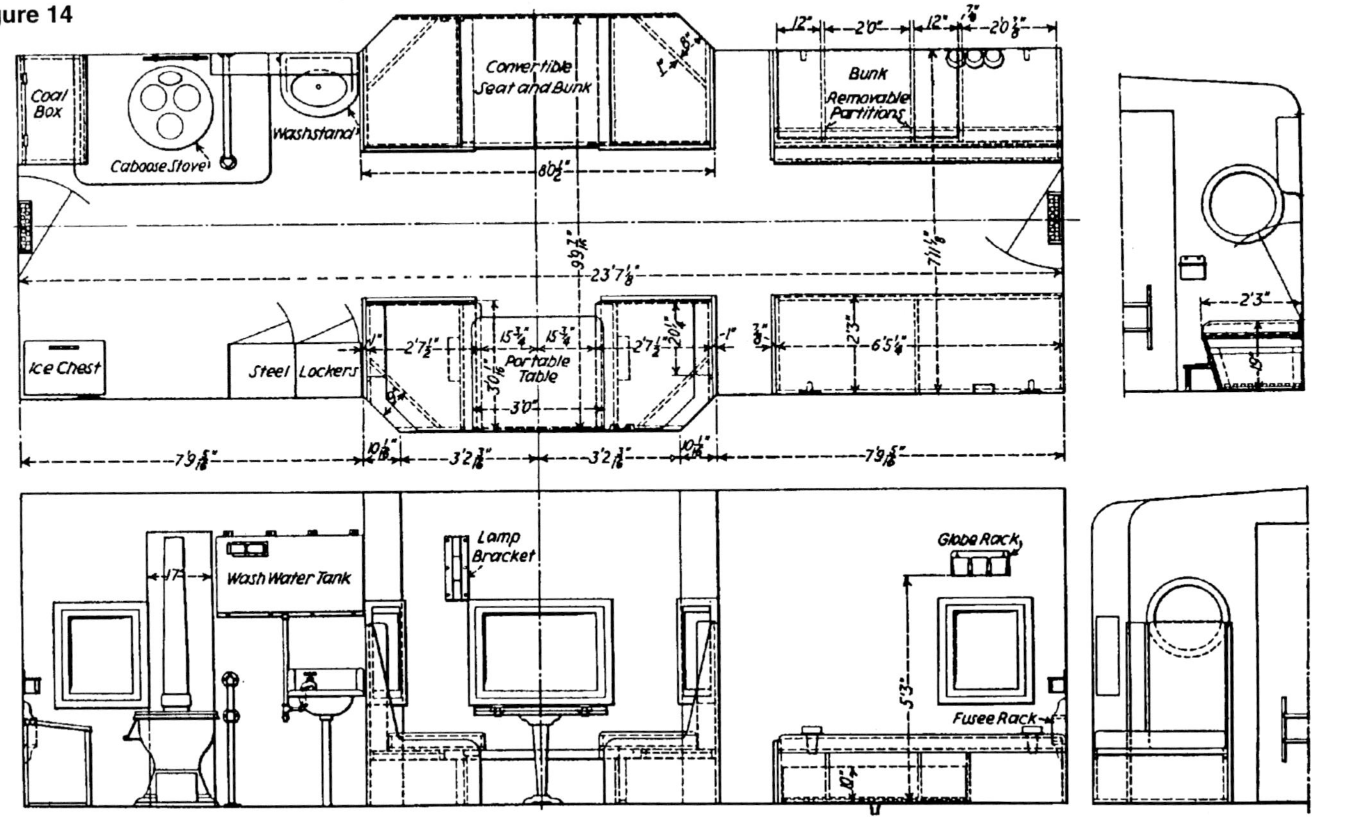

Class I-5BA Cabooses

Number Series   C-2502 to C-2507

The I-5BA caboose was a variation of the Class I-5B. As part of the 1940s program converting I-5 cars into I-5C and I-5D cabooses, the B&O also increased the distance between the truck centers on the I-5B cars from 15 feet to 19 feet to improve their performance in heavy pusher service. When this increase occurred, the railroad changed the car class to I-5BA. B&O records list only the C-2502, C-2506 and C-2507 as converted to Class I-5BA. However, photographs show that all the I-5B cabooses eventually received the modification.

After long service on the B&O and use as a restroom facility in West Virginia, the stripped carbody of C-2506 is now part of the B&O Railroad Museum's collection. Figure 15 is the clearance diagram for the Class I-5BA with the increased truck centers clearly indicated on the diagram.

J. J. Tatum: Designer of the Wagon Top

The man responsible for the development of the B&O's innovative wagon top caboose program was John J. Tatum. He began his career on the B&O as a messenger boy at the Mt. Clare shops in 1879, and served a four-year apprenticeship to become a Carbuilder in 1885. Tatum was thus formally trained in the construction of wood cars, and no doubt helped build Class K-1 cars during his time as a mechanic. By 1907, Tatum had become the B&O's Superintendent of Freight Car Equipment, and oversaw the successful design and construction of the I-1, and I-1A cabooses. In 1924, as Superintendent of the Car Department, he revised the I-1A to create the I-5. Immediately after the last of the 401 I-5 cabooses were completed in 1929, Tatum designed the B&O's first steel bay window caboose, the I-7. Built in 1930, the C-2500 was innovative for the time and a worthy successor to the I-5, but it was not reproduced. The Depression was deepening, and as carloadings dropped, so did the demand for new cabooses.

J. J. Tatum was a self-taught engineer who avidly followed advances in the mechanical disciplines. In response to the needs of the Traffic Department, advances in metallurgy, and a desire to do something new, Tatum and the B&O's engineering staff on the second floor of the Office Building at Mt. Clare designed fourteen freight cars in the mid-1930s utilizing various combinations of lightweight alloys, innovative fabrication techniques, and a very clever one-piece continuous rib design for the sides and roof. This family of experimental wagon top and corrugated-side cars promised several clear advantages. They were lighter in tare weight, meaning greater load carrying capacity on standard 50 and 70-ton trucks. Some were designed using aluminum or weathering steel alloys to reduce maintenance and last longer. Another goal was to fabricate as many of the parts as possible and build the cars in the Company's shops, so that the work could be kept "in the family" and employ B&O workers. Even second-hand steel was re-rolled into sheets and shapes at the company's rolling mill at Cumberland to produce needed parts and easily fabricated metal sections for roofs and sides. Some of the cars, because of their distinctive rounded roof corners resembling an old west covered wagon, were dubbed "wagon tops." The wagon top design was a qualified success, and the B&O produced hundreds of wagon top boxcars, covered hoppers, and cabooses, all of which served the railroad well for many years..

-John P. Hankey-

Upper Left: The last of the I-5BA cabooses, the C-2507, is seen at Cowen, West Virginia on October 10, 1976. Clearly visible in this photograph are the porthole end windows, a distinguishing feature found only on the Class I-5B/I-5BA cabooses. Also apparent are the extended truck centers and the resultant narrowed steps caused by the conversion from a Class I-5B to I-5BA. (Robert Hubler)

Middle Left: The only I-5BA caboose to receive the standard Chessie System paint scheme was the C-2505. In this case, the painting was done by the Chillicothe, Ohio shops, which accented the window frames in orange. This in turn caused the end portholes of the I-5BA to stand out in sharp relief in this photograph taken at Zanesville, Ohio on September 3, 1977. (Robert Hubler)

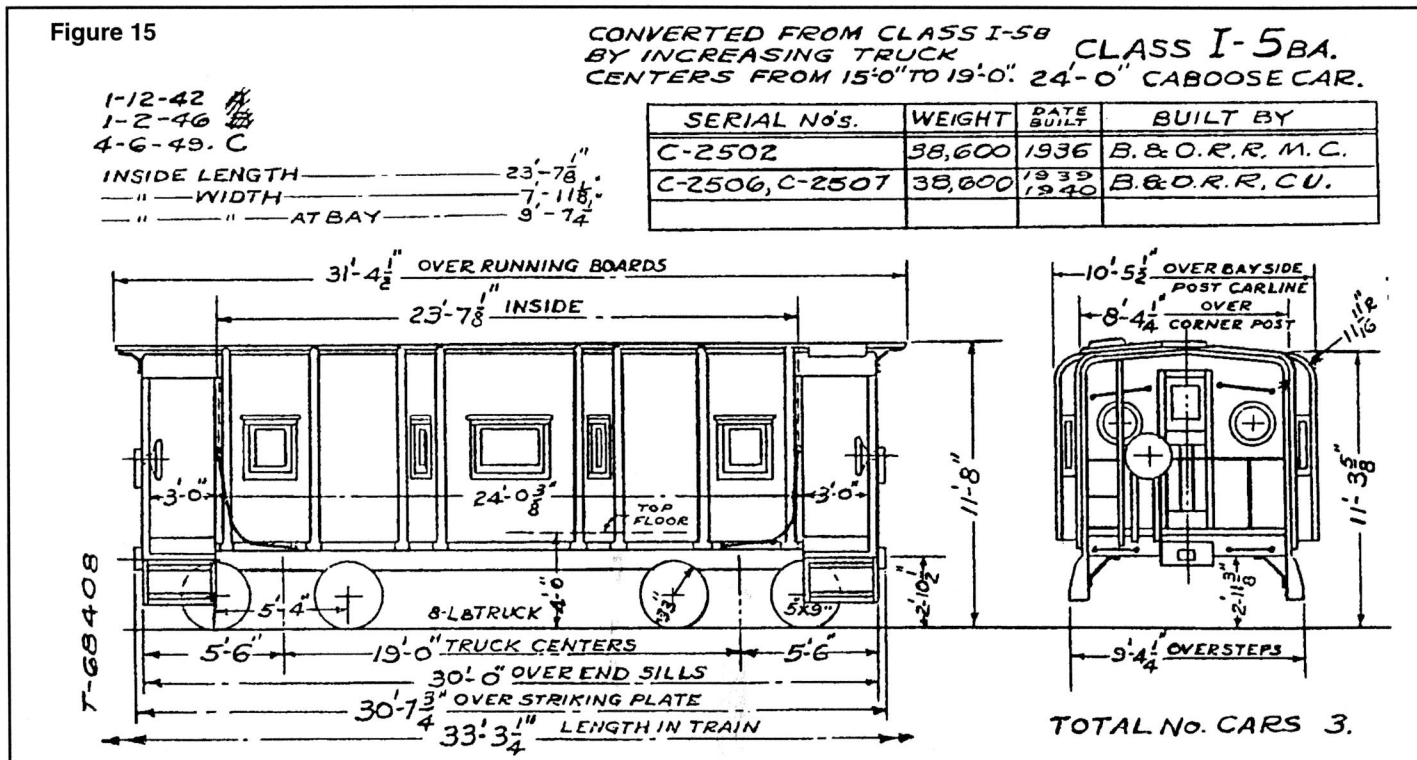

Figure 15

Class I-5C Cabooses

Number Series   C-1903 to C-2281

During 1940, the B&O began a formal program to modify Class I-5 cabooses to make them more suitable for use in heavy pusher service. Depending on what modifications were made, the railroad reclassified the cars as either I-5C or I-5D. In the case of the I-5C, the modification consisted only of increasing the distance between the truck centers from 15 to 19. As built, Class I-5 cars had truck kingpins seven and a half feet from the end of the car to clear the wide steps. On straight track or with trains typical of the 1920s, placing helper locomotives behind the caboose caused no difficulty. The steel center sill was adequate for the heaviest buff and draft forces. But as train weights and the tractive effort of helper locomotives increased, such a relatively large overhang caused special problems in districts with both heavy pushers and curving track. As the helper locomotives shoved against the caboose on curves, a combination of too much coupler swing and the short truck center-to-center distance permitted angular or lateral forces to develop, which acted to lift the car from the rails. Occasionally excessive lateral forces pushed the car sideways off the track. By moving the trucks outward the overhang was reduced, effectively reducing both the lever arm and the lateral force on the caboose. The cars converted to Class I-5C were not ballasted and thus weighed the same as the I-5. The steps on the Class I-5C were narrowed to allow room to clear the journal boxes when the trucks pivoted outward on curves. Many I-5C cabooses eventually returned to the shops for further modification into Class I-5D cars. Figure 16 is the clearance diagram for the Class I-5C cabooses.

Right: Class I-5C caboose C-1949 is seen at Willard, Ohio on February 27, 1965. Comparison of this photograph with that of Class I-5 C-1952 on page 54 shows the distinguishing feature of the I-5C cabooses. The movement of the trucks outward towards the end of the car and, the resulting narrowing of the steps to allow for the swing of the trucks on curves is very obvious in this photo. (Julian W. Barnard, The B&O Railroad Historical Society Collection)

Lower Right: On a gray and gloomy February 27, 1966, B&O I-5C C-1915 was in Willard, Ohio. By this date I-5C cabooses were a bit hard to find. They were never numerous, because most Class I-5 cars were converted directly into I-5D cabooses and many I-5Cs were later further modified into far more common I-5D cabooses. (Julian W. Barnard, The B&O Railroad Historical Society Collection)

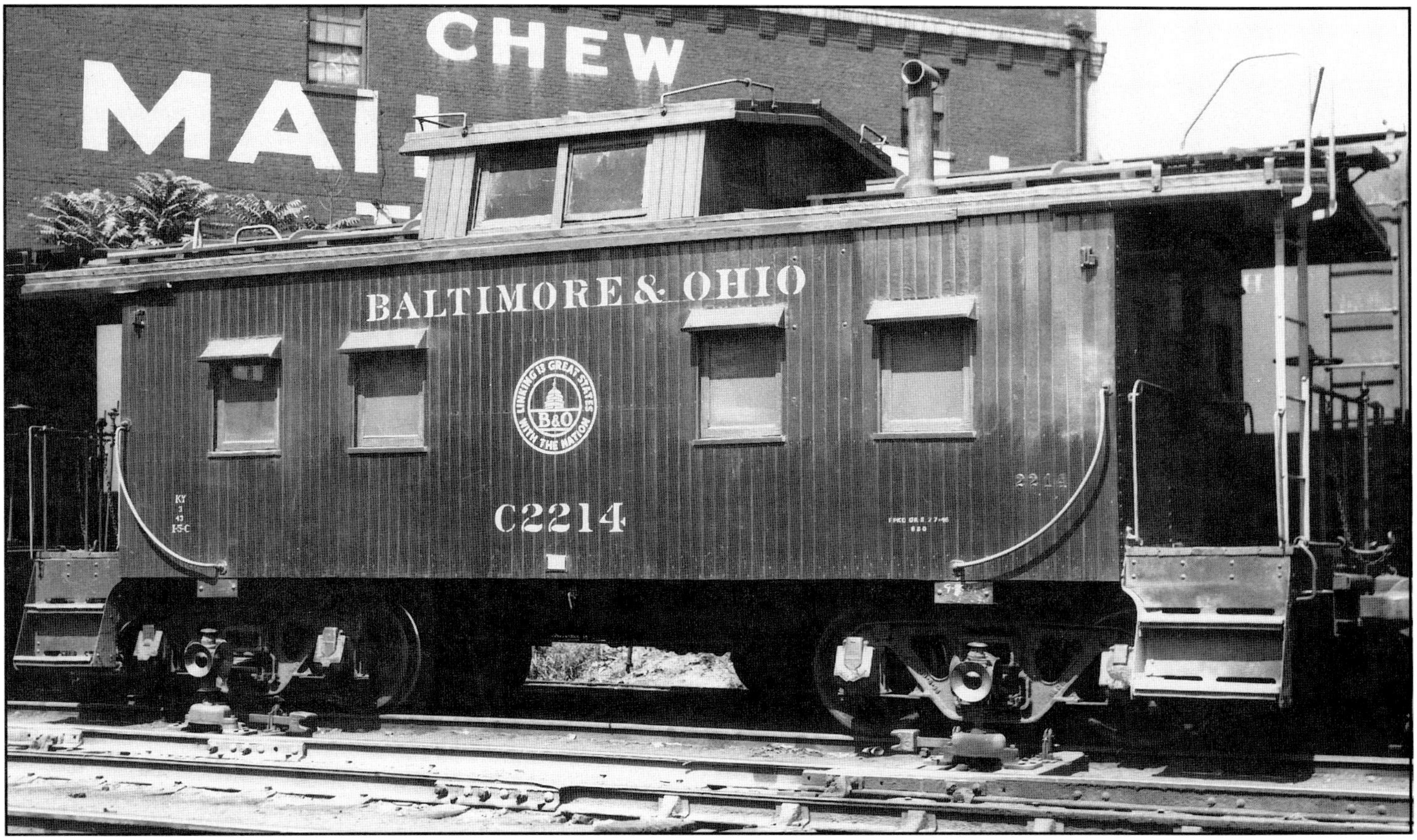
CHEW
MAI
BALTIMORE & OHIO
C2214

Above: This is a very clean photograph of Class I-5C C-2214 (later converted to a Class I-5D) at Parkersburg, West Virginia in 1946. It was one of the earlier I-5C conversions. The treatment of the steps is quite interesting. The movement of the trucks outward to the end of the car is obvious, requiring narrower steps to provide proper clearance for the trucks. However, rather than narrow the entire step as was usually done, the top of the step at the end platform was untouched and the steps were only narrowed at the bottom. This produced a very unusual curved step. (Paul Dunn, Robert Hubler Collection)

Figure 16

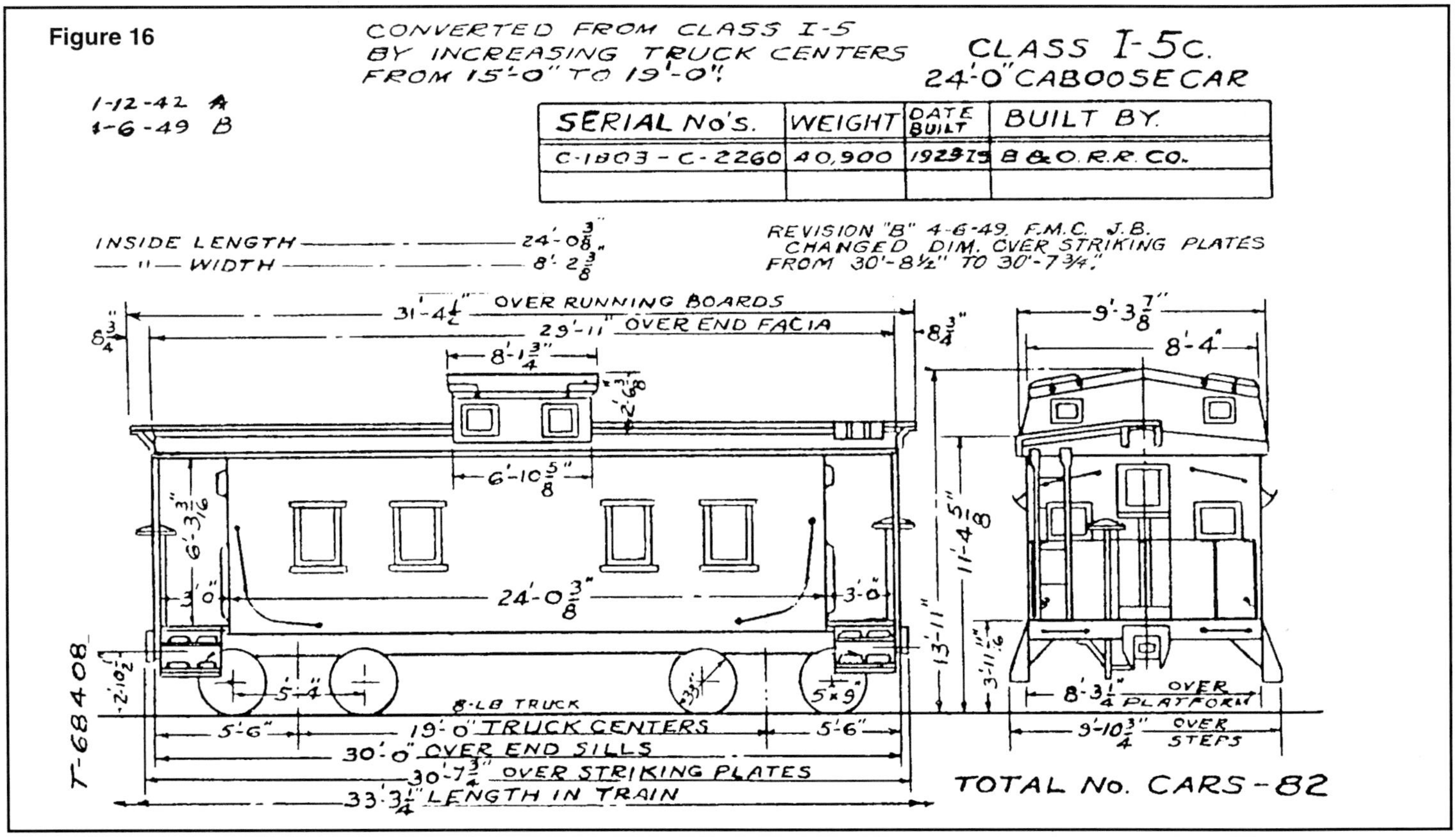
CONVERTED FROM CLASS I-5
BY INCREASING TRUCK CENTERS
FROM 15'-0" TO 19'-0".
CLASS I-5C.
24'-0" CABOOSE CAR
1-12-42 A
4-6-49 B
SERIAL No'S. | WEIGHT | DATE BUILT | BUILT BY
C-1803 - C-2260 | 40,900 | 1923-25 | B & O. R.R. CO.
INSIDE LENGTH — 24'-0 3/8"
— " — WIDTH — 8'-2 3/8"
REVISION "B" 4-6-49. F.M.C. J.B.
CHANGED DIM. OVER STRIKING PLATES
FROM 30'-8½" TO 30'-7¾".
31'-4½" OVER RUNNING BOARDS
29'-11" OVER END FACIA
8 3/4"
8'-1 3/4"
2'-6 3/8"
6'-10 5/8"
6'-3 3/16"
3'-0"
24'-0 3/8"
2'-10 1/2"
5'-4"
5 x 9
8-LB TRUCK
5'-6"
19'-0" TRUCK CENTERS
30'-0" OVER END SILLS
30'-7 3/4" OVER STRIKING PLATES
33'-3 1/4" LENGTH IN TRAIN
T-68408
9'-3 7/8"
8'-4"
11'-4 5/8"
13'-11"
3'-11 11/16"
8'-3 1/4" OVER PLATFORM
9'-10 3/4" OVER STEPS
TOTAL No. CARS - 82

Class I-5D Cabooses

Number Series   C-1900 to C-2298

As early as 1931, the B&O experimented with individual I-5 cabooses to improve their ability to withstand the in-train forces generated by helper locomotives in "heavy" pusher service. The railroad found that by both increasing the distance between the truck centers and ballasting the cars, it materially reduced the risk of intense buff forces lifting the cars and derailing them on curves. The B&O initially did not reclassify these experimental cars. At the beginning of the 1940s program to modify Class I-5 cabooses for use in heavy pusher service, the railroad reclassed the Class I-5 cars modified since 1931 to I-5D cabooses. The railroad classified newly modified cars as either I-5C, as described above, or I-5D. The modification of I-5s to I-5D consisted of increasing the distance between the trucks from 15 to 19 feet as was done to the I-5C cabooses. In addition, approximately 10 tons of concrete and steel scrap were added under the floor to bring the car's weight up to approximately 31 tons. The object of the extra weight was to improve the caboose's ability to withstand lateral forces acting to lift it off the rails when used in pusher service. Again, the underframe strength of the Class I-5 was not an issue, since the center sills had more than adequate cross-section and strength to resist the simple buff forces found in helper service. At least for the Class I-5C cars, the B&O found that increasing the truck center distance was necessary, but not sufficient, to make the cars track well in the heaviest service typified by eastbound coal trains on the West End of the Cumberland Division. The I-5D modifications largely solved the problem. Some Class I-5D cabooses were rebuilt from I-5C cars while others were rebuilt directly from Class I-5 cars.

During their long careers on the B&O, Class I-5D cars received additional modifications characteristic of all the I-1 and I-5 caboose cars. Betterments included replacement of the trucks, air brakes, hand brakes, and safety appliances. Many cars underwent a general interior rearrangement, including the addition of toilet compartments, the addition of extra lockers, and the blanking of some of the eight side windows. The railroad re-sided the cars as necessary, in later years applying plywood over the tongue and groove car siding. The B&O Railroad Museum, with the assistance of the B&O Railroad Historical Society, has preserved I-5D C-2222 in its permanent collection. Unfortunately, the car's interior had been removed by the previous owner. The B&O's clearance diagram for the Class I-5D caboose is shown in Figure 17.

Middle Right: Photographed at Cincinnati, Ohio on January 9, 1965, the C-2239 is a typical I-5D caboose. The increased length between truck centers is very apparent in this photo. Also visible are the modernized air brakes and grab irons that most I-5D cars had acquired by this time. However, decidedly atypical is the smoke jack, no doubt a local design. (Eileen Wolford Barnard, The B&O Railroad Historical Society Collection)

Lower Right: Class I-5D caboose C-2074 shows an early example of plywood sheeting used to cover deteriorated tongue and groove siding. On this particular car, all the side windows were retained when the siding was covered over. On many cars, the railroad took the opportunity to blank one or more windows, creating an almost endless number of permutations in combination with other individual modifications. This car was photographed at Grafton, West Virginia on July 25, 1973. (Robert Hubler)

Left: In later years the B&O equipped a few Class I-5D cars with a belt driven electrical generator to supply power for lights and radios. However, the majority of the I-5D cabooses were never equipped with electricity. Beginning in the 1960s, non-electrically equipped cabooses carried highly reflective paddles which could be mounted in the old marker lamp brackets. These paddles were green on one side and red on the other, and were used instead of flags or marker lights in some situations. While on the main line, the cars used battery powered flashing markers. The C-2283 is seen at Zanesville, Ohio in June, 1968. (Paul Dunn, Robert Hubler Collection)

Middle Left: This view from above of Class I-5D C-1994 provides a look at the roof details. Some features to note include the metal roof, wooden roof walks and wood planked end platforms, all of which were original equipment on Class I-5 and I-5D cabooses. This photograph was taken at Benwood, West Virginia on July 16, 1973. (Robert Hubler)

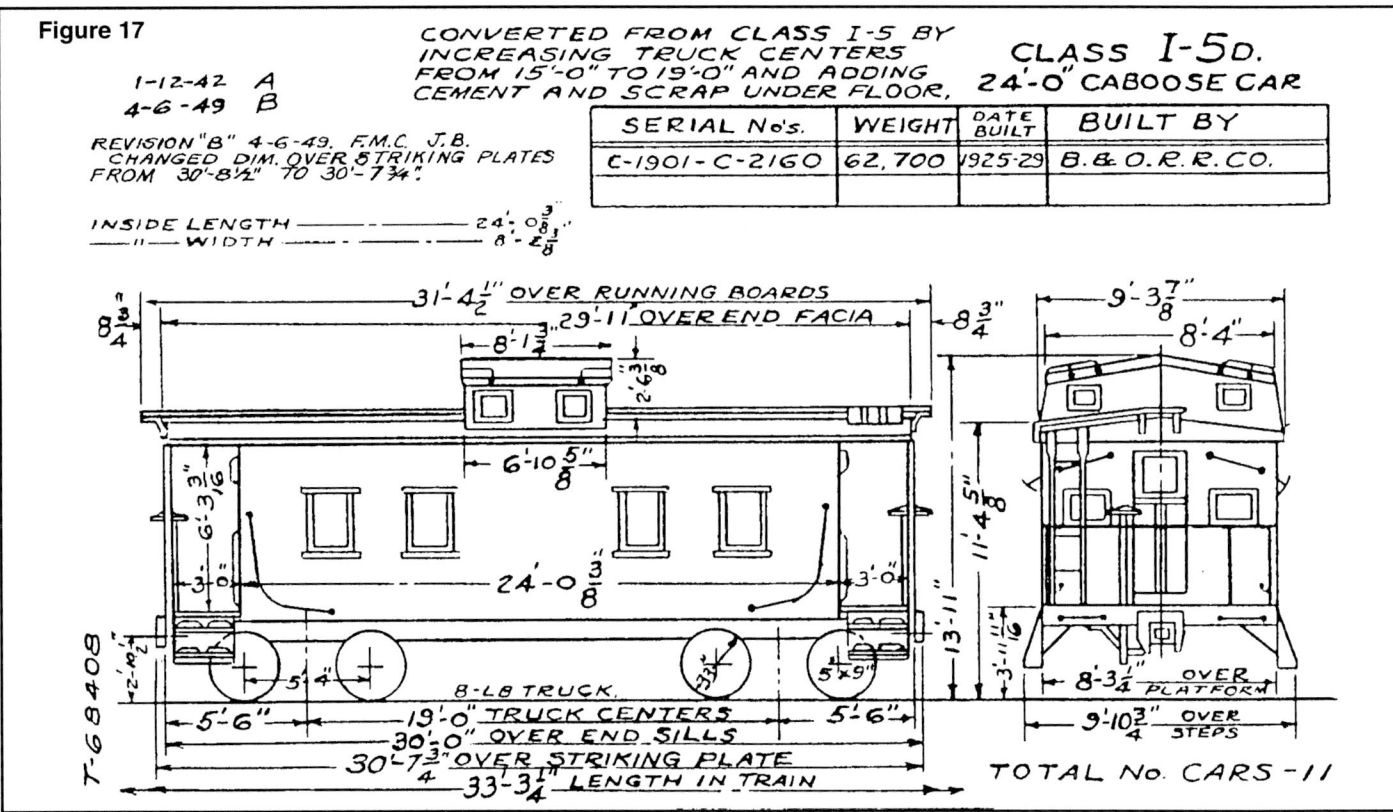

Figure 17

Upper Right: Class I-5D caboose C-1926 was found between runs at Willard, Ohio on June 27, 1965. If there was a "standard" B&O caboose, one would have to nominate the I-5D for that role. Even though wagon top cars were uniquely B&O and visually distinctive, the I-5D cars were far more numerous. Class I-5 cabooses comprised the second largest class of B&O cabooses (only the K-1 cars were produced in greater numbers). Most of the I-5 cars were eventually converted into I-5D cabooses. Thus, statistically at least, a B&O freight train of this era was more likely to be trailed by an I-5D than by any other type of caboose. With this in mind, the C-1926 can be considered as representative of the "standard" B&O caboose. (Julian W. Barnard, The B&O Historical Society Collection)

Middle Right: This I-5D, with seven windows, was photographed at Gassaway, West Virginia on August 10, 1978. The seven window variant is far more common on I-5Ds than among unmodified I-5s. Like a number of wooden cabooses remaining in service at this time, the C-1934 had plywood placed over its original siding. Except for these items, the C-1934 displays the typical I-5D features with the extended truck centers especially prominent in this broadside view. (Robert Hubler)

Lower Right: The C-1901 was the first of the "production model" I-5s built at the Washington, Indiana shops and was placed in service in November 1925. Photographed at Chillicothe, Ohio on July 5, 1976, well into its 51st year, it was also one of the last to see service. It was converted to a Class I-5D in the 1940s and in September 1961 it was extensively rebuilt at the DuBois shops. At this time Dubois was reworking I-5 and I-10 cabooses to comply with recently enacted Maryland and Pennsylvania laws which required sanitary facilities on all cabooses operating within these states. In the case of the I-5s this meant installing toilet facilities (note vent) and a large water tank, resulting in the covering of all four windows on one side. Other internal modifications caused two of the four windows on the other side to be covered. DuBois also installed AAR vertical hand brakes and characteristic "J" shaped grab irons on all wooden cabooses put through this program. The final paint scheme applied to wooden B&O cabooses by the Chillicothe shops between 1975 and 1977 is displayed by C-1901—the initials "B&O" and the number in black on a yellow body. (Robert Hubler)

Class I-6 Cabooses

Number Series   C-1676 to C-1699

The Class I-6 cabooses were acquired with the Cincinnati, Indianapolis & Western Railway (CI&W) in 1927. The CI&W owned twenty-four cabooses numbered 1 through 24. The B&O assigned Class I-6 and numbered them C-1676 through C-1699. The I-6 was an eight-wheel, end cupola, wood caboose originally equipped with arch bar trucks. CI&W cabooses 1 to 20 were built new for that road and had steel center sills, while CI&W 21 to 24 were converted by the CI&W from old Cincinnati, Hamilton & Dayton (CH&D) equipment of all wood construction. Only twenty-three of the cabooses received B&O numbers, as CI&W 22 was retired before being renumbered to B&O C-1697. The railroad retired the last I-6 caboose in 1956. During their careers they received many modifications, including the replacement of the arch bar trucks and either replacement or repositioning of side windows. There is no known diagram for the Class I-6.

Above: This rare photo shows CI&W caboose 17 at an unknown date and location, apparently in its original configuration and paint scheme. Note the ornate oval CI&W herald. This caboose would later become B&O Class I-6 caboose C-1692. Refer to the photo of B&O C-1692 below to see how the caboose was modified over the years. (The B&O Railroad Historical Society Collection)

Left: The photograph shows B&O Class I-6 C-1692 (ex-CI&W 17) at an unknown location on September 9, 1945. The windows were replaced and the first two windows repositioned in the carbody. The steps and end ladders also appear to have been replaced. The cupola bracing also appears to have been removed. Curiously, it retained arch bar trucks. (C. W. Abbott Collection)

Right: CI&W caboose 19, at an unknown date and location, seemed to be trailing a mixed train. The old photo shows the car in its original appearance with the distinctive CI&W oval herald. This caboose would later become B&O Class I-6 caboose C-1694. (Jim Henry Collection, via Dave Oroszi)

Middle Right: B&O Class I-6 C-1676 (ex-CI&W No. 1) was at Zanesville, Ohio in May, 1942. It appeared to have received only minimal modification since it was acquired with the CI&W. The most obvious change was the replacement of the original arch bar trucks. The car is a typical end-cupola I-6 and carries the 1916 caboose paint scheme which did not use a herald. Notice how the words "Baltimore & Ohio" have been broken to clear the very tall side windows. (Paul Dunn, Robert Hubler Collection)

Lower Right: In this photograph we see B&O Class I-6 C-1689 (ex-CI&W No. 14) at Chillicothe, Ohio on January 15, 1946. It was substantially different from the other Class I-6 cabooses pictured in this book, with a shorter body, taller cupola, and fewer side windows. The car is similar to CH&D cabooses pictured in the Class I-2 section of this book. One possible explanation is that the original CI&W 14 was wrecked, and the B&O or CI&W replaced it with a former CH&D caboose. (S. P. Davidson)

Class I-7 Caboose

Number Series   C-2500

In January 1931, the B&O's Mt. Clare shops turned out the only Class I-7 caboose, C-2500. The I-7 was an all steel, cushion underframe, bay window caboose, the first of its type on the B&O and one of the first on any railroad. The C-2500 was built using the frame and trucks of Class I-5 C-1911, damaged in a wreck at Altamont, Maryland on March 2, 1930. The remains were eventually taken to Mt. Clare where the B&O scrapped the body and built a new steel body on the frame. The underframe itself was modified with the addition of Duryea cushioning equipment. When it was new, the C-2500 shared many characteristics with the I-5 caboose from which it was created, including arch bar trucks, a tool box, and tall "L" shaped grab irons, all of which were replaced or removed over the years. Unlike Class I-5A, I-5B, I-5C, and I-5D cabooses, the C-2500 never had the distance between the truck centers increased, even though it was fitted out for pool service and given the 1965 blue paint scheme (which the I-5A and I-5B cars did not receive).

Although one of a kind, the design was successful and the I-7 caboose remained in service for 48 years. It was dismantled due to wreck damage in November, 1979. At the time of its construction, the Great Depression was worsening, and the B&O had begun massive employee furloughs and an economic retrenchment as business plummeted. Had conditions been more favorable, the railroad might have experimented further with similar cabooses, as it did a few years later in constructing the first wagon top cars. Ironically, the I-17 and I-17A cars built between 1952 and 1965 resembled the C-2500 and shared many dimensions and construction details. Figure 18 is the B&O clearance diagram for the Class I-7 caboose and Figure 19 is the interior arrangement of the I-7.

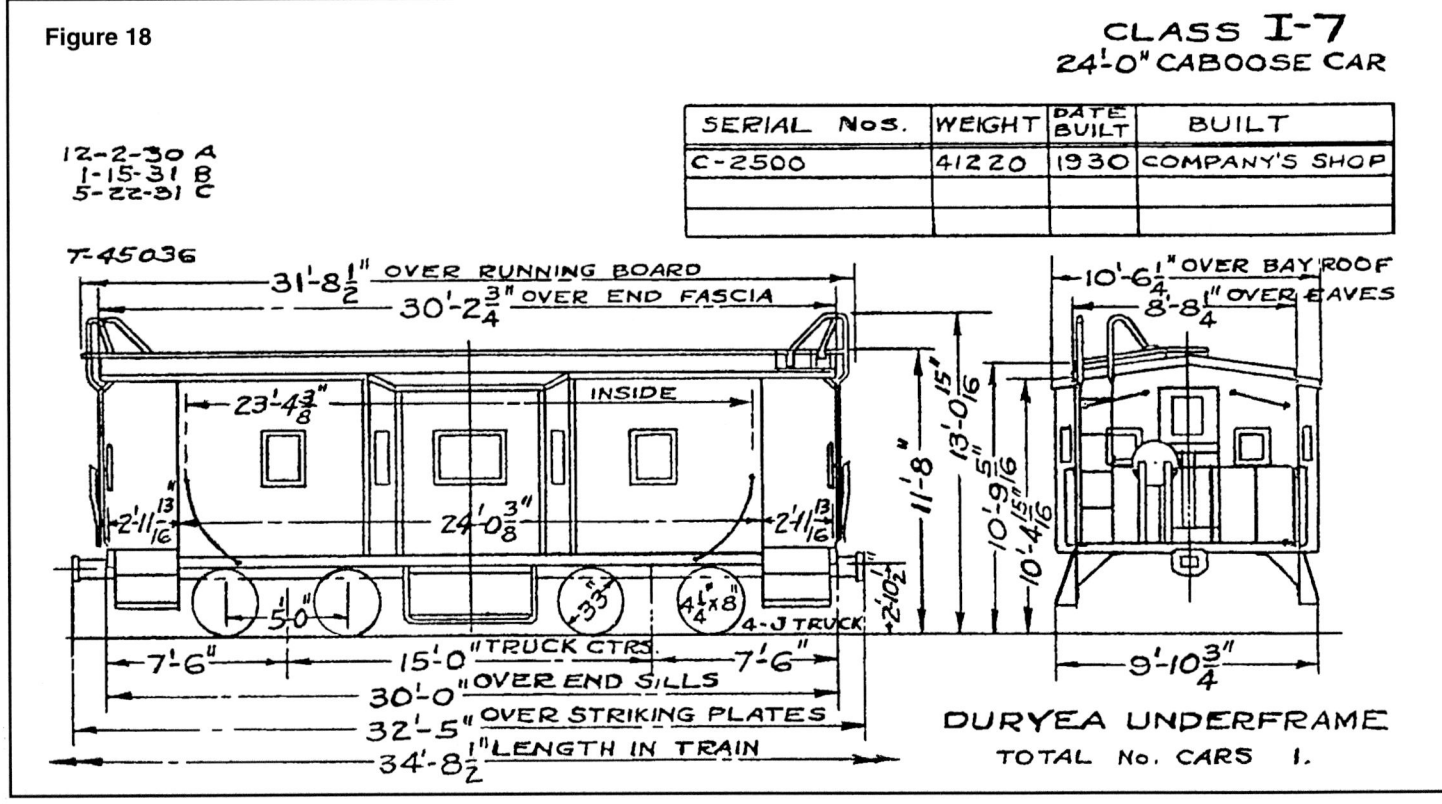

Figure 18

Left: This photo shows I-7 caboose C-2500 at Cumberland, Maryland in August, 1959. The C-2500 changed over the years in subtle ways. Most obvious were new side grab irons and paint. Less obvious was the replacement of the K brake system with AB air brakes. The near end of the car rides on an AAR double-truss truck; the far end on an Andrews truck. For some unknown reason it never had its truck centers lengthened four feet as did the Class I-5 wood and wagon top cars. (E. C. Kirstatter)

Right: This is a company photo of B&O I-7 caboose C-2500 taken in January, 1931. John J. Tatum, at that time in charge of the railroad's freight equipment, created the car from the remains of wrecked I-5 C-1911. This prototype B&O bay window car retained many features of the original I-5 which were nearly obsolete in 1931. They included the diamond arch bar trucks, style of the side grab irons, steps, K brake system, and stem hand brake wheels. However, Tatum added the new Duryea cushion underframe, a slack adjuster for the foundation brake rigging, and modern Ajax hand brakes, the latter apparently added just after this photograph was taken. Superficially, the car resembled the Class I-17 bay window cars built by the B&O in the early 1950s. Notice the adaptation of the standard B&O caboose paint scheme, notably the words "Baltimore & Ohio" in two lines to fit on the bay window. (The B&O Railroad Museum Collection)

Middle Right: Apparently this is another company photo of B&O Class I-7 caboose C-2500, taken at Mt. Clare, in January, 1931. Like so much of the experimental equipment built by the B&O at Mt. Clare, the C-2500 is a transitional piece mixing traditional and new features. A few other railroads (like the Milwaukee Road) were testing bay window cabooses. Characteristically, the B&O created a contemporary car with obsolete features. In comparing this with an earlier company photo, the only difference seems to be that the stem brake wheel has been replaced with an AAR vertical hand brake. (The B&O Railroad Museum Collection)

Figure 19

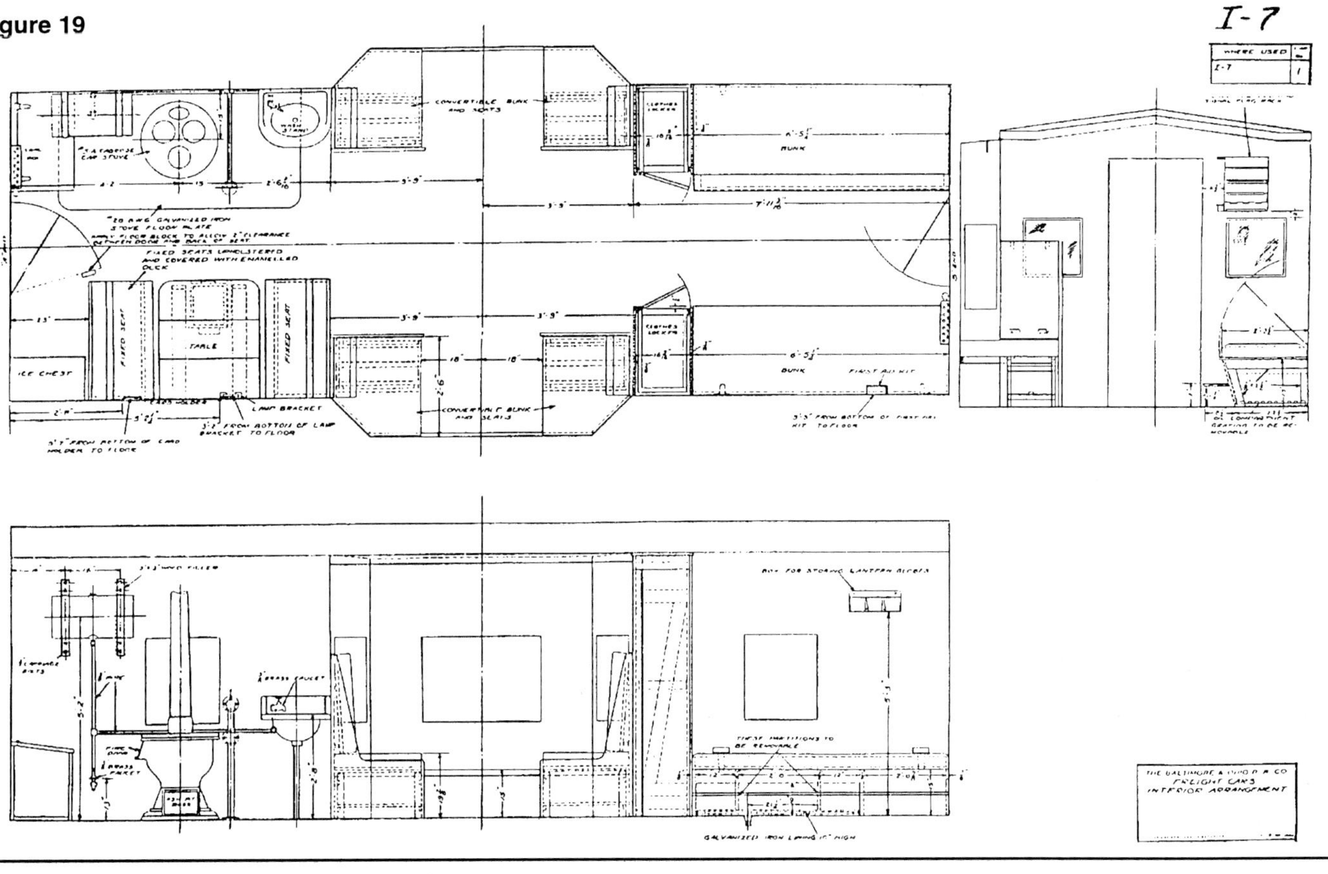

Class I-8 Cabooses

Number Series   C-1750 to C-1772

The B&O acquired the Buffalo, Rochester & Pittsburgh Railway (BR&P) in January 1932. At the time of the merger, there were 23 four-wheel, center cupola, wooden cabooses remaining on the BR&P roster - BR&P numbers 2, 12, 14, 18, 20, 27, 43, 44, 48, 55, 63, 68, 81, 101, 105, 107, 108, 109, 112, 115, 117, 118, and 119. They were built in the BR&P shops at DuBois, Pennsylvania and Lincoln Park (Rochester), New York, between February 1898 and December 1915. They were the BR&P's standard caboose before the acquisition of the eight-wheel cars which eventually became B&O Class I-10. The B&O assigned the four-wheel cars Class I-8 and numbers in the series C-1750 through C-1772. Only BR&P 107 actually received a new number; it became B&O C-1765 at East Salamanca, New York on June 5, 1934. All other Class I-8 cabooses were retired before they received B&O numbers. The C-1765 was retired on August 15, 1937. Figure 20 reproduces a late BR&P clearance diagram for the Class I-8 cars.

Figure 20

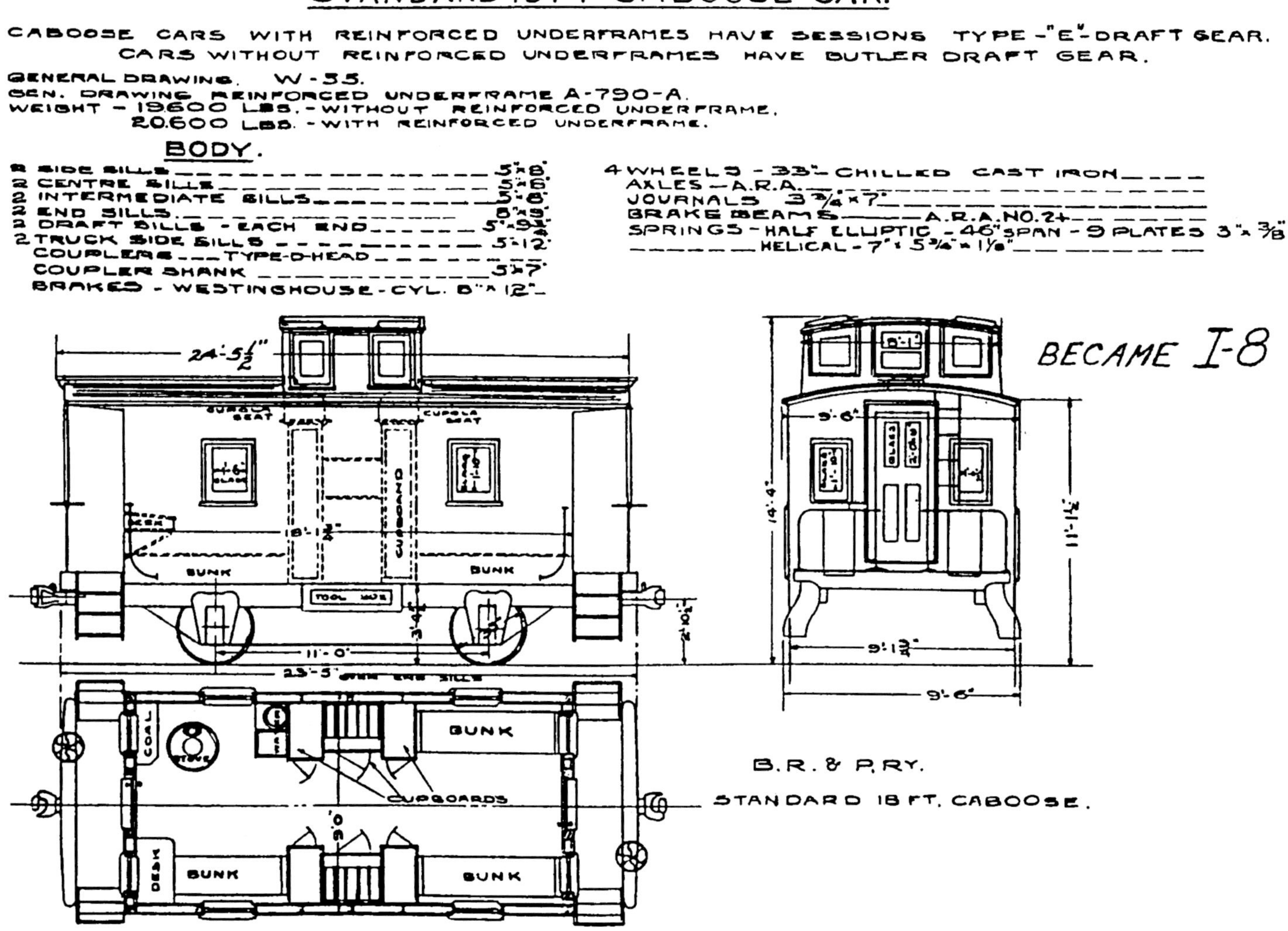

Left: This photo shows a Buffalo Rochester & Pittsburgh (BR&P) four-wheel caboose at an unknown location. The B&O acquired twenty-three such BR&P cabooses and assigned them Class I-8. As its number is not visible, there is no way to tell if the B&O acquired this particular caboose. The car does, however, illustrate the general appearance of the class. (Gary Schlerf Collection)

Above: Although technically not a Class I-8 since it was destroyed in a wreck on January 14, 1916, long before the B&O acquired the BR&P and its cabooses, BR&P 38 does illustrate the general appearance of the class on the B&O between 1932 and 1937. (Stanley Ames Collection)

Class I-9 (1st) Cabooses

Number Series   C-1594 to C-1599

The Class I-9 (1st) cabooses were also former BR&P cars. At the time of the merger, the BR&P had a group of six old eight-wheel, all wood, off-center cupola cabooses on the roster numbered BR&P 6, 9, 32, 36, 46 and 49. They were very old, predating even the four-wheel cabs mentioned previously.

They had been built by the BR&P's Lincoln Park shops and the LaFayette Car Works between July 1887 and December 1890. Although assigned B&O Class I-9 and numbers C-1594 to C-1599, none received B&O numbers before being retired. The last I-9 caboose (BR&P 9) was dismantled in December 1934. The only known photograph representing the appearance this class is found on page 158 of *Buffalo Rochester & Pittsburgh Railway* by Paul Pietrak. A BR&P clearance diagram for the Class I-9 cabooses is shown below.

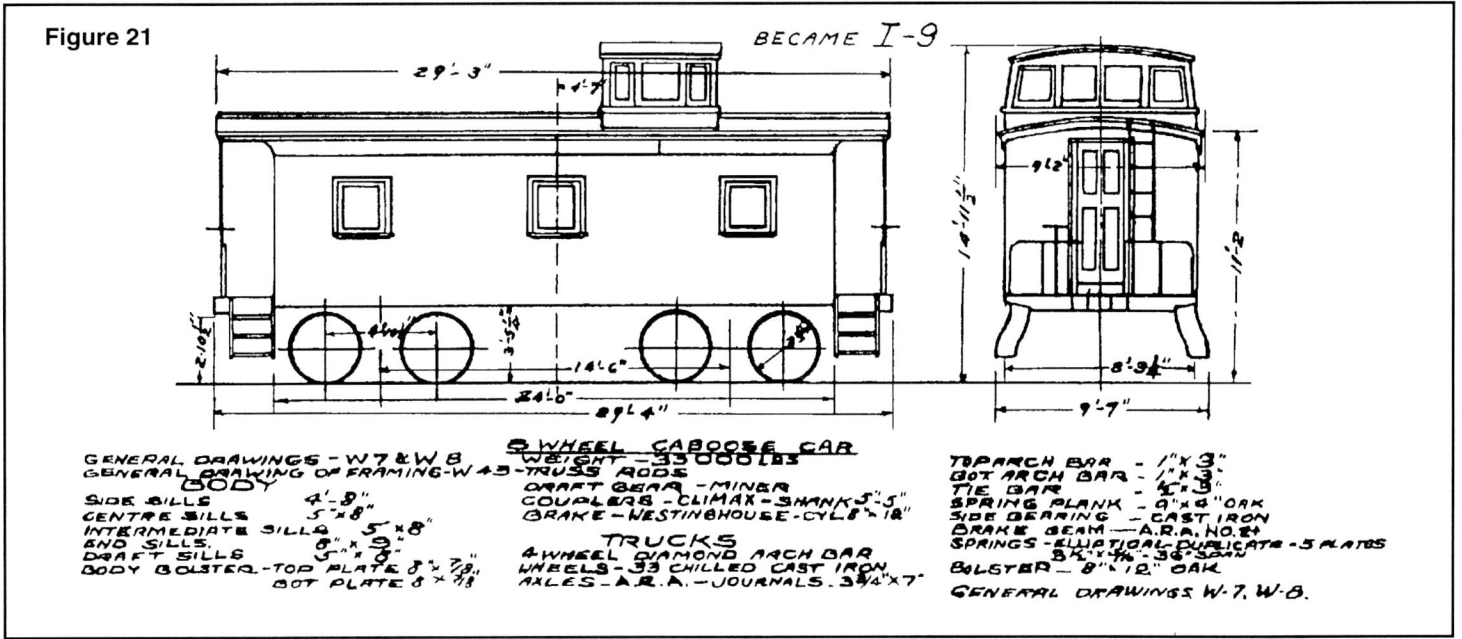

Figure 21

Class I-8 and I-9 Cabooses

Over the years the B&O maintained detailed records covering the origin and disposition of its cabooses. Unfortunately many of the detailed records concerning B&O cabooses have been lost. Surprisingly however, many of the BR&P history files covering the early BR&P cabooses have survived. The following cars were obtained by the B&O when they took over the BR&P.

Class I-8 Cabooses

BR&P Number	B&O Number	Builder	Date Built	Dismantled	Date
2 (fourth)	C-1750	DU	12/30/11		4/35
12 (second)	C-1751	LN	1/6/04	ES	6/8/33
14 (second)	C-1752	LN	2/3/98	BA	5/23/34
18 (third)	C-1753	UN	12/23/15		11/34
20 (third)	C-1754	LN	12/5/01		11/34
27 (second)	C-1755	LN	9/8/00	ES	8/7/33
43 (second)	C-1756	LN	5/4/05		11/34
44 (third)	C-1757	LN	11/10/13	BA	5/23/34
48 (second)	C-1758	LN	11/13/13	DU	10/10/33
55 (second)	C-1759	LN	10/7/98	DU	11/22/33
63 (second)	C-1760	LN	11/18/13	GW	6/2/33
68 (second)	C-1761	UN	10/14/12	ES	1/8/34
81	C-1762	LN	1/30/00	DU	5/8/33
101	C-1763	LN	8/4/03	ES	8/7/33
105	C-1764	LN	7/21/05	DU	9/19/33
107	C-1765	LN	8/16/05	See Note	
108	C-1766	LN	8/26/05	DU	7/26/33
109	C-1767	LN	8/26/05		4/35
112	C-1768	LN	10/27/05	ES	1/18/34
115	C-1769	LN	8/7/06	DU	11/22/33
117	C-1770	LN	8/8/07	ES	1/9/34
118	C-1771	LN	8/8/07	DU	7/19/33
119	C-1772	LN	8/10/07	ES	1/17/34

Class I-9 Cabooses

BR&P Number	B&O Number	Builder	Date Built	Dismantled	Date
6 (second)	C-1594	LN	7/26/90	DU	11/22/33
9 (second)	C-1595	UN	12/9/90		12/34
32 (second)	C-1596	LF	3/88	DU	9/19/33
36	C-1597	UN	7/87	DU	11/22/33
46	C-1598	UN	9/87	DU	10/10/33
49	C-1599	LF	4/88		11/34

Legend of Shop Symbols:

BA = Brook Avenue Yard Rochester, New York
DU = BR&P Shops DuBois, Pennsylvania
ES = East Salamanca, New York
GW = Glenwood Yard Pittsburgh, Pennsylvania
LF = LaFayette Car Works
LN = BR&P Shops Lincoln Park, New York
UN = BR&P Shops location not recorded

General Notes:

Only BR&P 107 ever received its new number. BR&P 107 renumbered to B&O C-1765 at East Salamanca, New York on June 5, 1934. B&O C-1765 leased to Castleman River Railroad and dismantled by them at Grantsville, Maryland on August 15, 1937.

Class I-9 (2nd) Caboose

Number Series   C-1594

When the B&O assumed operation of the BR&P Railway in 1932, numbers and classes were assigned to all BR&P equipment on hand at the time. In 1936, the B&O found an eight-wheel wooden caboose numbered BR&P 1 operating on the railroad, but not listed in the accounting records. An investigation revealed that the caboose was the former Reynoldsville & Falls Creek number 1. This small line had gone bankrupt and its equipment obtained by the BR&P. The caboose had been renumbered BR&P 1 at DuBois, Pennsylvania on July 31, 1929 but not entered in the equipment records. Hence, it was not assigned a B&O class or number when the B&O acquired the BR&P. Once this had been sorted out, the caboose was assigned the Class I-9 (2nd) and renumbered to B&O C-1594 at Punxsutawney, Pennsylvania on April 1, 1936. It remained in service for ten more years, finally being scrapped at DuBois, Pennsylvania on December 16, 1946.

Class I-10 Cabooses

Number Series   C-2600 to C-2665

The Class I-10 cabooses were also former BR&P cars. At the time of the B&O takeover, the BR&P had sixty-six first-line, steel underframe, center cupola cabooses, numbered BR&P 150 and 250 through 314. They were built in three groups: BR&P 150 at its DuBois, Pennsylvania shops in January 1914, BR&P 250 to 264 by the Mt. Vernon Car Company, at Mt. Vernon, Illinois in April and May 1918, and BR&P 265 to 314 by Standard Steel Car of Butler, Pennsylvania, between September and December 1923. The B&O assigned Class I-10 to these cabooses, and numbers C-2600 through C-2665. Only 62 cars actually received B&O numbers, as BR&P 260, 261, 271, and 297 were wrecked and retired before they could be renumbered to B&O C-2611, C-2612, C-2622, and C-2648.

The I-10s were well-constructed, main line cabooses and remained in service on the B&O for many years. They were in every respect the equal of the B&O's I-5s. In 1961, the B&O began a program at the DuBois shops to modernize the I-10 cabooses, in part to comply with a Pennsylvania law requiring sanitary facilities. The changes included covering side windows, modifying the toilet facilities, adding water tanks, replacing the steps, changing the stem brakes to an Ajax or other vertical hand brake type, and modifying the cupola windows. In 1967, Class I-10 cabooses C-2650, C-2653, C-2663, C-2660, C-2637, C-2616, C-2604, C-2613, C-2635, C-2617, C-2636, C-2601, C-2609, and C-2642 were sold to the C&O and renumbered C&O 90357 through 90370. In 1971, the C&O sold eight of them back to the B&O, but they were not returned to their old numbers. They were simply relettered B&O 90363 through 90370. The B&O retired the last I-10 in 1977. Figure 22 reproduces the BR&P clearance diagram for the third and largest group of Class I-10 cabooses. Aside from insignificant differences in a few dimensions (fractions of an inch), the diagram represents the entire series of cars despite their construction by three builders.

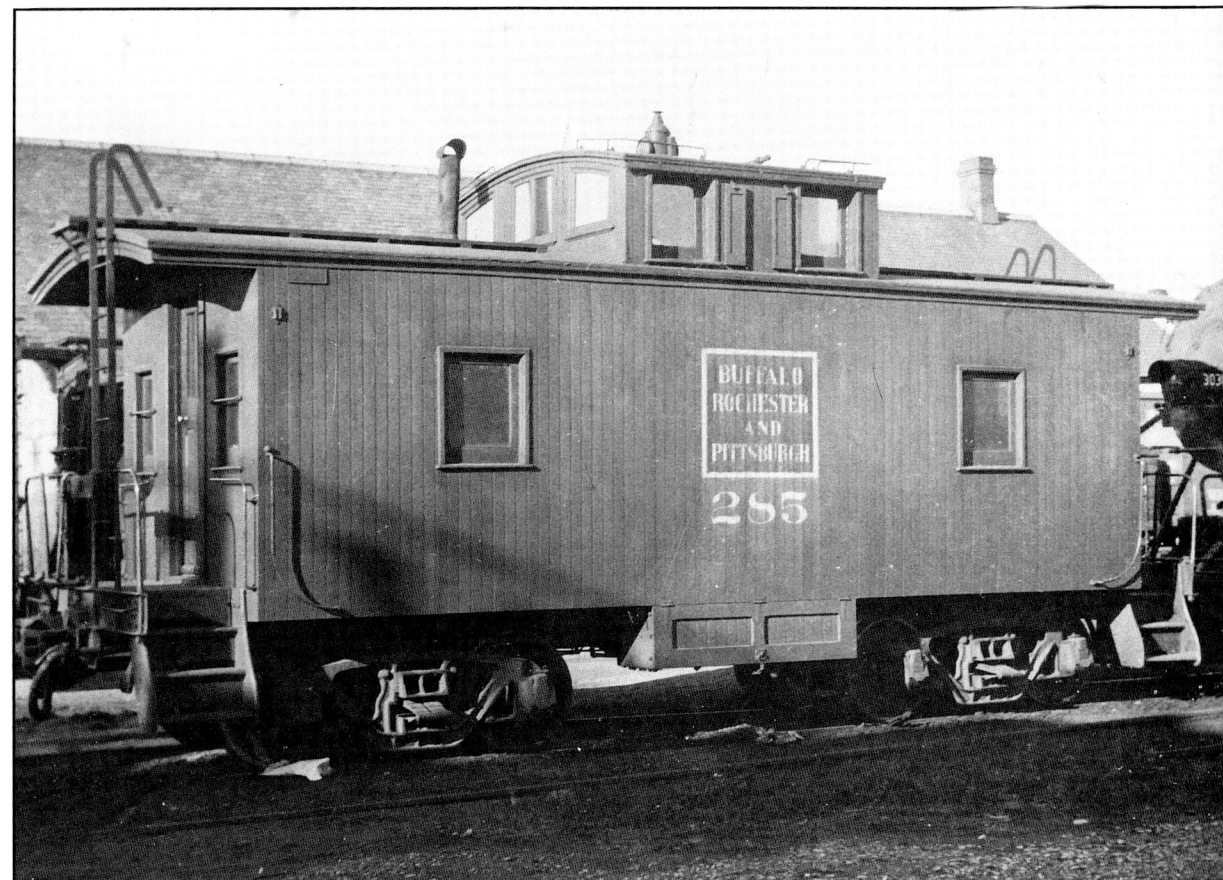

Right: BR&P caboose 285 later became B&O Class I-10 caboose C-2636. It is about 10 years old in this photograph and presumably represents the original appearance of these cars. Note the built-in marker light on the roof of the cupola; the crew could change the aspect of the light from inside the car. The 285 was photographed at Rochester, New York in 1933, just after the B&O formally acquired the BR&P. (John Woodbury, S.P. Davidson Collection)

Figure 22 — Standard 8 Wheel Steel Frame Caboose Car, No's 265 to 314, Built Sept. to Dec. 1923, by Standard Steel Car Co., Butler, PA. C-2616–C-2665 Class I-10.

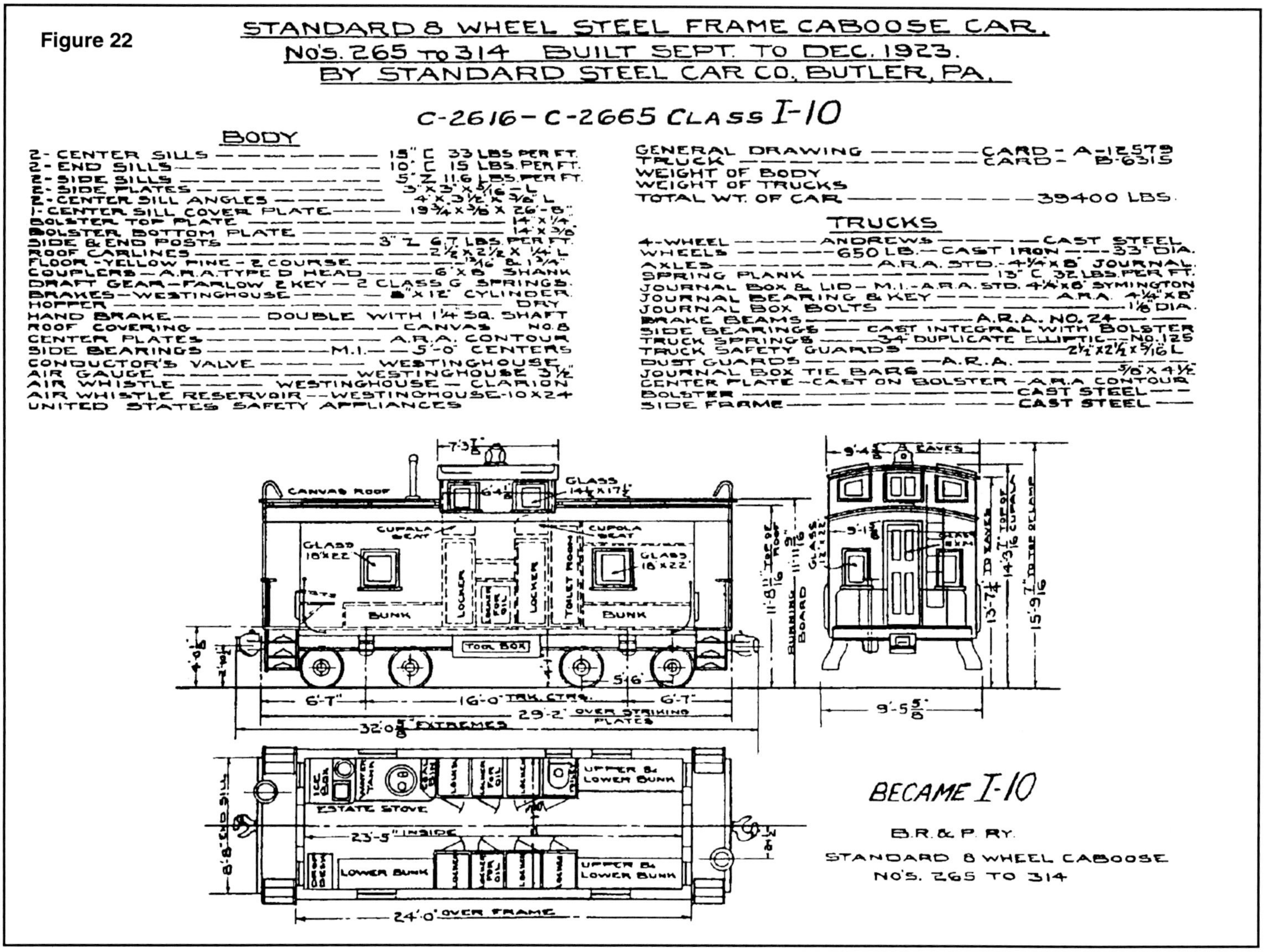

Middle Right: B&O I-10 caboose C-2601 (ex-BR&P 250) at Perry, New York on October 14, 1951, appears to have received few modifications after 33 years in service. The light on the cupola roof is gone and the steps have been replaced, but the rest of the caboose seems to be unaltered from BR&P days. At this point, it had been a B&O car longer than it had been a BR&P car. The addition of several coats of B&O paint, window awnings, and other small details had not masked its heritage. (J. W. Brauner)

Above: B&O Class I-10 C-2639 (ex-BR&P 288) was still in its original B&O paint scheme at the time of this photograph in May, 1939 at Buffalo, New York. The only change from its "as built" appearance seemed to be the removal of the light on the cupola roof. The lettering scheme was standard for this era, featuring only the railroad name with no herald, with the car's former initials and number (in this case, BR&P 288) in small letters below. Unlike the roughly contemporaneous B&O Class I-1 and I-5 cars, the BR&P cabooses had toilet compartments as built, shown by the small window. Having a shorter tool box on each side instead of a single deep one on one side made it easier for carmen to get under the car. (J. W. Brauner, Robert Hubler Collection)

Above: Beginning in 1961 the DuBois shops overhauled a number of I-10s to comply with a new Pennsylvania law requiring sanitary facilities on all cabooses operating in the state. The C-2621 (ex-BR&P 270) at Chillicothe, Ohio in April 1976 illustrates the effect of this overhaul. It received improved toilet facilities, which caused the former narrow toilet compartment window to be covered (note vent), and a large drinking/wash water tank which required the covering of the right window. DuBois also installed AAR vertical hand brake wheels and characteristic "J" shaped grab irons as part of this program. The railroad also combined the two cupola side windows into one with aluminum sliding window frames. Many, but not all of the I-10s had the center cupola window covered during this shopping. Curiously, many of the I-10s retained their tool boxes even though they had been removed from original B&O cabooses decades before. (Robert Hubler)

Lower Right: B&O caboose C-2646 (ex-BR&P 295) at Chillicothe, Ohio on October 16, 1976 is another example of a car rebuilt in the early 1960s. It survived almost until the very end of the operation of wood (technically, composite) cabooses on the B&O. The C-2646 was later sided with plywood and repainted into the final 1975 yellow scheme with only the initials B&O and the caboose number. The silver roof paint greatly decreased the heat build-up inside during summer. Sharp-eyed readers might notice the different kinds of transoms or truck bolsters in each truck, more evidence of the "mix and match" nature of railroad equipment in service for a long time. (Robert Hubler)

Class I-11 Cabooses

Number Series   C-1773 to C-1781

The Class I-11 cabooses were acquired in 1932 with the Buffalo & Susquehanna Railroad (B&S). At the time of the B&O takeover, the first line B&S cabooses were a group of nine four-wheel wood cars with steel center sills and a center cupola, numbered B&S 1 to 9. The B&O assigned Class I-11 and numbers C-1773 through C-1781. The last Class I-11 (C-1775) was retired in 1956 and preserved at the B&O Railroad Museum in Baltimore, Maryland. No diagram is available for the Class I-11.

Above: The C-1774 is one of nine similar cars acquired when the B&O absorbed the Buffalo and Susquehanna Railroad (B&S) in 1932. This one, the ex-B&S 2, is a four-wheel, center cupola caboose built with a steel center sill. It is otherwise similar to the B&O Class K-1 and virtually all four-wheel cabooses. The I-11s were the only former B&S cabooses to see service on the B&O. It is in its original B&O paint scheme when it was photographed at Mt. Jewett, Pennsylvania, on July 19, 1938. (J. W. Brauner, Robert Hubler Collection)

Middle Left: The B&O had its own "bicentennial" caboose, the C-1776, a Class I-11. Unfortunately, it was destroyed in a wreck at Buffalo Creek, New York in December, 1945, 30 years too soon to be caught up in the bicentennial craze. The C-1776 was originally B&S 4. This photograph was taken at Wellsville, New York on September 10, 1938. (J. W. Brauner)

Lower Left: This is an excellent photograph of B&O I-11 C-1775 (ex-B&S 3) taken at Bradford, Pennsylvania on March 31, 1946. The steel center sills under these attractive little cabooses probably account for their longevity, especially compared to the other B&S cabooses obtained by the B&O. The C-1775 was preserved and can be found today on display at the B&O Railroad Museum in Baltimore. (J. W. Brauner, Robert Hubler Collection)

Class I-12 (1st) Cabooses

Number Series   C-1782 to C-1799

The B&O also acquired 18 wood four-wheel cabooses from the B&S, which it classed I-12 (1st). On the B&S, they were numbered in the series 70 through 98. The B&O assigned numbers C-1782 through C-1799 to these cabooses, but retired them in 1932 and 1933 before actually relettering them. No photographs or diagrams of these cabooses have been found. Beyond the fact that they were four-wheel cabooses, nothing is known of their appearance.

Class I-12 (2nd) Cabooses

First Number Series	C-2400 to C-2499 & C-2800 to C-2824
Second Number Series	902403 to 902498 & 902800 to 902824

By 1941, the seven experimental wagon top cabooses had proven themselves and J. J. Tatum had become Assistant Chief of Motive Power and Equipment under George H. Emerson. The Depression had ended, the railroad was busy with traffic from World War II mobilization, and the B&O was ready to produce wagon top cabooses in quantity. However, looming wartime shortages permitted the construction of only 100 cars numbered C-2400 to C-2499. They were built at the Keyser, West Virginia shops, in December 1941 and January 1942.

Since the original group of Class I-12 B&S cabooses were long gone the B&O assigned the Class I-12 to the new group of wagon top cars. The production wagon top cabooses had nineteen-foot truck centers, AAR trucks, Ajax or other modern vertical hand brakes, Duryea cushioned underframe, and all-steel construction, although the interior was framed and finished in wood. They were rugged, successful, and distinctive. The round end windows of the earlier Class I-5Bs were not used on the I-12s, which utilized a square end window like the I-5A.

Near the end of the War, the railroad studied available data and made projections of traffic, revenue, and equipment needs. As the Class I-13 and I-16 cabooses converted earlier in the war had held up well, the railroad predicted a need for relatively few additional I-12s. By 1945, the B&O was able to obtain the material to construct 25 more I-12s at Keyser. They were numbered C-2800 through C-2824 and finished between August and October, 1945.

Most of the I-12 wagon top cars were later modified with the addition of electric lights and toilet facilities. Also, as with most cabooses which saw many years of service on the B&O, variations could be found in the trucks, grab irons and other details. Cars remaining in service in 1982 were renumbered into the "902400" and "902800" series by dropping the "C" prefix and adding the digits "90" before the car number. The B&O Railroad Museum in Baltimore has two I-12s in its collection, C-2452 and C-2478. The B&O's clearance diagram for the Class I-12 wagon top cabooses is shown in Figure 23.

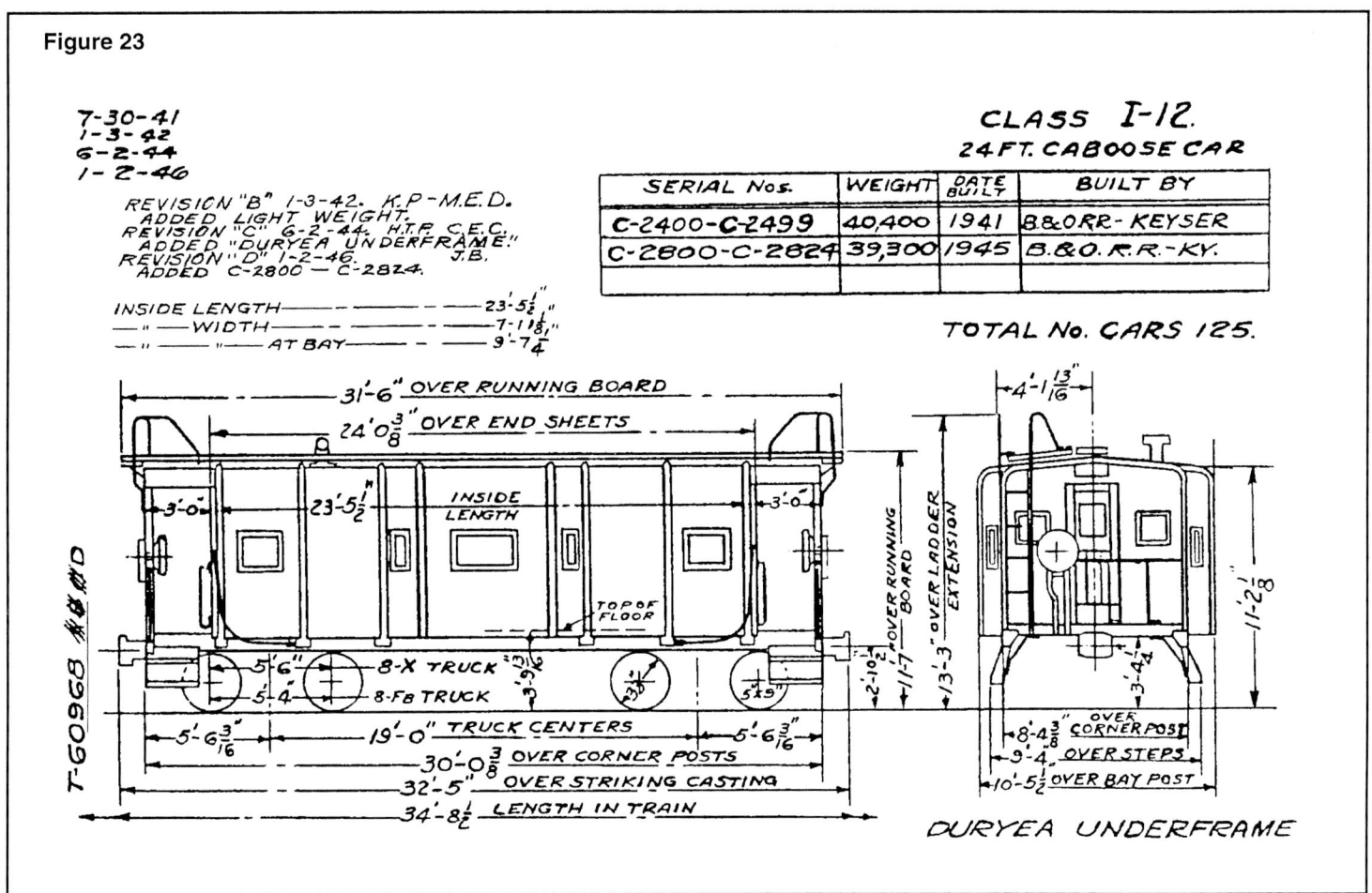

Figure 23

Above: Keyser shop forces built the C-2807 in the second lot of wagon top cabooses. At Philadelphia in July, 1951, the C-2807 appears essentially "as built." As World War II came to a close, the B&O mustered the materials to begin the post-war re-equipment of the entire railroad. Some parts, such as trucks, were in extremely short supply, resulting in long delivery times from manufacturers. As before, the B&O reused frames, bolsters, and perhaps wheel sets from older or scrapped equipment. This car rides on Andrews trucks, usually used under heavy cars and tenders. It has a Duryea cushion underframe, 19 foot truck centers for unrestricted use on any main line or with helpers, and a variety of special devices on the platform. One handle permitted the trainmen to close the angle cock without reaching down; a chain connected directly to the coupler lock lifter, allowing the man on the platform to safely uncouple the caboose even while moving. Another chain connected to the glad hand of the trainline air hose, so that the train crew could break that connection if needed. These devices enabled helpers to cut off "on the fly," a technique perfected by the B&O in the 1890s on the electrified Baltimore Belt Line. (Paul Dunn, Robert Hubler Collection)

Right: Galvanic corrosion—the ordinary oxidation of steel accelerated by the presence of water and minute, stray electrical currents—became a common problem among steel freight cars. Often, the mere fact that two slightly different kinds of steel were riveted together and exposed to the atmosphere was sufficient to cause a "battery" effect and relatively rapid corrosion. Because they were made of whatever steel was on hand, and partly due to their riveted construction, permeability to water, and the presence of minute electrical currents, I-12 cabooses corroded

severely near the riveted seam between the lower side sheets and the side and end sills. This was an important part of the car's structure, so the B&O repaired the damage as the cars were shopped in the 1960s. C-2802 shows the standard fix: cut between a few inches and a foot from the bottom of the side and end sheets, weld new steel onto the remaining good material, and re-rivet the sheets to the sills. By the end of their service life, few wagon top cabooses had escaped side sheet repair, just as few wood cabooses retained their original siding. (Robert Hubler)

Middle Left: Twenty years after the B&O built the last wagon top cars and just before they were modified for pool service, the C-2433 waits between runs on the caboose track at Willard, Ohio in December, 1965. It displays the usual variations in grab iron detail, stencilling, and placement of the bad order card holder. The car now has an oil stove, as evidenced by the oil fill pipe to the right of the right-hand side window. It also carries a few of the body sheet crinkles which characterized almost all wagon top cabooses toward the end of their active service. Dents in the soft carbon steel sheets sometimes resulted from contact with slings and cables used to pick the cars up. Other ripples or dents might be the results of derailments, collisions, or extremely hard couplings. While they were light, strong, and stiff overall, the carbodies were weak in certain areas and not terribly resistant to deformation between the ribs. (Julian W. Barnard, The B&O Railroad Historical Society Collection)

Lower Left: At Dubois, Pennsylvania in May, 1976, I-12 C-2448 provides an example of a wagon top caboose converted to pool service in the mid-1960s. Features to note include the small globular electric marker lights at each corner of the caboose, and the installation of a toilet, indicated by the small vent just to the left of the bay window. The cushion underframe of the I-12 cars is particularly apparent from this angle. An unusual feature can be observed by comparing this caboose with the C-2433 shown above. Note that the side grab irons on the C-2433 are quite tall as compared to C-2448, extending fully half-way up the end of the caboose. The distribution of tall and short grab irons seemed to be about equal among the I-12 cars. Photos from the 1940s and 1950s (well before cabooses were pooled on the B&O) indicate that I-12 cabooses used on the Cumberland Division had short grab irons, while those used on the Pittsburgh Division had tall grab irons. If this was more than just a coincidence, it would be interesting to know why the shops went to such trouble to implement a seemingly trifling variation in the same class of caboose. (Robert Hubler)

Right: Newer cabooses had replaced most of the wood cars and many of the I-12 cars on main line freights by early 1974, when the C-2485 posed in the local yard at Martinsburg, West Virginia. The B&O still maintained many small terminals from which branch and switching jobs operated, almost always with a caboose. From Martinsburg, crews worked the Frog Hollow Branch; switching jobs to Pearson Yard and Cumbo to the west; work trains in both directions; and "turn arounds" to Brunswick and Cumberland as necessary. As the I-12s aged, they increasingly served on these local jobs, continuing the practice of "cascading" older but otherwise fit cars to less rigorous assignments. In this way, crews returned to assigned cars, for a caboose could remain on certain runs for years and carry the same men day after day. (J. R. Quinn, Robert Hubler Collection)

Above: The C-2478, shown in Akron, Ohio on June 26, 1977, wears what would be its final Chessie paint scheme. The vicious sport of throwing rocks at trains, once an almost exclusively urban phenomenon, began to occur all over the railroad by the 1960s. Before the Federal Railroad Administration mandated the use of heavy penetration-resistant safety glass, Chessie installed heavy rock screens on all road cabooses. Their use permitted trainmen to get some air circulation and see out reasonably well, but protected them from most missiles. Beneath the car is a battery box similar to those carried by passenger cars. The I-12s received axle-driven generators and sizeable battery sets, which permitted the installation of electric lights, more powerful Motorola railroad radio packs, and flashing rear-end markers. The C-2478 is now part of the permanent collection of the B&O Railroad Museum in Baltimore, where it received an earlier red paint scheme while being partially returned to "as built" condition. (Robert Hubler)

Figure 24

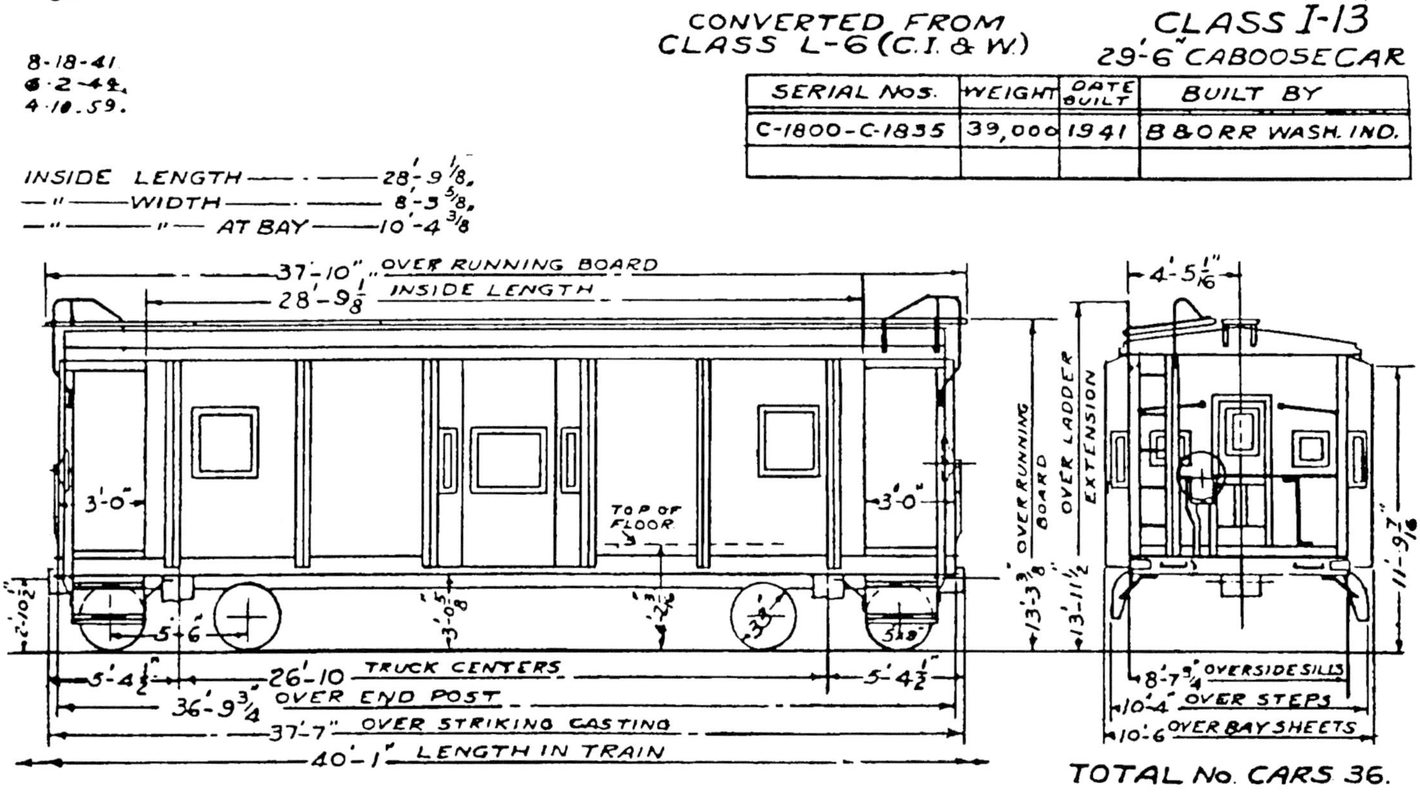

Class I-13 Cabooses

Number Series   C-1800 to C-1835

The I-13 was a steel-framed, wood bodied caboose converted from a stock car. The B&O set a fabricated steel bay window into what had been the door openings, and shortened the carbody to create end platforms. During 1941, in order to ease the wartime shortage of cabooses, the B&O created thirty-six of these cars from stock cars originally acquired with the Cincinnati, Indianapolis, and Western Railway (CI&W). The cars were built by Haskell & Barker in 1916 and carried CI&W numbers 651 through 700. In 1927 and 1928, the forty-nine surviving stock cars were renumbered B&O 13000 through 13048 and assigned Class L-6. In 1941, the B&O converted the remaining cars to cabooses. The first two (C-1800 and C-1801) were converted from B&O 13041 and 13046 at Mt. Clare shops in April 1941. The B&O converted the remaining 34 cabooses (C-1802 to C-1835) at the Washington, Indiana shops between June and August 1941. The I-13s continued to see service on the B&O for many years after the war. In later years some cars were assigned to yard service with their bay windows removed. Figure 24 is the clearance diagram for the Class I-13 cabooses.

Above: This official railroad photo is of the first Class I-13 caboose, C-1800 (former B&O Class L-6 stock car 13041, originally CI&W stock car 692), taken at Mt. Clare in April 1941. Note the narrow step and stirrup next to it rather than the wide step with journal box access door found on later Class I-13 cabooses. Also note the outward facing brake wheel on only one end of the caboose, rather than the dual brake wheels of later cars. The car wears a variation of the 1941 lettering scheme with the capitol dome herald instead of the later "13-states" herald. Since the bay window was so much narrower than that of the wagon top bay window cabooses, the words "Baltimore & Ohio" would not fit, and had to be placed on the body of the caboose, in this case with the unusual lines above and below the company's name. (The B&O Railroad Museum Collection)

Right: Well-worn Class I-13 Caboose C-1824 is seen late in its career at Cincinnati, Ohio on January 9, 1965. This photograph provides a good view of some of the unique characteristics found on the I-13 cabooses. Note that the external siding has been nailed on top of the old stock car siding. Also evident are the characteristic external steel braces of the original stock car. (Eileen Wolford Barnard, The B&O Railroad Historical Society Collection)

Class I-13 Cabooses

As noted, many detailed records concerning B&O cabooses have been lost. However, the history files covering the Class L-6 stock cars have survived. Since these cars were converted into Class I-13 cabooses it is possible to document the origins of this particular class. As additional archival resources become available in the future, it may be possible to reconstruct similar records for additional classes.

Haskell & Barker built stock cars 651 to 700 for the Cincinnati, Indianapolis, & Western Railroad at Michigan City, Indiana in 1916. CI&W 697 was retired before the B&O assumed control of the railroad in 1927, but the surviving 49 cars were renumbered to B&O Class L-6 stock cars 13000 to 13048 at various B&O shops in 1927 and 1928. 36 cars survived until 1941, when they were rebuilt to Class I-13 cabooses as detailed below.

CI&W Number	L-6 Number	Shop	Date	I-13 Number	Shop	Date
692	13041	WA	11/7/27	C-1800	MC	4/19/41
698	13046	WA	1/31/28	C-1801	MC	4/21/41
651	13000	WA	7/19/27	C-1802	WA	6/24/41
654	13003	PV	9/10/27	C-1803	WA	7/1/41
655	13004	IV	1/27/28	C-1804	WA	7/2/41
657	13006	GA	10/8/27	C-1805	WA	7/25/41
658	13007	NE	12/13/27	C-1806	WA	7/14/41
659	13008	PV	7/21/27	C-1807	WA	6/18/41
660	13009	PV	9/9/27	C-1808	WA	7/22/41
664	13013	WA	8/24/27	C-1809	WA	7/5/41
665	13014	WA	11/8/27	C-1810	WA	7/25/41
667	13016	WI	7/13/27	C-1811	WA	6/19/41
668	13017	MC	11/25/27	C-1812	WA	8/5/41
670	13019	NE	10/22/27	C-1813	WA	7/30/41
672	13021	WA	11/8/27	C-1814	WA	7/3/41
673	13022	WA	11/21/27	C-1815	WA	7/7/41
674	13023	CE	12/10/27	C-1816	WA	7/5/41
675	13024	LP	2/2/28	C-1817	WA	6/21/41
677	13026	PV	9/10/27	C-1818	WA	7/14/41
678	See Note			C-1819	WA	7/14/41
679	13028	MD	10/15/27	C-1820	WA	7/19/41
680	13029	WA	11/2/27	C-1821	WA	6/20/41
681	13030	BW	11/30/27	C-1822	WA	7/16/41
683	13032	WA	7/8/27	C-1823	WA	7/30/41
684	13033	CE	11/29/27	C-1824	WA	6/14/41
685	13034	PV	11/2/27	C-1825	WA	8/2/41
686	13035	MD	1/12/28	C-1826	WA	7/1/41
687	13036	WA	7/22/27	C-1827	WA	8/6/41
688	13037	WA	6/29/27	C-1828	WA	7/17/41
689	13038	MD	10/20/27	C-1829	WA	8/5/41
691	13040	MD	12/19/27	C-1830	WA	7/12/41
694	13043	GA	11/23/27	C-1831	WA	7/26/41
695	13044	MD	9/20/27	C-1832	WA	7/15/41
696	13045	BW	11/20/27	C-1833	WA	7/18/41
699	13047	MD	10/12/27	C-1834	WA	8/1/41
700	13048	CE	10/29/27	C-1835	WA	6/23/41

The first date shown is the date that car was renumbered to B&O L-6 number. The second date shown is the date that the car was placed in service as a Class I-13 caboose.

Legend of Shop Symbols:

BW = Brunswick, Maryland
CE = Chillicothe, Ohio
GA = Garrett, Indiana
IV = Ivorydale, Ohio
LP = Locust Point (Baltimore), Maryland
MC = Mt. Clare (Baltimore), Maryland
MD = Moorefield Yard, Indianapolis, Indiana
NE = Newark, Ohio
PV = Painesville, Ohio
WA = Washington, Indiana
WI = Willard, Ohio

NOTE: CI&W 678 changed to B&O 12027 in error at Chillicothe, Ohio on December 2, 1927. Number corrected to B&O 13027 at Moorefield Yard, Indianapolis, Indiana on December 8, 1927.

Above: B&O I-13 C-1818 is in fresh paint at Brunswick, Maryland on July 22, 1950. By comparing this view to the photograph of C-1800 on page 81, we may note several characteristics of the production run I-13 cars that differ from the prototype C-1800. The C-1818 has full width steps. Because of its stock car heritage, the trucks are set closer to the ends of the underframe than on most cabooses. This, in turn, necessitated a small door in the back of the steps to provide access to the outermost journal boxes. The C-1818, like almost all cabooses, has two brake wheels—one at each end of the car. This is a change from the prototype I-13, which originally had only one as a carryover from its freight car past. (L. W. Rice, John R. King, Jr. Collection)

Figure 25

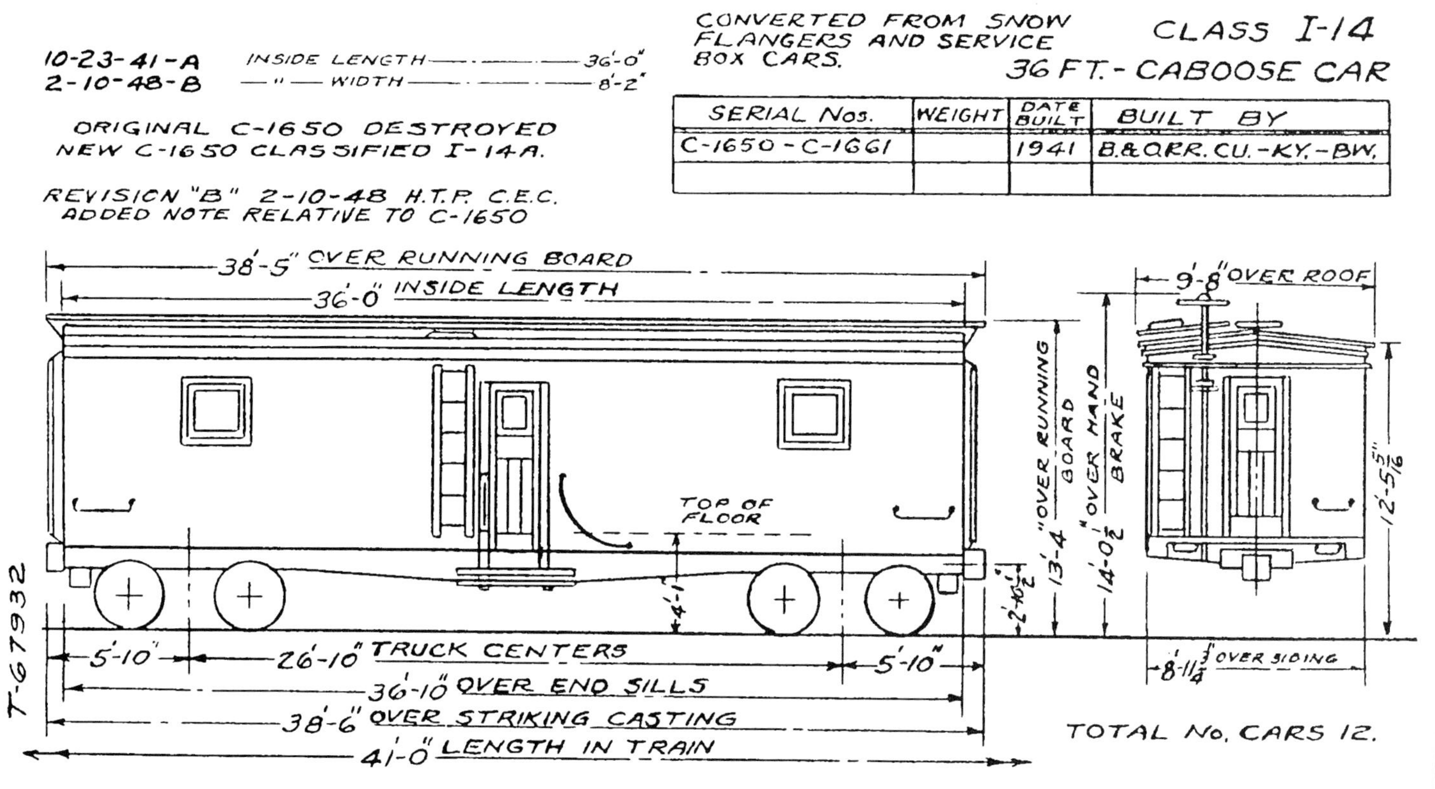

Class I-14 Cabooses

Number Series   C-1650 to C-1661

Also to ease wartime caboose shortages, the B&O converted snow flangers and service box cars to cabooses designated Class I-14. These cars were side door cabooses with no end platforms, cupolas or bay windows. The first ten (C-1650 to C-1659) were renumbered from snow flangers, SF-19, SF-42, SF-43, SF-13, SF-14, SF-10, SF-11, SF-12, SF-45, and SF-41. The last two (C-1660 & C-1661) were converted from service box cars X-2235 and X-2628. The conversions were accomplished by shops at Keyser, West Virginia (C-1650 to C-1653), Cumberland, Maryland (C-1654), and Brunswick, Maryland (C-1655 to C-1661). Most of these cars were originally Class M-8 boxcars, built between 1897 and 1900. In the teens, the B&O rebuilt the cars with steel center sills and reclassed them M-8B. Finally, in 1927 and 1929, they were converted to non-revenue service equipment.

After the war, all the former snow flangers were returned to that service and renumbered with their original snow flanger numbers. The exception was C-1650, which had been wrecked. The C-1660 and C-1661 retained their caboose numbers until retirement. Figure 25 shows the B&O's diagram for the Class I-14 cabooses.

Above: B&O Snow Flanger SF-43 was at M&K Junction, West Virginia on October 11, 1976, at the ripe old age of 79 years. This ancient car had a long and varied career on the B&O including a stint as one of the unusual Class I-14 cabooses. It was built as B&O Class M-8 boxcar 42005 by the Pullman Company on September 2, 1897, renumbered to 82005 on October 11, 1901 and converted to Class M-8B boxcar 98294 by application of a steel center sill on January 4, 1913. The car was converted to snow flanger SF-43 on March 22, 1929, changed to Class I-14 caboose C-1652 on June 7, 1941, and changed back to snow flanger SF-43 on December 11, 1945. Notice the lack of any sort of cupola, bay window or end platforms. The car still had its arch bar trucks and truss rods. (Robert Hubler)

Class I-14A Caboose

Number Series   C-1650

In October 1942, the Keyser, West Virginia shops produced the sole Class I-14A caboose. This car also carried the number C-1650 which had been vacated when the Class I-14 caboose of that number was destroyed. Like the I-14, the I-14A was a side door caboose with no end platform, cupola, or bay window. The car was originally B&O Class M-13A boxcar 182072, built by Standard Steel Car and delivered to the B&O in February 1910. The 182072 was converted to tie car X-6198 at Cumberland, Maryland on November 29, 1940. The X-6198 was rebuilt to the C-1650 at Keyser, West Virginia, placed in service on October 23, 1942, and retired from service in February 1954. The clearance diagram for the Class I-14A caboose is shown in Figure 26.

Class I-14 Cabooses

As noted, many of the detailed records concerning B&O cabooses have been lost. However, some of the history files covering the B&O Class M-8 boxcars have survived. Since most of the Class I-14 cabooses originated as Class M-8 boxcars, it has been possible to partially reconstruct information on the origins of this class.

C-1650: Built as Class M-8 41017 by Pullman Company, Pullman, IL 7/14/1897.
Number changed to 81017 at Locust Point, MD 4/7/01.
Rebuilt to Class M-8B 89081 by Ryan Car Co., Chicago, IL 10/26/14.
Converted to Snow Flanger SF-19 at Locust Point, MD 11/9/29. Converted to Class I-14 C-1650 at Keyser, WV 6/7/41.

C-1651: Built as Class M-8 42550 by Pullman Company, Pullman, IL 10/25/1897.
Number changed to 82550 at Mt. Clare, MD 5/23/01.
Rebuilt to Class M-8B 89793 by Ryan Car Co., Chicago, IL 12/2/15.
Converted to Snow Flanger SF-42 at Locust Point, MD 3/22/29. Converted to Class I-14 C-1651 at Keyser, WV 6/7/41.

C-1652: Built as Class M-8 42005 by Pullman Company, Pullman, IL 9/2/1897.
Number changed to 82005 at South Chicago, IL 10/11/01.
Rebuilt to Class M-8B 98294 by Ryan Car Co., Chicago, IL 1/4/13.
Converted to Snow Flanger SF-43 at Locust Point, MD 3/22/29. Converted to Class I-14 C-1652 at Keyser, WV 6/7/41.

C-1653: Built as B&OSW Boxcar 4948 placed in service in 11/1883.
Number changed to B&O 97783 at location not recorded.
Rebuilt to Snow Plow X-24 at Keyser, WV 11/20/05.
Converted to Snow Flanger SF-13 at Locust Point, MD 11/9/29. Converted to Class I-14 C-1653 at Keyser, WV 6/7/41.

C-1654: Built as Class M-8 Boxcar 80072 by Pullman Company, Pullman, Il 2/9/1900.
Rebuilt to Class M-8B 97314 by South Baltimore Car Company, Curtis Bay, MD 1/25/13.
Converted to Snow Flanger SF-44 at Locust Point, MD 3/22/29. Converted to Class I-14 C-1654 at Cumberland, MD 6/7/41.

C-1655: Built as Class M-8 56160 by Pullman Company, Pullman, IL 10/21/1898.
Number changed to 86160 at South Chicago, IL 8/13/04.
Rebuilt to Class M-8B 95079 by South Baltimore Car Co., Curtis Bay, MD 3/1/15.
Converted to Snow Flanger SF-10 at Locust Point, MD 11/29/29. Converted to Class I-14 C-1655 at Brunswick, MD 6/11/41.

C-1656: Built as Class M-8 78986 by Missouri Car & Foundry Co. St. Louis, MO 2/17/1898.
Rebuilt to Class M-8B 93125 by Ryan Car Co., Chicago, IL 3/9/14.
Converted to Snow Flanger SF-11 at Locust Point, MD 11/29/29. Converted to Class I-14 C-1656 at Brunswick, MD 6/10/41.

C-1657: Built as Class M-8 56398 by Pullman Company, Pullman, IL 11/2/1898.
Number changed to 86398 at Chillicothe, Ohio 8/24/04.
Rebuilt to Class M-8B 87816 by Ryan Car Co., Chicago, IL 10/31/14.
Converted to Snow Flanger SF-12 at Locust Point, MD 11/29/29. Converted to Class I-14 C-1657 at Brunswick, MD 6/12/41.

C-1658: Built as Class M-8 64378 by South Baltimore Car Co., Curtis Bay, MD 11/28/1899.
Number changed to 69628 at Sandusky, Ohio 4/12/02.
Rebuilt to Class M-8B 90745 by South Baltimore Car Co., Curtis Bay, MD 1/11/15.
Converted to Snow Flanger SF-45 at Locust Point, MD 3/22/29. Converted to Class I-14 C-1658 at Brunswick, MD 6/9/41.

C-1659: Built as Class M-8 57052 by Michigan Peninsular Car Co., Detroit, MI 8/26/1898.
Number changed to 87052 at Grafton, WV 9/5/04.
Rebuilt to Class M-8B 90098 by Ryan Car Co., Chicago, IL 1/4/13.
Converted to Snow Flanger SF-41 at Locust Point, MD 3/22/29. Converted to Class I-14 C-1659 at Brunswick, MD 6/9/41.

C-1660: Built as Class M-8 B&OSW 15001 by Pullman Company, Pullman, IL 7/7/1898.
Number changed to B&O 70001 at Locust Point, MD 1/24/05.
Rebuilt to Class M-8B 88171 by Ryan Car Co., Chicago, IL 11/11/14.
Converted to Service Box Car X-2235 at Painesville, Ohio 8/9/29. Converted to Class I-14 C-1660 at Brunswick, MD 6/9/41.

C-1661: Built as Class M-8 67781 by Pullman Company, Pullman, IL 5/16/1898.
Rebuilt to Class M-8B 87473 by South Baltimore Car Co., Curtis Bay, MD 3/1/16.
Converted to Service Box Car X-2628 at Locust Point, MD 6/3/27. Converted to Class I-14 C-1661 at Brunswick, MD 6/9/41.

Figure 26

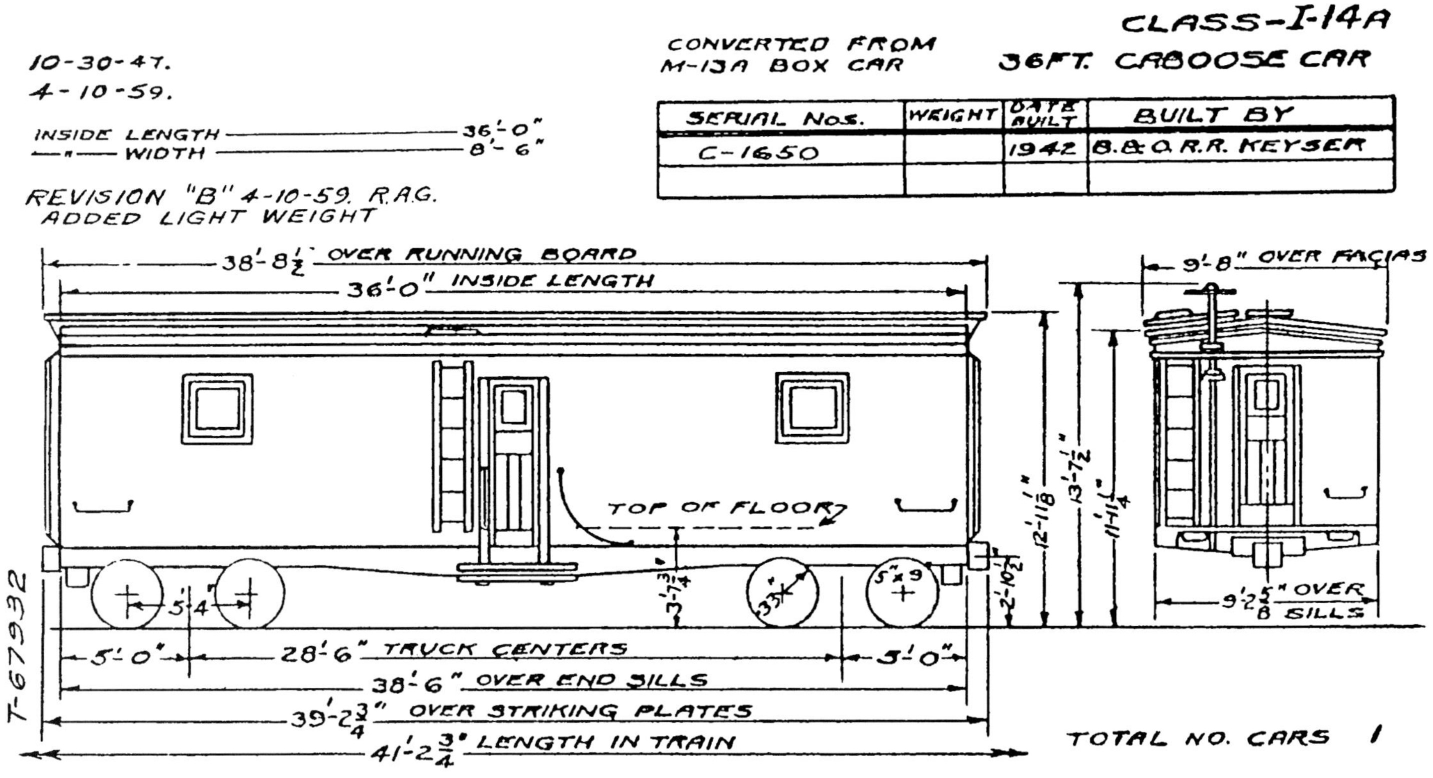

[Drawing: Class I-14A 36 Ft. Caboose Car, converted from M-13A Box Car. Serial No. C-1650, built 1942 by B.&O.R.R. Keyser. Dated 10-30-47, revised 4-10-59. Inside length 36'-0", width 8'-6". Over running board 38'-8½". Truck centers 28'-6". Over end sills 38'-6". Over striking plates 39'-2¾". Length in train 41'-2¾". Over fascias 9'-8". Over sills 9'-2⅝". Height 13'-7½". T-67932. Total No. Cars: 1.]

A Mystery and Speculation

Why was there no Class I-15 caboose?

The B&O coped with increased World War II traffic by building as many new cabooses as it could (the bay window I-12 cabooses), and by converting stock cars, snow flangers and box cars to Class I-13, I-14 and I-16 cabooses. Note that Class I-15 was not used, prompting the question of why the B&O skipped this class.

To look at this question in another way, consider these classes chronologically in terms of when the first car of each class was put into service.

Class	First Car	Date Placed in Service
I-13	C-1800	April 19, 1941
I-14	C-1650	June 7, 1941
I-12	C-2400	December 1, 1941
I-16	C-2300	October 1942

When viewed in this respect, it invites speculation that the B&O intended to assign Class I-15 to the C-2400 series wagon top cabooses. Perhaps, before this could happen, someone noticed that the Class I-12 was vacant and assigned it to the wagon top cars. Of course this does not resolve the question of why the I-17s were not designated Class I-15 which was vacant when the I-17s were built in 1952. The Society welcomes any additional information that anyone could provide on this subject.

Class I-16 Cabooses

Number Series   C-2300 to C-2374 & C-2700 to C-2799

In 1942, the B&O began to produce the Class I-16 caboose. They were yet another wartime emergency measure to alleviate a critical shortage of cabooses. Boxcars of the M-13, M-13A and M-13B Classes formed the raw material for the conversions. The result was a wooden bodied, steel underframe caboose with a steel bay window set into each door opening. The I-16 Class totaled 175 cars produced in two groups. The B&O produced the first group of 75 cars, numbered C-2300 through C-2374, in late 1942. The railroad converted the second group, consisting of 100 cars numbered C-2700 through C-2799, in the summer of 1943. These conversions were made by B&O shops at Mt. Clare, (Baltimore) Maryland (C-2300 through C-2324 and C-2700 through C-2724), DuBois, Pennsylvania (C-2325 through C-2349 and C-2725 through C-2749) and Washington, Indiana (C-2350 through C-2374 and C-2750 through C-2799).

Although they were wartime emergency conversions, the Class I-16 cabooses remained in service on the B&O for many years after the war. Some were assigned to yard and transfer service with their bay windows removed, with many later being transferred to maintenance of way service. The clearance diagram for the Class I-16 cabooses is shown in Figure 27.

Right: B&O I-16 caboose C-2701 was seen at Forest Hill yard in Chicago, Illinois on November 7, 1965. It was leased to the B&OCT, and, since it was used for transfer service, the bay window was removed and an additional regular window was installed in the side of the car. Other instances have been noted where the bay window was removed from I-13 and I-16 cabooses, but on many occasions the opening was simply covered over with no new windows provided. (Eileen Wolford Barnard, The B&O Railroad Historical Society Collection)

Figure 27

Left: This low angle photograph of B&O caboose C-2784 affords a good look at the "fishbelly" underframe of the Class I-16 and also the triangular supports for the bay window which replaced the original boxcar door opening. (S. P. Davidson, Robert Hubler Collection)

Middle Left: This excellent photograph of C-2363 was taken at Zanesville, Ohio in August 1949. In this view, it is easy to visualize the boxcar heritage of the C-2363 with the bay window set into the old boxcar door opening and the new platforms cut into the ends. Clearly distinguishable from this angle are the small doors in the steps to permit access to the journals. Notice also the small square end windows cut quite low into the ends of the car. (Paul Dunn, Robert Hubler Collection)

Lower Left: The B&O photograph of caboose C-2306 at Mt. Clare in October, 1942 documents the newly constructed Class I-16 cars. As on the I-13's, the bay window was so narrow that the words "Baltimore & Ohio" would not fit, forcing their relocation to the body of the car. These cabooses were built from Class M-13 box cars and retained some original characteristics, such as the fishbelly underframe and arch bar trucks. Like cars of the I-13 class, the steps have a small door to permit access to the journal boxes. (The B&O Railroad Museum Collection)

Class I-17 Cabooses

First Number Series   C-2850 to C-2861
Second Number Series 902850 to 902861

Because so many cabooses were created by conversions during the war years, it was 1952 before the B&O found itself in need of new cabooses. The last cabooses built new by the B&O were the second series of I-12s in 1945. By the 1950s, the B&O no longer favored the wagon top style of construction, although cabooses of that size and length were still adequate for the B&O's needs. The Class I-17 was the successor to the B&O's wagon top design. The configuration of the I-17 was virtually identical to that of the earlier Class I-12 wagon top car. At least dimensionally, the Class I-17 cabooses were similar to the wagon top cabooses but built with a conventional roof design and carbuilding technique. Except for the position of the side windows and the distance between the truck centers, the I-17 was similar to the I-7 of 1930-31. The I-17s were built at the Washington, Indiana shops during December 1952 and January 1953. The series consisted of 12 cars numbered C-2850 through C-2861.

The I-17s were distinguishable from later I-17A cars by their square, wooden sash end windows and slotted steps. When the company later replaced the wooden sash end windows with the same type of sealed end windows used on Class I-17A cabooses, the steps remained the only consistent spotting feature of the original cars.

In 1970 and 1971, the B&O rebuilt all the Class I-17s at the shops in DuBois, Pennsylvania. The rebuilding had two effects on the external appearance of the I-17. First, due to a rearrangement of the interior fixtures, one of the side windows was plated over. Second, the leaf spring trucks of the Class I-17 cars were replaced with coil spring trucks. Those cars which remained in service in 1982 were renumbered to the "902850" series by dropping the "C" prefix and substituting the digits "90" preceding the car number. The last two I-17s in service on CSXT, 902850 and 902855, were retired at Connellsville, Pennsylvania in 1993. Figure 28 shows the clearance diagram for the Class I-17 cabooses.

Above: Class I-17 cars were functionally identical to their predecessor I-12 cars, but structurally more modern. By the early 1950s, the B&O was still traditional, conservative, and committed to building its own cars whenever advantageous. But Dan Willard and J. J. Tatum were gone, the post-World War II prosperity was well underway, and the B&O had embarked on a program of modernization and rationalization still being carried on by CSX Transportation. In some ways, the I-17 was merely the I-12 constructed with a different style carbody with the same size and general arrangement. Yet, it also represents a new philosophy, for the cars were not "home made," but assembled from stock parts. Almost all major pieces, from the ride control trucks to the safety tread roof walk, were purchased items cut to size and assembled like a kit. The car sides, structural shapes, and many interior elements came from outside carbuilders instead of Cumberland Bolt and Forge or the Mt. Clare sawmill. The C-2858, shown in a shop portrait at the Washington, Indiana shops where it was built, exhibits a degree of fit and finish lacking in the Keyser-built I-12 cars. (The B&O Railroad Museum Collection)

Figure 28

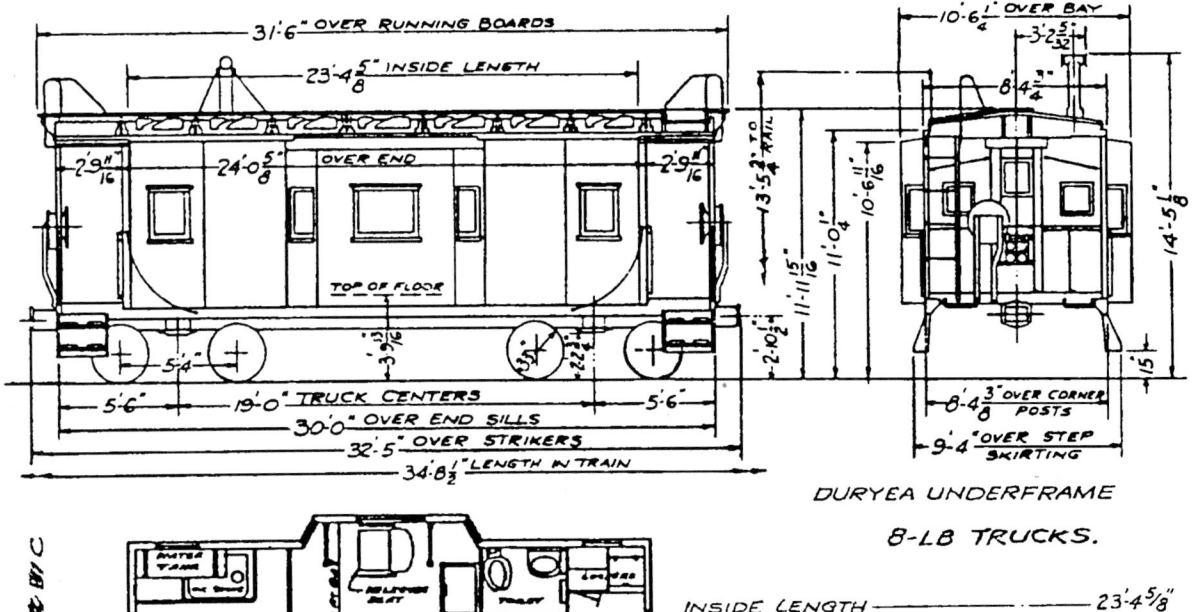

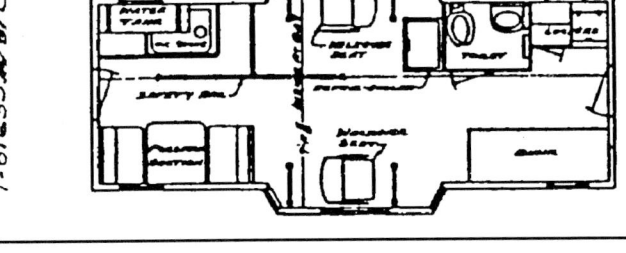

Left: This view illustrates the appearance of the I-17 cars as they approached the end of their career on the B&O. The C-2855 was equipped with a retention-type toilet, which in turn forced the relocation of the battery box to the opposite side. At some point, the original grab irons were replaced with the unusual "J" style. The B&O replaced the original leaf springs with coil springs, although the trucks retained friction-bearings. Finally, the end windows were replaced with sealed windows of the style used on the newer Class I-17A cars. The C-2855 was photographed at Benwood, West Virginia on September 3, 1977. (Robert Hubler)

Right: In 1970 and 1971, all I-17 cabooses were put through a rebuilding program at the DuBois, Pennsylvania shops, emerging with the 1970 blue-and-yellow scheme seen on the C-2861. The B&O replaced the truck's leaf springs with coil springs, and replaced the original end windows with sealed windows identical to those on Class I-17A cabooses. This modification left the slotted steps as the only consistent identifying feature of Class I-17s. The C-2861 was photographed at Cincinnati, Ohio on January 2, 1978. (Robert Hubler)

Figure 29

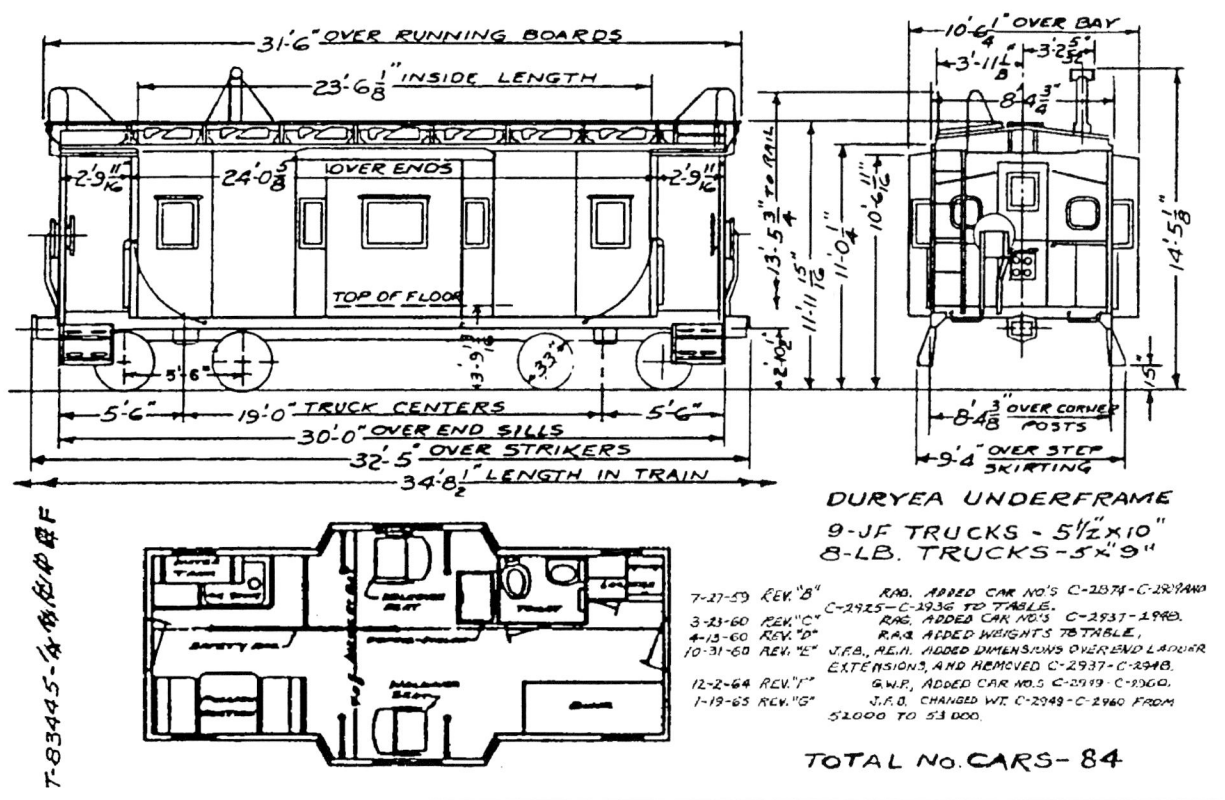

Class I-17A Cabooses

First Number Series   C-2862 to C-2909 & C-2925 to C-2960

Second Number Series   902862 to 902909 & 902925 to 902960

The I-17A caboose varied only slightly from its predecessor, the I-17. The B&O used sealed rubber gasket end windows and solid rather than slotted step backs. Since all Class I-17 cabooses were later fitted with the new sealed end windows, the distinction became even more blurred in later years with only the steps as a consistent spotting feature. The I-17A class totalled eighty-four cars numbered C-2862 through C-2909 and C-2925 through C-2960. They were built in seven groups of twelve cars each with only small variations between them. For example, through car C-2885, the side of the bay window was cut from a single sheet of steel like the Class I-17 cars. Starting with the C-2886, the side of the bay window was cut from two sheets riveted together. The group of I-17A cabooses from C-2886 to C-2897 were built with an unusual side grab iron shaped like a "J." The Washington, Indiana shops built all the Class I-17A cabooses except for the last twelve cars. C-2949 through C-2960 were assembled at the DuBois, Pennsylvania shops and completed at Mt. Clare. This last group of I-17A cabooses, completed in 1964 and 1965, were the last road cabooses built by the B&O in its own shops.

As in the case of the I-17 cabooses, in 1970 and 1971 the B&O rebuilt the I-17A cabooses at the DuBois shops. This rebuilding affected their external appearance in two ways. First, due to a rearrangement of the interior fixtures, one of the side windows was plated over. Second, the railroad replaced the truck leaf springs with coil springs. Sometime in the early 1970s, one Class I-17A caboose, the C-2905, was equipped with roller bearing trucks as an experiment. So far as is known, the C-2905 was the only I-17A caboose ever equipped this way. Cars remaining in service in 1982 were renumbered to the "902862" and "902925" series by dropping the "C" prefix and substituting the digits "90" preceding the car number. Two I-17As have been preserved for the B&O Railroad Museum, C-2884 and C-2943. The B&O's clearance diagram for the Class I-17A cars is shown in Figure 29.

Above: B&O caboose C-2939 was from the second to the last group of I-17A cars built at the B&O's Washington, Indiana shops in December 1960. This photograph illustrates the original appearance of the C-2939 and serves to highlight the differences from the earlier I-17 cabooses. Note that the C-2939 had sealed, rubber gasket end windows rather than the wooden framed windows of the I-17 cars, while the step backs were solid instead of slotted. In common with the I-17 cars, the C-2939 had leaf spring trucks and no window screens. (Julian W. Barnard, The B&O Railroad Historical Society Collection)

Right: The C-2889 is an example of a class I-17A car modified in the pool caboose program of the mid-1960s. Note the new window screens and the electric marker lights applied as part of its conversion to pool service. It is one of the group of Class I-17A cabooses built with the unusual "J" shaped grab irons and this feature stands out clearly in this view. The C-2889 was photographed at Willard, Ohio on July 17, 1966. (Julian W. Barnard, The B&O Railroad Historical Society Collection)

Middle Right: In 1970 and 1971, all surviving I-17A cabooses were put through a rebuilding program at the DuBois, Pennsylvania shops. C-2890 in the 1970 blue with yellow paint scheme illustrates the results of this overhaul. On this side of the caboose, the change of trucks springs was the most visible evidence of the shopping. On the opposite side of the car, the window on the left was covered by a steel plate, because of a rearrangement of some interior equipment. It is one of the group of I-17A cars built with the "J" shaped grab irons. This photograph was taken at Dayton, Ohio in October, 1973 by Robert Hubler.

Lower Right: This photograph of C-2869 illustrates the appearance of the I-17A cars as they ran out their final years on the B&O. Due to government mandates, the C-2869 was equipped with a retention type toilet (on the other side of the car from that shown here). This, in turn, required the battery box to be relocated to the opposite side of the caboose where it can be seen in this photograph. As a result of the 1970 rebuilding program, the original leaf springs were replaced with coil springs, although the trucks still had friction bearings. The C-2869 was photographed at Grafton, West Virginia on September 4, 1977 by Robert Hubler.

Class I-18 Cabooses

First Number Series   C-3000 to C-3045
Second Number Series   903000 to 903045

Late in 1965 and early in 1966, the railroad received its first Class I-18 cabooses. They were the first new B&O bay window cars with 30-foot carbodies (40 feet over platforms), and the first B&O cabooses in almost sixty years to be purchased from an outside builder. The International Car Company at Kenton, Ohio built 46 cars numbered C-3000 through C-3045. They rode on Barber swing-motion roller bearing trucks and a Waugh "floating center sill" cushion underframe, a conceptual descendent of the Duryea underframe the B&O was so fond of. The body of the car was connected to the center sill through a complex arrangement of springs and damping devices, so that the carbody acted like a seismic mass while the part of the center sill attached to the couplers moved almost independently and absorbed much of the slack action. Inside, the cars had fewer bunks and more seats, automatic oil stoves, a 70 gallon water tank with stainless steel sink, electric refrigerator, and flushing toilet. They weighed almost twice as much as the I-1 cars of 1913, and represented the state of the caboose-building art in the mid-1960s. The I-18s were also the last B&O cabooses to be built with roof walks, and to be classified under the B&O system. All future cabooses would be classified according to the C&O/B&O classification system.

The B&O experimented at times with deadheading crews to or from their work assignments in cabooses, which was one of the reasons for a car capable of seating six men. For example, Trailer Jet trains (the B&O term for expedited piggyback trains) could make the run from Baltimore to Brunswick in under three hours, making it technically feasible to deadhead train and engine crews between those terminals in the cabooses of the Jets. Especially with the reduction in passenger service in the 1960s, the railroad was searching for ways to gain flexibility in assigning and transporting manpower, and cabooses offered one possible means. For a few years, several modern cabooses also carried fare-paying passengers on the Ohio River Sub-division. Until relieved of the responsibility in 1971 by the creation of Amtrak, the B&O operated a little-known mixed train between Parkersburg and Huntington, West Virginia. The cushioned, rest room-equipped cabooses with coach-like seats permitted the railroad to dispense with the passenger car and carry the few people holding transportation with the crew.

The cars remaining in service in 1982 were renumbered to the "903000" series numbers by dropping the "C" prefix and substituting the digits "90" preceding the car number. In 1993, the B&O Railroad Museum acquired I-18 C-3014 for its collection. Figure 30 is the clearance diagram for the Class I-18 cabooses.

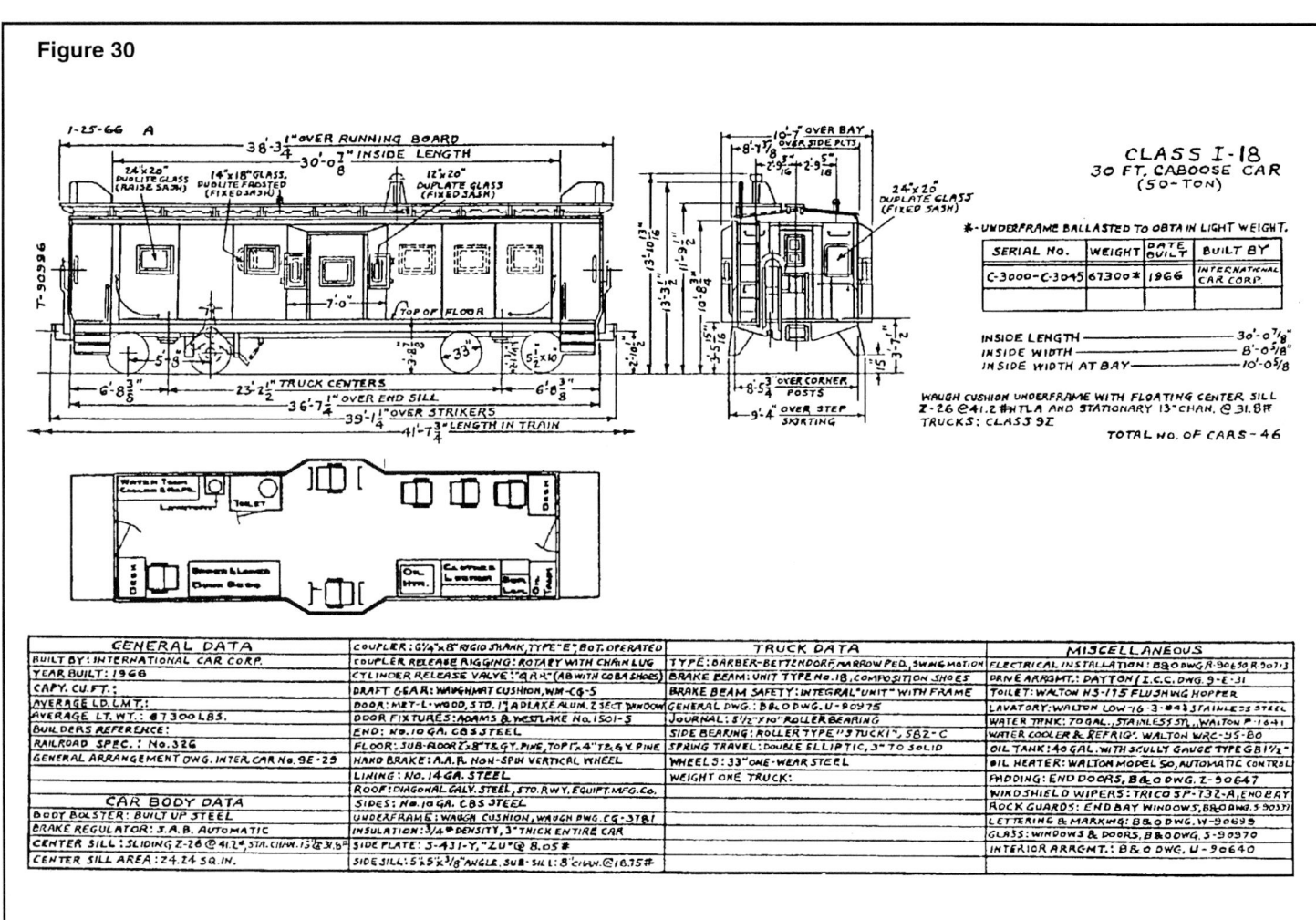

Figure 30

Above: The most obvious differences between the I-18 and its predecessors include an increase in length to 40 feet; all-welded construction; modern sealed roller bearing trucks, and a full package of amenities including window screens, oil stove, toilet, and improved water systems and ice boxes. The carbody "floated" on a full-cushion underframe, meaning that a sprung-and damped continuous draft gear connected both couplers, allowing the car itself to act something like a seismic mass. Such draft gears were the latest in a long succession of mechanical means to attenuate or lessen harsh slack action, and partly reflect the B&O's earlier fascination with the Duryea underframe used on many freight cars and cabooses. In a collision or extremely hard coupling, full-cushion underframes were designed to fail by absorbing as much energy as possible. If there was still sufficient force, the coupler was shoved through the draft pocket and underframe. When one coupler was hit hard enough to break the draft gear, the other coupler was pushed out the other end while the shock felt inside the car would be considerably lessened. In later years, cars damaged in that fashion were the first of the "new" cabooses to be retired, as the repair was costly. (J. W. Brauner, Robert Hubler Collection)

Below: This photograph of C-3031 was taken seven years after the preceding one. In the intervening years, the caboose received the Chessie System colors, but, more importantly, this shot affords a look at the other side of the caboose, illustrating the differences in window arrangements on opposite sides of the car. Note that there were only two windows to the left of the bay window on this side, not three as on the other side. Also, the wall to the right of the bay window was completely blank on this side of the car. Photographed at Chillicothe, Ohio on December 26, 1977. (Robert Hubler)

Left: The last of the B&O shop-built I-17 cars of 1965 contrast greatly with the first International Car Company I-18 cars of the same year. The last I-17s represented the end of a long B&O caboose-building tradition and the end of a capital equipment program initiated by the railroad while it was still independent. By the time the I-18 order was approved in 1964 as part of the 1965 capital budget, the coordination of the C&O and B&O Mechanical Departments was well underway. These cars reflect both the availability of more money for equipment purchases and the railroad's desire to acquire modern, state-of-the-art cars. The C-3014 was analogous to the GP-35 in that both marked the end of B&O corporate independence and beginning of the most recent phase of technological innovation on the railroad. (Julian W. Barnard, The B&O Railroad Historical Society Collection)

Middle Left: The C-3045 was the last car of the I-18 class. By this time it has been modified with a retention toilet, indicated by the box under the frame just ahead of the rear truck directly below the window of the toilet compartment. Also apparent in this end view is the roof walk. The I-18 cars were the last B&O cabooses built with this feature. The C-3045 was photographed at Dayton, Ohio on May 22, 1976. (Robert Hubler)

Class C-15B Caboose

First Number Series	C-3050
Second Number Series	903050

In 1965 and 1966, the B&O began to implement a pooled caboose system for its mainline trains. The DuBois, Pennsylvania shops upgraded the Class I-7, I-12, I-17 and I-17A cabooses for service as pool cabooses, and the B&O purchased the I-18s to supplement the pool caboose fleet. In spite of this, the B&O apparently found itself one caboose short of the number needed for the pool. Thus, in September 1967, the B&O acquired C&O steel cupola caboose 90099, built by the Magor Car Corporation in April 1941. It was overhauled at the DuBois shops and renumbered B&O C-3050. This caboose was not given a B&O Class, but when the C&O/B&O classification system was instituted, C-3050 was designated Class C-15B. In the early 1980s it was renumbered 903050. The C&O/B&O clearance diagram for the Class C-15B caboose is shown in Figure 31.

Right: In 1967, when the B&O needed one additional caboose for a road pool, it purchased C&O 90099 and refurbished it at the DuBois, Pennsylvania shops. The result was B&O C-3050, shown in blue paint at Newark, Ohio in June, 1972. This 1941 steel car invites speculation as to what form the Class I-12 cars might have taken had the B&O chosen to build a conventional steel cupola caboose derived from the Class I-5 rather than the wagon top bay window car. It remained in service until the mid-1980s. (J.W. Brauner, John C. La Rue, Jr. Collection)

Figure 31
MECHANICAL DEPARTMENT
HUNTINGTON, W. VA.   DATE: 6-3-70

RR	SERIES	CLASS
B&O	C-3050	C-15B

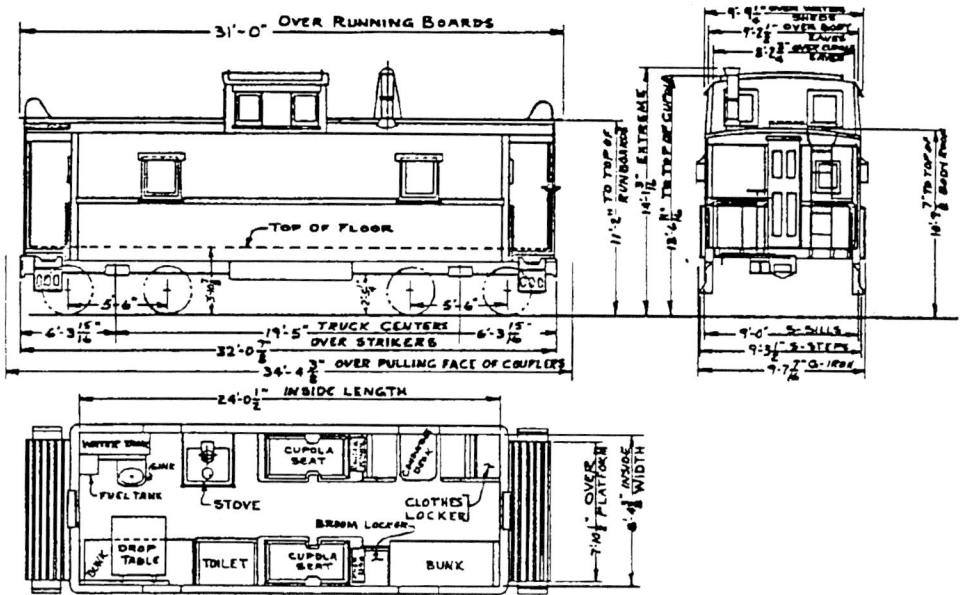

GENERAL DATA	CAR BODY DATA	TRUCK DATA	MISCELLANEOUS
BUILT BY - MAGOR CAR CORP.	BRAKE ARRANGEMENT - 112-11-192	LINING - 13/16" T.&G. WOOD	ALTERNATOR -
YEAR BUILT - 1941-REBUILT 1967 R.C.S.	END DOOR - 26" X 6'-1-1/4" WOOD	UNDERFRAME - DURYEA	BATTERY -
AVERAGE LT WT. - 41700	SUB-FLOOR 13/16" T.&G. WOOD	TYPE - INTEGRAL BOX	DRINKING WATER -
BUILDERS REFERENCE - P-9680	HAND BRAKE -	GENERAL DWG. - 184-5-89	ELECTRIC DRIVE -
GENERAL ARRANGEMENT DWG - 139-11-288	INSULATION - 1/2" SIDE, 3/4" TOP, HAIR BESTOS	JOURNAL - 4-1/4" X 8" FRICTION	HEATER - CABAN OIL BURNING
CLEARANCE - PLATE "B"	ROOF - 3/32" C.B. STEEL	SPRING TRAVEL -	OIL TANK CAPY. -
CURVATURE - UNCOUPLED -	SHEATHING - 3/32" C.B. STEEL	WHEELS - 33" DIA. I.W.W.S.	RADIO ANTENNA -
COUPLED TO BASE CAR -	SASH - WOOD FRAMES	WEIGHT ONE TRUCK -	REFRIGERATOR - METAL ICE BOX
	BRAKES - AB CONVENTIONAL	BRAKE SHOES - CAST IRON	SEATS -
	CENTER SILL - (2) 25.3 LB. CHANNELS		TOILETS - FLUSH
	COUPLER - 6-1/4" X 8" TYPE "E"		WATER TANK CAPY.
	DRAFT GEAR - DURYEA		
	END - 3/32" C.B. STEEL		
	FLOOR - 13/16" T.&G. WOOD		

Class C-5 Cabooses

Number Series　　　　　　90363 to 90370

In 1967, when the C&O Railway was experiencing a shortage of cabooses, Class I-10 cabooses C-2650, C-2653, C-2663, C-2660, C-2637, C-2616, C-2604, C-2613, C-2635, C-2617, C-2636, C-2601, C-2609 and C-2642 were "sold" to the C&O, renumbered to C&O 90357 to 90370, and assigned Class C-5 in the C&O/B&O classification system. In 1971, when the B&O experienced its own shortage of cabooses, the C&O "sold" eight of these cars back to the B&O. They were not restored to their B&O numbers, but were simply relettered B&O 90363 to 90370, retaining the C-5 classification. Figure 32 is the C&O/B&O clearance diagram for the Class I-10 cabooses sold to the C&O in 1967 (indicated as class C-5 on the diagram). Note that the car drawing is a copy of the obsolete BR&P diagram for these cars, right down to the long-gone lamp on the cupola roof.

Class C-8 Cabooses

Number Series　　　　　　90689 to 90998

In 1971, to fill assignments for cabooses in yard and local service, the B&O acquired 25 wood-bodied, steel underframe cabooses from the C&O. Their numbers were 90689, 90697, 90743, 90746, 90747, 90748, 90764, 90771, 90800, 90831, 90837, 90846, 90848, 90850, 90855, 90860, 90877, 90915, 90922, 90951, 90957, 90963, 90966, 90969, and 90998. The B&O relettered the cars, but did not give them B&O numbers. On the C&O, the cars were designated Class C-8 under the C&O/B&O classification system; they retained that class when transferred to the B&O. The 90700 series cabooses were built by Standard Steel Car in November 1924, and the 90800 series by Standard Tank Car in February and March 1926. The 90680 and 90900 series cars were built for the C&O by the Hocking Valley Railway from August to November 1929. The C&O/B&O clearance diagram for the Class C-8 cabooses is Figure 33.

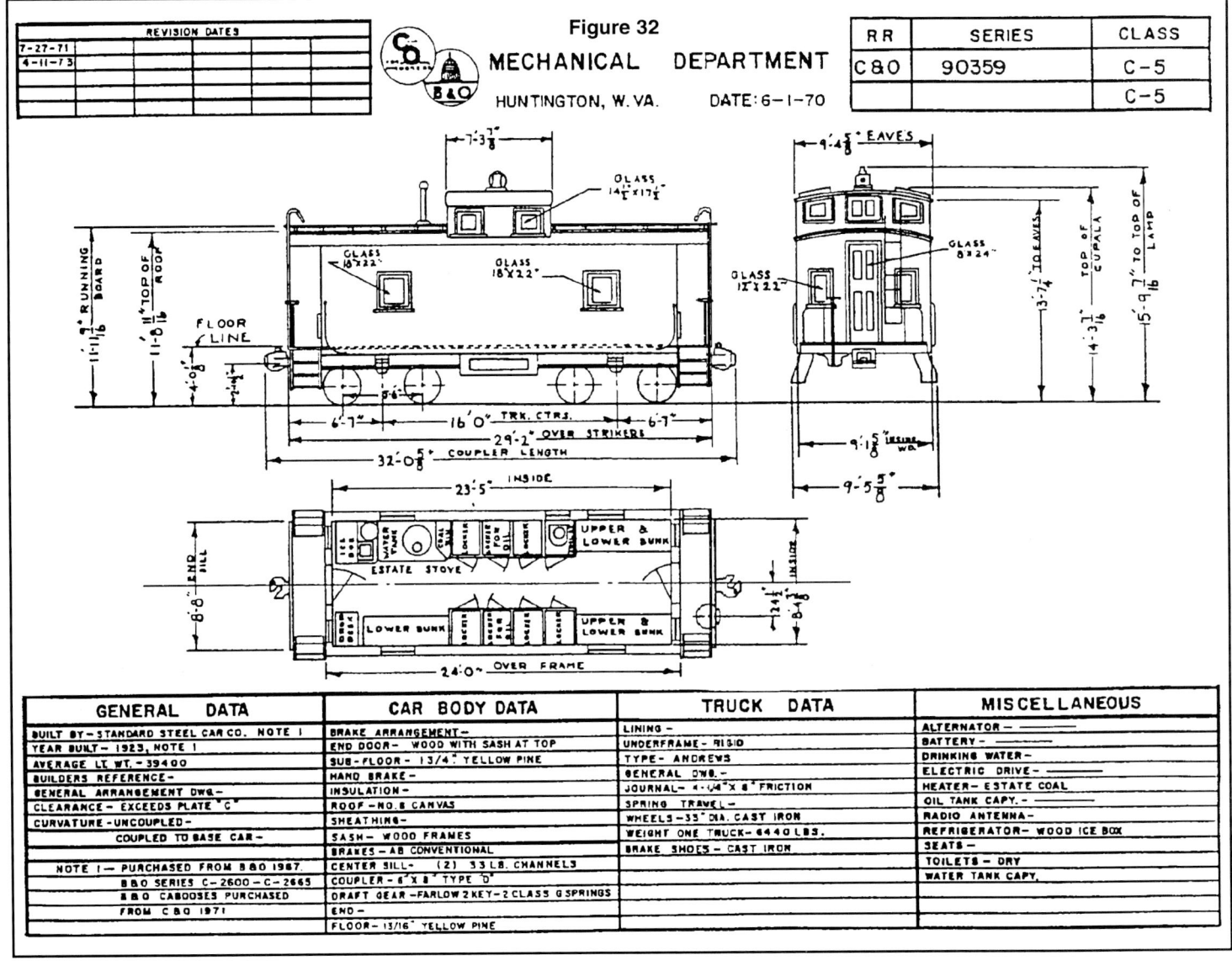

Right: In 1971, the B&O purchased a number of cabooses secondhand from the C&O. Included were eight cars from a group of fourteen I-10 cabooses the B&O sold to the C&O in 1967. They retained their C&O numbers during their remaining service on the B&O. They were also referred to by their C&O class, rather than the original B&O classification. This photograph shows Class C-5 caboose 90369 (the former B&O I-10, C-2609, and originally BR&P 258), at Chillicothe, Ohio on August 20, 1977. (Robert Hubler)

Below: Class C-8 90855 (a former C&O car of the same number) was at the Chillicothe, Ohio shops on July 23, 1978. This 52-year-old caboose was one of a number acquired from the C&O in 1971 to relieve a temporary caboose shortage on the B&O. The 90855 saw relatively little modification in its career, most noticeably, replacement of the car's original arch bar trucks and the application of plywood siding to the outside. This broadside view also illustrates the off-center cupola typical of C&O cabooses. (Robert Hubler)

Figure 33 — MECHANICAL DEPARTMENT
HUNTINGTON, W. VA. DATE: 6-1-70

RR	SERIES	CLASS
C&O	90681-90999	C-8

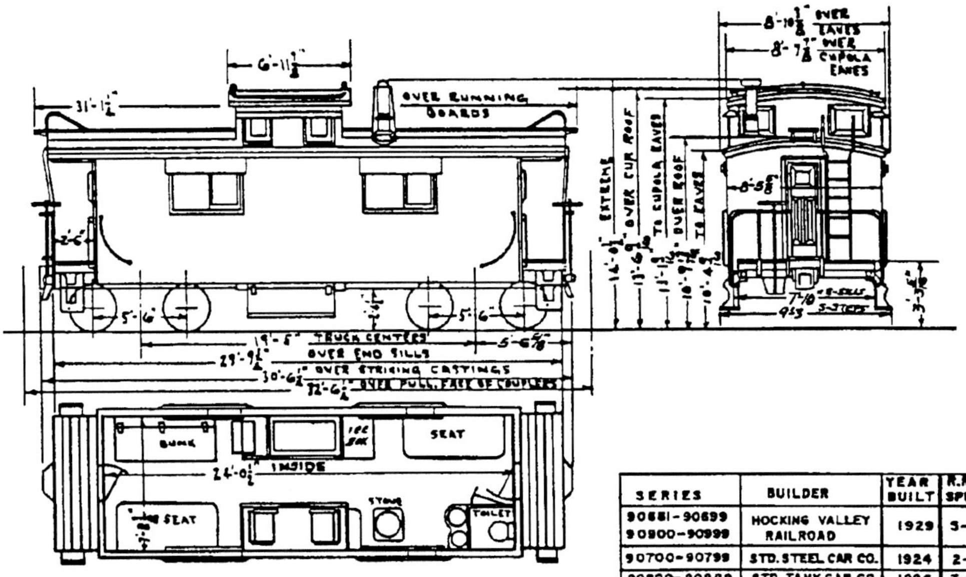

SERIES	BUILDER	YEAR BUILT	R.R.CO. SPEC. NO.	LIGHT WEIGHT	WEIGHT OF 1-TRUCK
90681-90699 / 90900-90999	HOCKING VALLEY RAILROAD	1929	3-CCA	41,500	6612
90700-90799	STD. STEEL CAR CO.	1924	2-CCA	40,300	6320
90800-90899	STD. TANK CAR CO.	1926	3-CCA	40,500	8400

GENERAL DATA	CAR BODY DATA	TRUCK DATA	MISCELLANEOUS
BUILT BY - SEE TABLE	BRAKE ARRANGEMENT - 112-8-370	LINING - 13/16" WOOD-SIDE & END	ALTERNATOR -
YEAR BUILT - SEE TABLE	END DOOR - 26" X 5'-11 7/16" WOOD	UNDERFRAME - STEEL	BATTERY -
AVERAGE LT WT. - SEE TABLE	SUB-FLOOR - 1" WOOD	TYPE -	DRINKING WATER -
BUILDERS REFERENCE -	HAND BRAKE -	GENERAL DWG. - C&O 20556 NOTE 1	ELECTRIC DRIVE -
GENERAL ARRANGEMENT DWG - C&O 18713, NOTE 1	INSULATION -	JOURNAL - 4 1/4" X 8" FRICTION	HEATER - STOVE - COAL
CLEARANCE - PLATE "B"	ROOF - WOOD & CANVAS	SPRING TRAVEL -	OIL TANK CAPY. -
CURVATURE - UNCOUPLED -	SHEATHING - 13/16" WOOD	WHEELS - 33" DIA. CAST IRON	RADIO ANTENNA -
COUPLED TO BASE CAR -	SASH - WOOD FRAMES	WEIGHT ONE TRUCK - SEE TABLE	REFRIGERATOR - WOOD ICE BOX
	BRAKES - AB CONVENTIONAL	BRAKE SHOES - CAST IRON	SEATS -
NOTE 1 - GEN. ARRG'T. DWG. 17255 & TRUCK ARRG'T. DWG. 17258 FOR SERIES 90700-90799.	CENTER SILL - (2) 44.5 LB. CHANNELS		TOILETS - DRY
	COUPLER - TYPE "E" 6 1/4" X 8" SHANK		WATER TANK CAPY.
	DRAFT GEAR - M-901		
	END - 13/16" WOOD		
	FLOOR - 13/16" WOOD		

Above: B&O Class C-8 caboose 90771 (formerly same number on the C&O) is seen in the dead line at the Chillicothe, Ohio shops on December 28, 1975, showing evidence of fire damage. Notice that even at this late date it is still equipped with its original arch bar trucks. (Robert Hubler)

Class C-9 Cabooses

Number Series   90619 & 90631

Another group of cabooses acquired from the C&O in May 1971 for use in yard and local service were wooden, steel underframe cars numbered C&O 90619 and 90631. Again, they were not given B&O numbers, but were relettered B&O. The C&O cars of this type were known as Class C-9 under the C&O/B&O classification system in effect at the time. This class was retained by the cabooses transferred to the B&O. The Hocking Valley Railway built the cabooses at their Logan, Ohio shops in April 1926. Figure 34 is the C&O/B&O clearance diagram for the Class C-9 cabooses.

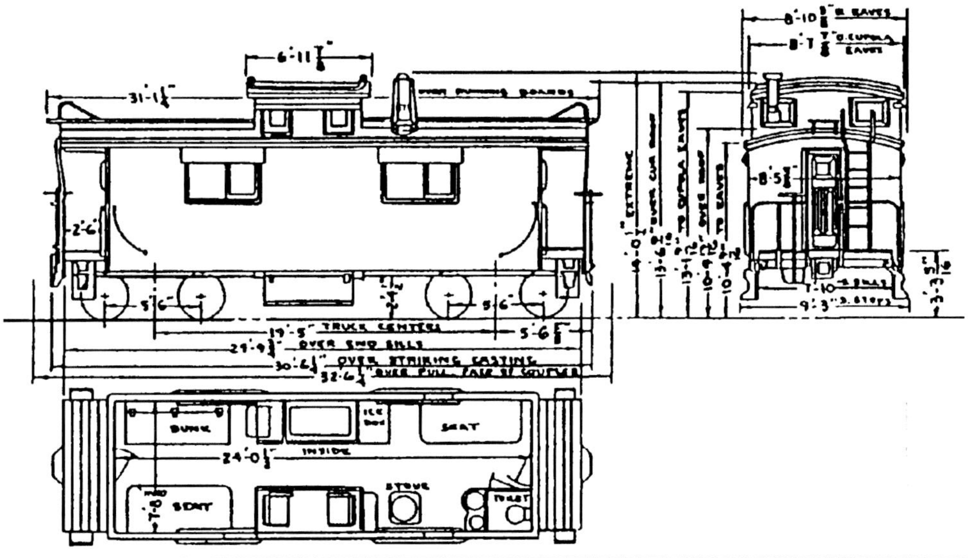

Right: When the B&O purchased a group of second-hand cabooses from the C&O in 1971, two class C-9 cabooses were included, originally built by the Hocking Valley Railroad and subsequently acquired by the C&O. The cars had steel underframes, wooden bodies, an off-center cupola and were identical to Class C-8 cabooses. The 90631 is seen at Chillicothe, Ohio on December 28, 1974. (C. W. Abbott)

Class C-26 Cabooses

First Number Series	C-3700 to C-3827
Second Number Series	903700 to 903827

The Class C-26 cabooses were noteworthy in several respects. They were the first group built for the B&O to be classified under the new C&O/B&O system and the last to be delivered painted in a B&O scheme. The International Car Company at Kenton, Ohio built 128 C-26 cars in two groups. The first group of 75 (C-3700 through C-3774) was built between March and May 1971, while the second group of 53 cabooses (C-3775 through C-3827) was built in November and December of the same year. The car itself was an evolution of the earlier Class I-18 design, with similar dimensions and equipment, including the sliding center sill, Barber swing motion trucks, and crew amenities. However, on the Class C-26 cars the bay window was more squared off, and they were the first modern B&O cabooses built without roof walks.

Unlike previous cabooses, which featured as many bunks as the railroad could squeeze in, the I-18 through C-27A cars had comfortable high-backed, vinyl upholstered walk-over seats for four men in addition to the "working" seats at the bay windows and table. Much of the space previously occupied with bunks was used for the toilet compartment, stove and sink, lockers, and a table with two facing seats. The cars had only an upper and lower bunk, reflecting the fact that few trainmen lived aboard the cars while off duty, and sleeping in any position while on duty was cause for immediate dismissal. In reality, the presence of even one bunk could be sore temptation for a trainman working long hours, or who had just come in to the warmth from flagging in sub-freezing weather.

The cars remaining in service in 1982 were renumbered to the "903700" series numbers by dropping the "C" prefix and substituting the digits "90" preceding the car number. The C-3808 was donated by CSXT to the B&O Railroad Museum and delivered for display in September 1994. The C&O/B&O clearance diagram for the Class C-26 cabooses is shown in Figure 35.

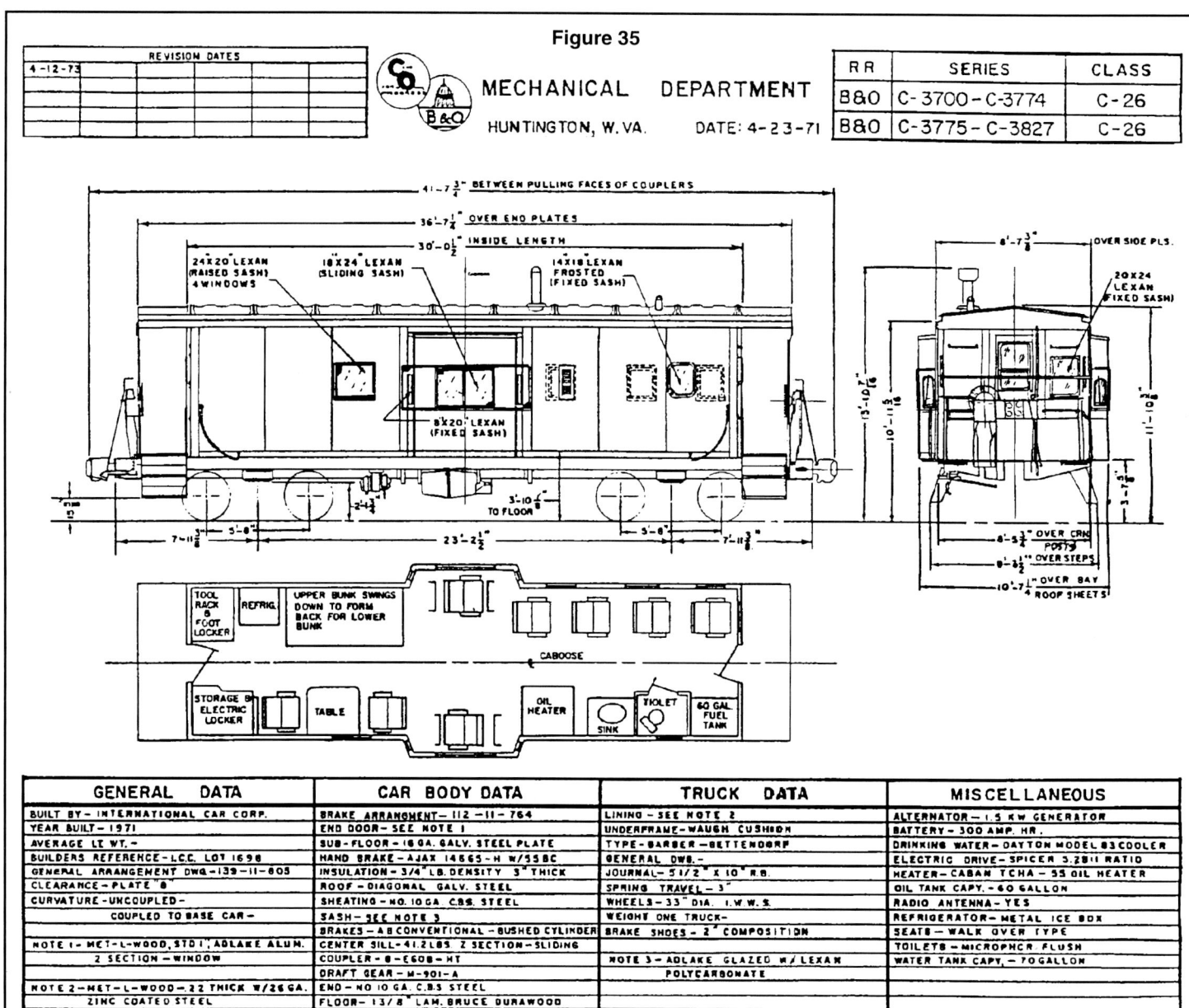

Above: B&O Class C-26 caboose C-3753 trails a southbound freight through Dayton, Ohio on May 22, 1976. This photograph illustrates many of the features of the C-26 cars. They evolved from the earlier I-18 cabooses, also built by International Car at Kenton, Ohio. However, there were several differences between the two classes. The most obvious was the shape of the bay window, which had a squarer shape on the C-26 instead of the more angular style of the I-18. There are three windows to the left of the bay window on this side of the car, and the wall to the right of the bay window is blank due to the relocation of the toilet compartment to the opposite side of the car. Also apparent in this photo is the electrical generator driven by a Spicer shaft connected to one axle of the caboose. (Robert Hubler)

Below: In the eye of the Interstate Commerce Commission and later the Federal Railroad Administration, a caboose was a freight car subject to all applicable freight car standards in addition to special rules for cabooses. The Association of American Railroads drew up many of those standards and adopted rules for car construction and interchange which had the force of administrative law. By 1971, the AAR made roller bearing axles standard for new cars, and eliminated roofwalks and full-height side and end ladders. The C-26 cars were the first B&O cabooses built without access to the roof since the class K-1 cars of the early twentieth century. Twenty years had passed since B&O trainmen were required to "decorate the tops" of moving trains, and railroaders now were positively forbidden to occupy the tops of moving cabooses. (Robert Hubler)

Class C-26A Cabooses

First Number Series	C-3828 to C-3924
Second Number Series	903828 to 903924

In 1975, the B&O continued to add to its fleet of modern steel caboose cars with the purchase of C-26A cars C-3828 through C-3924. Like the C-26s, the C-26As were built by International Car Company at Kenton, Ohio. The order was for 97 cars, built between January and June 1975. Although they were near duplicates of the earlier C-26 cabooses, they were the first new cabooses to be delivered in the Chessie System paint scheme and were equipped with chevron-shaped window screens over the bay windows. The B&O had applied rock screens to caboose windows since the 1960s, and these were designed in such a way that the motion and vibration of the car tended to close the screens, providing a measure of safety for the crew inside.

Throughout the 1970s, the Chessie System upgraded existing train radio equipment and added new sets to locomotives, cabooses, and ground stations, culminating in the current network enabling virtually any employee anywhere on the railroad to have instant voice and data communications with operating headquarters in Jacksonville, Florida, and other stations throughout the system. Older cabooses received larger generator and battery sets to accommodate the powerful Motorola FM transmitter/receiver sets, while modern cars such as the C-26A cars had them as original equipment. Reliable, instantaneous voice communication between the head end and hind end profoundly changed the way the B&O operated trains, and helped pave the way to further automation of the railroad.

The cars remaining in service in 1982 were renumbered to the "903828" series by dropping the "C" prefix and substituting the digits "90" preceding the car number. The C&O/B&O clearance diagram for the Class C-26A cabooses is shown in Figure 36.

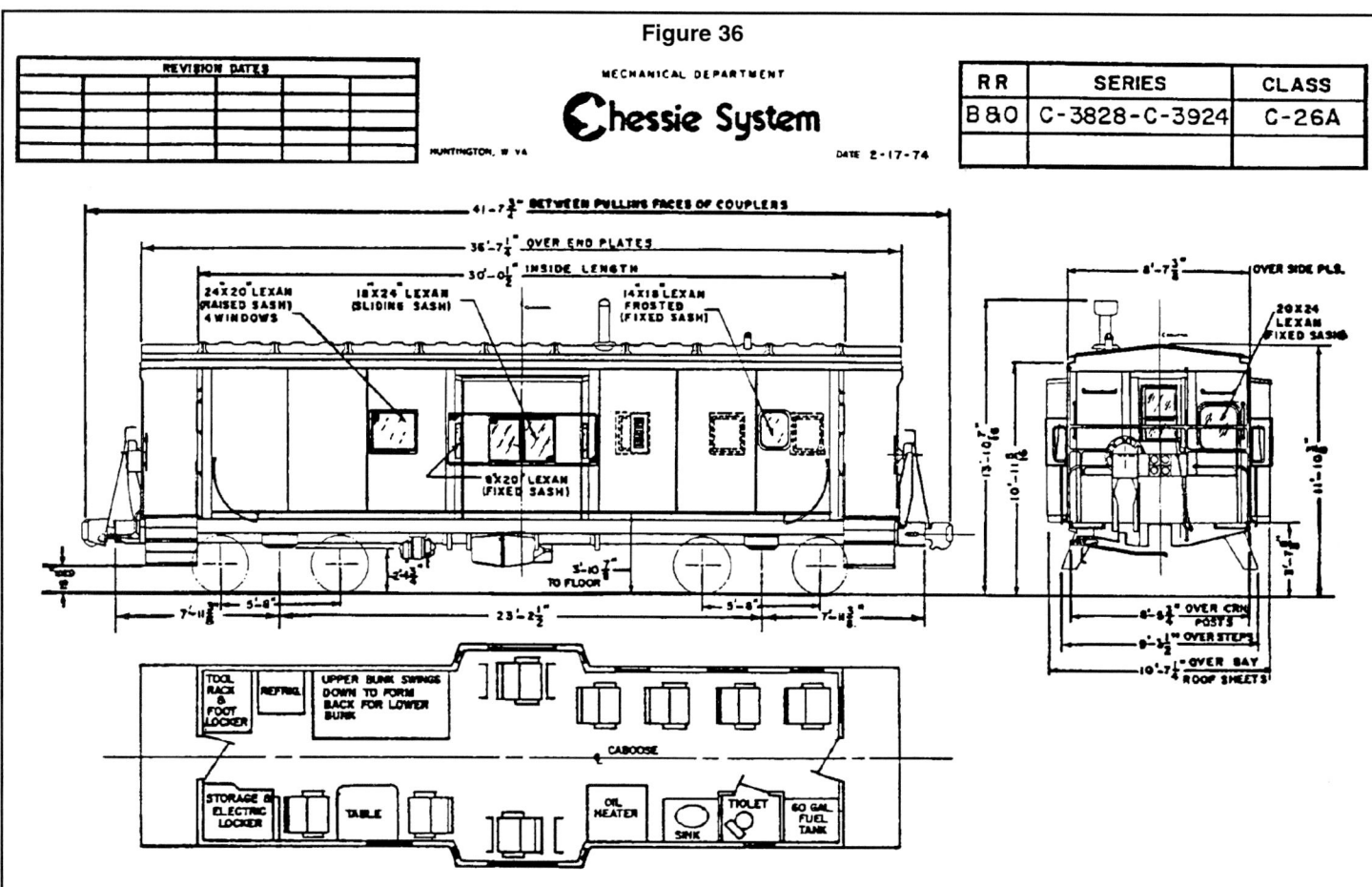

Above: The Class C-26A cars were the first B&O cabooses delivered in the Chessie System paint scheme and were near-duplicates of Class C-26 cars. C-3831 at Dayton, Ohio on August 18, 1976 illustrates the chevron-shaped screens for the bay windows which distinguish the C-26A from earlier cars. The screens were arranged in that fashion because the vibration of the moving car tended to close the screens and keep them shut as a safety measure for the crew. (Robert Hubler)

Below: This overhead view of C-26A C-3866 provides an opportunity to examine the roof arrangement on this class caboose. The C-26 and C-26A cars were never equipped with roof walks. Note the "X" panel roof sheets and how the relatively clean roof line is broken only by the exhaust pipe for the stove and the vent pipe for the toilet compartment. The end platforms were of non-skid open safety grating which provided an interesting view of of the track when the car was in motion. The C-3866 was photographed at Connellsville, Pennsylvania on August 8, 1978. (Robert Hubler)

Class C-28 Caboose

First Number Series	C-3051
Second Number Series	903051

Perhaps the oddest of all B&O cabooses was the one-of-a-kind C-3051, rebuilt at the DuBois, Pennsylvania shops from B&O M-56 boxcar 285084. It was the railroad's attempt to construct a caboose suitable for yard and transfer service. The conversion involved shortening the boxcar frame and body to form a short cabin resting on a much longer frame. The cabin retained the full boxcar height which resulted in a caboose with an extremely top heavy appearance. The boxcar trucks with friction bearings and coil springs were retained. It was released from DuBois in July 1976 shortly before the B&O closed the shop. When originally built, the caboose was not given a class, but after several years it was assigned Class C-28. Note that this is out of sequence since the class follows that of the C-27 cabooses built in 1978 even though this car was built in 1976. In the 1980s it was renumbered 903051. The Chessie System clearance diagram for the Class C-28 caboose is Figure 37.

Class C-27 Cabooses

First Number Series	C-3925 to C-3986
Second Number Series	903925 to 903986

Less than three years after the arrival of the Class C-26A cabooses, the B&O was again in the market for new equipment, leading to the purchase of the C-27 cabooses in 1978. For this group of cars the B&O turned to a new builder, the Fruit Growers Express Company (FGE), in Alexandria, Virginia. FGE was owned by a consortium of railroads, including the B&O, and built refrigerator cars at its well-equipped Alexandria Shop. By 1976, as a result of the association of the C&O, B&O, and Western Maryland in Chessie System, Chessie owned a substantial stake in FGE, and that company had begun taking orders for other types of cars. With refrigerator car loadings in a steep decline during the early 1970s, FGE management had sought to augment their business by going into commercial car building. The company's owners (including Chessie) would naturally have directed their new car orders to support this effort. Although FGE had built only refrigerator cars before the 1970s, it created a well-crafted, nicely finished group of cabooses. The railroad was pleased with the results.

The C-27 cars were numbered B&O C-3925 through C-3986 and were built between February and May 1978. Despite having been built by a different company, the C-27 cabooses were virtual twins of the previous C-26A. The most obvious external difference was a slight variation of the Chessie System paint scheme, i.e. the application of a large "track and safety cross" emblem on each side. Cars remaining in service in 1982 were renumbered to the "903925" series numbers by dropping the "C" prefix and substituting the digits "90" preceding the car number. The Chessie System clearance diagram for the Class C-27 cabooses is shown in Figure 38.

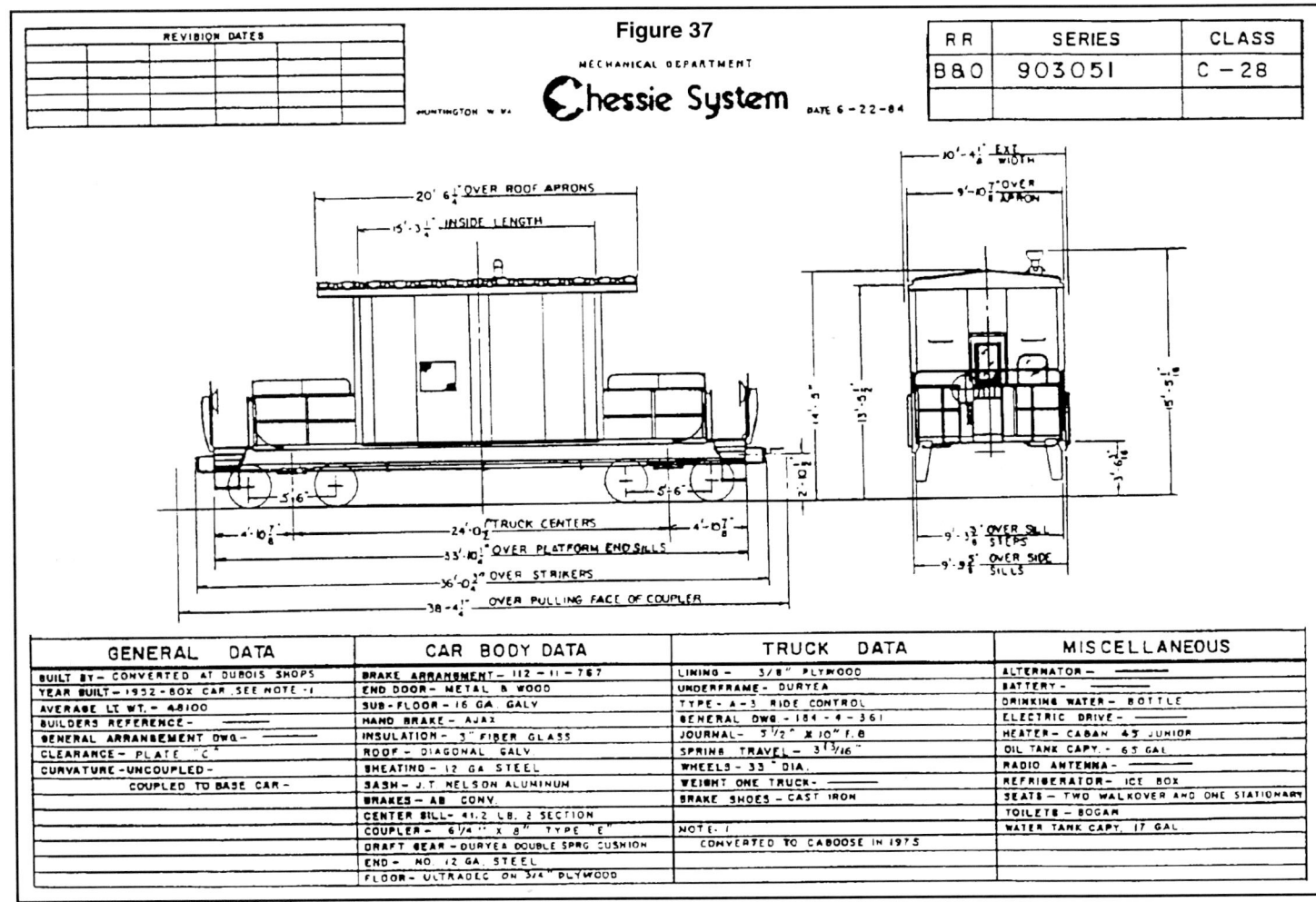

Right: Perhaps the strangest of all B&O cabooses was the C-3051. Rebuilt from a boxcar, the body and frame were shortened but the full height was retained. The resulting caboose presented a rather top-heavy appearance. Several years after it was built, the C-3051 was assigned Class C-28. This photograph was taken at the L&N yard in DeCoursey, Kentucky on July 4, 1978. (Robert Hubler)

Middle Right: Looking down on C-3954, we are provided with a view of the rooftop arrangement of the C-27 class. As noted, the C-27s were virtual twins of the C-26A cabs. This is also apparent in the roof design. The clean roofline is broken only by the stove stack, the toilet compartment vent, and what appears to be a rooftop ventilator for the interior of the caboose. Photographed at Altamont, Maryland on August 9, 1978. (Robert Hubler)

Lower Right: Although the Class C-27 cabooses were built by a different car builder (Fruit Growers Express) than the earlier C-26A class (built by International Car), the two classes were nearly identical. In this view of the single window side of the car, the only departure from the C-27 class is the lettering style, featuring the addition of a safety logo and subsequent repositioning of the railroad logo. The C-3934 was photographed at Dayton, Ohio on April 15, 1978. (Robert Hubler)

Figure 38

Chessie System — Mechanical Department, Huntington W.Va. Date: 2-10-78

RR	SERIES	CLASS
B&O	903925–903986	C-27

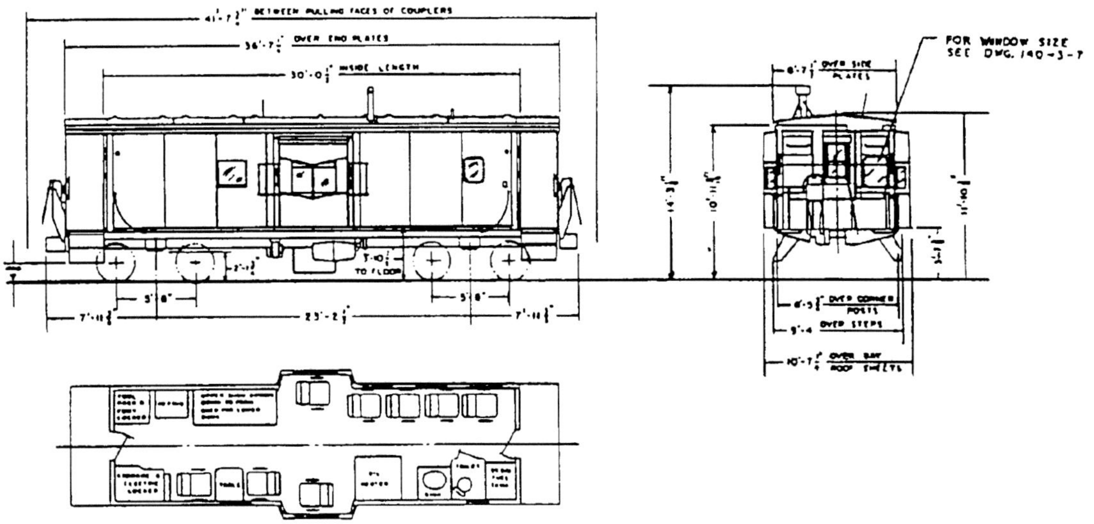

GENERAL DATA	CAR BODY DATA	TRUCK DATA	MISCELLANEOUS
BUILT BY - FRUIT GROWERS EXPRESS	BRAKE ARRANGEMENT -	LINING - NOTE 2	ALTERNATOR - 12 V. 1.5 K.W. GENERATOR
YEAR BUILT - 1978	END DOOR - NOTE 1	UNDERFRAME - WAUGH CUSHION	BATTERY - 330 AMP. HR.
AVERAGE LT WT. - 66,100 LBS.	SUB-FLOOR - 18 GA. GALV. METAL	TYPE - BARBER - BETTENDORF	DRINKING WATER - BOTTLED WATER
BUILDERS REFERENCE - SPEC. S-427	HAND BRAKE - AJAX No. 5 w/66 B.C.	GENERAL DWG. -	ELECTRIC DRIVE - SAFETY ELECT. END-OF-AX
GENERAL ARRANGEMENT DWG -	INSULATION - 1" DENSITY 3" THICK	JOURNAL - 5-1/2" x 10" R.B.	HEATER - CABAN TCHA - 55 OIL HEATER
CLEARANCE - PLATE "B"	ROOF - STANRAY X-PANEL C.B.S.	SPRING TRAVEL - 2-5/8"	OIL TANK CAPY. - 55 GALLON
CURVATURE - UNCOUPLED - 100 FT.	SHEATING - No 10 GA. C.B.S.	WHEELS - 33" DIA. 1 W.W.S.	RADIO ANTENNA - YES
COUPLED TO BASE CAR -	SASH - METAL FRAME	WEIGHT ONE TRUCK -	REFRIGERATOR - METAL ICE BOX
NOTE 1 MET-L-WOOD, STD 1" NELSON	BRAKES - CONVENTIONAL - ABDW 10 x 12	BRAKE SHOES - 2" COMPOSITION	SEATS - WALK OVER TYPE
ALUMINUM 2 SECTION WINDOW	CENTER SILL - 41.2 LB Z SECTION-SLIDING		TOILETS - MICROPHOR FLUSH
	COUPLER - E60C-HT		WATER TANK CAPY. 65 GAL.
NOTE 2 MET-L-WOOD 20 THICK w/26 GA.	DRAFT GEAR - M-901-A		
ZINC COATED STEEL	END - No. 10 GA. C.B.S.		
	FLOOR - 1-3/8 LAM. OAK (FRAMLOC)		

Left: The cabooses of classes C-26 through C-27A represented the final expression of a continually evolving car type and a century-and-a-half of car building experience. They were expensive, heavy, complex, and costly to maintain, which hastened their demise by the substitution of cheap electronics. These cars were also the Cadillacs of the caboose track, highly desired for their ride qualities, amenities, safety, and newness. Chessie System bought top-of-the-line caboose cars, just as it purchased its locomotives "fully loaded." The only option the railroad declined for both was air conditioning. That fact registered forcefully on former B&O trainmen when, toward the very end of the use of caboose cars on mainline trains, cars of the more southerly constituents of CSX Transportation began to make their way north. By comparison, the "south end" cabooses were spartan and not nearly so comfortable as even a modernized I-12. The C-3930 at Dayton in 1978 is the penultimate B&O caboose and a member of the last group to carry traditional C-numbers. (Robert Hubler)

Class C-27A Cabooses

Number Series   904000 to 904093

The very last cabooses to be built for the B&O were the C-27As. Like the earlier Class C-27, the Fruit Growers Express Company built the C-27A cabooses. By 1980, the merger of the Chessie and Seaboard Coast Line Industries holding companies meant that CSX Corporation (the parent company of the railroad operating units) owned a controlling interest (over 73%) in FGE. As the first group of C-27 cars had held up well in service, the company decided to keep the subsequent order for C&O and B&O cabooses "in the family." The B&O order, consisting of 94 cars numbered 904000 through 904093, was built between July and October 1980. The cars were almost identical to the earlier C-27 cabooses, with the only external differences being slight variations in the screens over the side windows.

The final order of cars incorporated every current car-building technique and safety standard, resulting in cars which would have astounded a typical train crew of a century previous. The Class I-18 through C-27A cars were heavier, safer, quieter, better-insulated, and generally more comfortable for the crew than anything else on rails. With thoughtfully placed hand grabs, AAR non-spin vertical hand brakes, whistles which sounded when the brakes released (giving audible warning that the car might move), Federal Railroad Administration-approved safety glazing, better steps, and many small details, the last few classes of B&O caboose made work on the hind end much easier and safer than it had ever been. Severe slack could still injure a man unprepared for it, but these cars even came with seat belts. In an industrial sort of way, they were attractive, with a bright paint scheme on the outside and smooth finishes, hardwood floors, and good lighting on the inside. Nostalgia notwithstanding, any working railroader would agree that the last B&O cabooses were indeed the best.

The Chessie System apparently intended to number the C-27A cabooses C-4000 through C-4093, but by the time they were built the railroad had adopted a new numbering scheme which assigned non-revenue equipment to the 900000 series. Accordingly, the cars were numbered into the 904000 series. The B&O Railroad Museum acquired 904032 for its permanent collection in 1993. The very last caboose built for the B&O, C-27A 904093, remains in service on CSXT in 1994 but has been proposed for donation to the B&O Railroad Museum upon its retirement. Figure 39 is the Chessie System clearance diagram for Class C-27A cabooses.

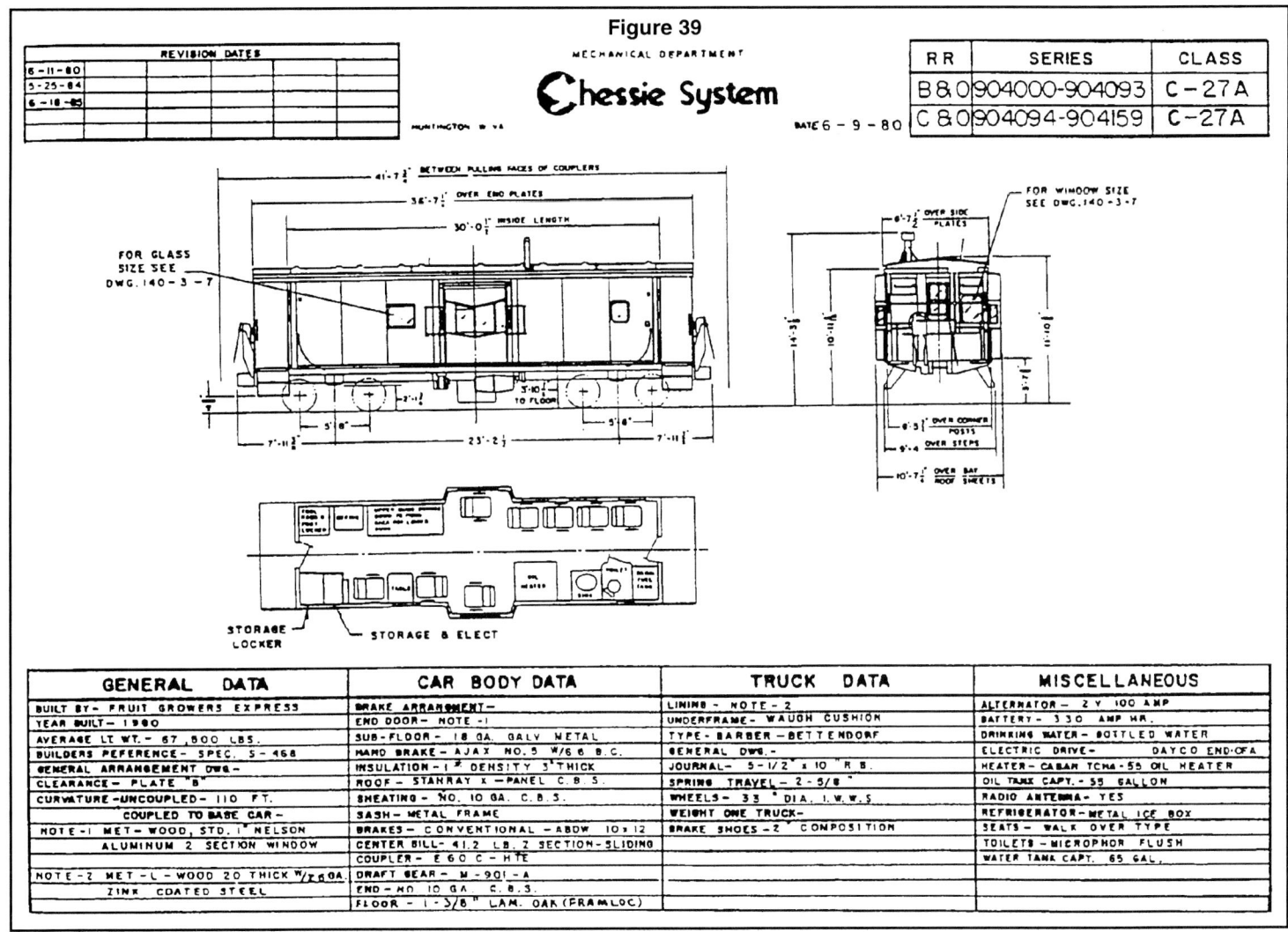

Above: B&O C-27A 904022 was found at M&K Junction, West Virginia on August 14, 1982. The combination of a low camera angle and a high sun made the window screens and their tracks stand out from the caboose in sharp relief. Notice the so-called "FRA light" and the characteristic external tracks to allow the side window screens to be raised. This angle also provides a good view of the arrangement of the grab irons and railings at the end of the caboose. There was little variation to the end arrangement from C-26 through the C-27A cabooses. (Robert Hubler)

Below: At Lima, Ohio, C-27A 904031 occupied the caboose track on June 2, 1984. Note the notch in the side sill providing access to and clearance for the belt-driven alternator. This was a return to the type of alternator found on the C-26A cabooses and a move away from the axle mounted alternator used on the class C-27 cabooses. (Robert Hubler)

Above: This, the last B&O caboose, is much more than an historical footnote—it may be regarded with some irony and used as an indicator of the accelerating rate of change within the railroad industry. As it and its 93 sister cars were taking shape on the erecting floor of the Fruit Growers Express shop in Alexandria, Virginia, various government agencies were giving their final approval to the merger of Chessie System and Seaboard Coast Line Industries holding companies. Within a few years, railroads across the country would negotiate a contract with the United Transportation Union virtually eliminating both flagmen and the vehicle which housed them over the road. Rapid advances in technology and a revolution in operating practice were combining to make the 904093 obsolete even before it was completed. Some of the earliest B&O cabooses lasted six decades in service. The biggest, best, and last cars essentially vanished within ten years. (Robert Hubler)

Below: Caboose 904054 after 7 years of service on the B&O. The only modification from the cars original condition, which can be seen in this photograph, is in the area of the alternator. Notice that the notch in the side sill has been widened considerably and a new piece of electrical gear has been mounted next to the belt drive on the axle. The 904054 was photographed at Chillicothe, Ohio on September 25, 1987. (Robert Hubler)

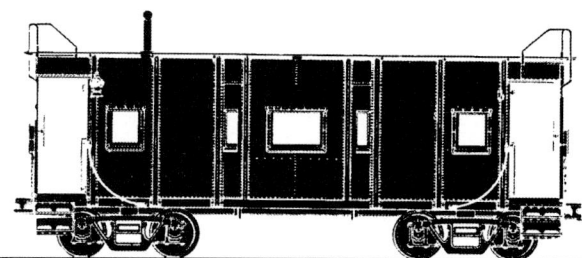

PAINTING AND LETTERING

General

Determining and describing how the B&O painted cabooses at a particular point in time is a difficult task, but one of importance to many people. In a variety of places in the United States, individuals and organizations have original B&O caboose cars to restore or renovate, and they need to know what paint scheme is appropriate for their artifact. In addition, there are thousands of hobbyists, and manufacturers, who wish to accurately decorate models of B&O cabooses. The B&O maintained specifications describing how the cars were to be painted and lettered so that, in theory, the entire fleet presented a reasonably uniform appearance. However, in practice, a wide variety of factors influenced how individual classes, groups of cars (for example, cars maintained or modified at a particular shop), and specific cars actually appeared in service. Available evidence supports the conclusion drawn by most observers of the B&O's car fleet: while there was a "family resemblance" between caboose cars and the railroad applied "standard" painting and lettering schemes, there was a great deal of variety in the color and lettering of cabooses. The data presented in this chapter should be used for general guidance in determining the appropriate color scheme for a particular period. The appearance of individual cars, especially those in service for a number of years, often varied from the standard scheme of the period.

In the nineteenth century, the B&O seems to have left many decisions as to painting and lettering cars up to the local shops, crews, and management directly responsible for the cars. The railroad did favor certain styles and arrangements of lettering, such as the block lettering outlined in white widely used on freight equipment and illustrated in the photograph of caboose 1871 on page 30. Nevertheless, what little evidence exists suggests that nineteenth century cabooses were painted much like house cars (box cars) and other freight equipment, with a body of freight car red or brown with white lettering. Because there were no formal requirements for reporting marks, lettering probably was minimal, with only the car number and railroad name or initials applied.

After the Pennsylvania Railroad assumed control in 1901, the B&O began an administrative reorganization which resulted in much more standardization and centralized decision making than had been present before. About this time, the B&O adopted the Roman-style serif letter forms applied to all classes of equipment until C&O control in the 1960s. The Mechanical Department in Baltimore began issuing formal directives specifying how cabooses were to be painted and lettered. Such directives may have been issued prior to the early 1900s, but the evidence is sparse and inconclusive. The B&O issued both painting and lettering diagrams for cabooses, but the railroad apparently did not retain a complete file and available sources are incomplete. Caboose paint and lettering schemes for the twentieth century may be described by referring to company diagrams, company memoranda, and photographs.

Note the distinction between painting and lettering diagrams. A lettering diagram indicated the size and placement of the lettering as applied to a particular type of car. In general, lettering diagrams did not give information about the type or colors of paint applied to the car shown. Conversely, painting diagrams described the color and stock number of the paint to be applied to a particular car, without reference to the lettering. In the C&O/B&O and Chessie System eras, the railroad issued diagrams which gave both painting and lettering information.

The earliest lettering diagram available to the Society dates from 1916 (see diagram W-33265, Figure 42, page 149). Some information about earlier B&O caboose lettering schemes can be inferred from photographs, and this will be discussed where appropriate. B&O caboose color schemes are not nearly as easy to document. The earliest painting diagram available to the Society was issued in 1954 (see diagram T-83278, Figure 40). Some earlier painting instructions (not diagrams) have been located, but the exact shade for a particular color cannot be determined from these instructions. Unfortunately, photographs of B&O cabooses in early paint schemes are unreliable for determining color, since they are black & white.

Several general statements apply to the painting and lettering of virtually all B&O equipment, and especially to cabooses. Over the twelve decades covered in this book, the B&O Railroad owned and operated hundreds of thousands of cars and employed tens of thousands of Car Department, Mechanical Department, and shop craft employees to build and maintain them. While the railroad attempted (especially in later years) to standardize and control the appearance of all of its equipment, simply maintaining such a large fleet was a massive undertaking. A number of factors combined to produce wide variety in the appearance of cabooses in particular.

Perhaps most basic is color. In the nineteenth and early twentieth centuries, paint was a locally produced commodity which the railroad purchased from many manufacturers and vendors. Not until the rise of national paint brands and markets before World War I would the B&O even have been able to specify an inexpensive, widely available, standard color for the cars. Instead, local car foremen, storekeepers, or whoever was in charge of painting procured whatever paint met their needs and met applicable company guidelines. Those guidelines were often vague as to actual color, instead requiring a "good freight car paint" or simply "brown paint." Journeymen car painters often mixed their own paints from dry pigment and vehicle, and a thorough empirical education in paint chemistry was part of the apprentice painter's education. Even as late as 1954, B&O specifications directed painters to mix lamp black and oil for interior caboose lettering.

So-called "freight car red" was widely used by the B&O and other railroads because it was cheap, available almost everywhere, and it protected wood and metal surfaces well. The base of the paint was any of several polymerizing oils such as fish oil, linseed oil, and later, petroleum oils. The pigment was iron oxide, yielding shades from yellow-brown all the way to dark red-brown. Depending on the particular oxide of iron, how it was processed, and the type of vehicle, the paint produced anything from a fine, glossy finish to a dull, thick, crude surface. Much of the outcome depended on the skill and knowledge of the painter. That was true almost everywhere on the B&O in the 1800s, and at remote repair facilities as late as the 1950s.

Even as the B&O refined its testing capability and standardized its paint ordering procedures in the twentieth century, vendors still supplied paint which varied slightly from batch to batch, and manufacturer to manufacturer. At the point of application, painters might combine paints or add drying oils, thinners, or other additives which could affect the finish on individual cars. The result was that even though the railroad maintained a "standard" color, the result could vary from year to year, car to car, and any description of color or reference to a particular color must be regarded as a *range* of colors.

That was particularly true for the bright red paints used by the B&O on its cabooses after 1941. Even though the railroad established a standard for B&O Caboose Red and tested samples of paints at the Testing Department Laboratory at Mt. Clare, many different shades of red passed for the standard color. In reality, it did not matter if the paint precisely matched some arbitrary standard, so long as it was a deep, bright red. The intent clearly was to be to make the caboose as visible as possible, and only snow plows and wreck train cars were also painted in this shade of very bright red. The carbody color was described as "Caboose Car Red," but it was also known as "Devil's Red" and used by the railroad for safety related structures like fire hose sheds. As different red paints weathered, they faded to a kind of pink, or changed to more of a brown shade through the action of grime and the environment. A freshly-painted bright red caboose was bright indeed, while a car in service for some time often looked dull and brown even if it had once been bright. Please refer to the color section for examples.

When the railroad rebuilt cabooses for pool service beginning in 1965, it specified "Enchantment Blue" for the carbodies to differentiate them from non-pool equipped cars. Dark blue had been an "official" color for the B&O since the railroad inaugurated the "Royal Blue" trains in 1895, although even at the time there was considerable debate as to what constituted the B&O color "Royal Blue." In the mid-1930s, when the B&O dabbled with lightweight and streamlined passenger equipment, it revived "Royal Blue" under the Dupont Dulux enamel color name "Bando Blue" (a contraction of B and O). Bando Blue became a standard B&O color, used on steam and diesel locomotives, passenger equipment, some freight cars, and miscellaneous equipment.

Enchantment Blue, however, was the Chesapeake and Ohio Railway's designation for its standard dark blue. The C&O also had adopted a deep, dark blue for locomotives and cars after World War II. In the course of several extensive car restorations at the B&O Railroad Museum in the late 1970s, the staff examined samples of unweathered Bando Blue and Enchantment Blue, and found them to be indistinguishable. In practice, the railroad freely substituted the two colors, so that no doubt some B&O cabooses were painted with Bando Blue if that is what the shop had on hand.

Dark blue is a difficult color paint to manufacture, and it generally does not weather well. Depending on whether Dupont, PPG, the Columbia Paint Company, or any of several other companies supplied the paint, Bando/Enchantment Blue varied slightly in color and faded, chalked, and oxidized differently. When new, Bando/Enchantment Blue was very dark and looked almost black in certain light. As it aged, it would either fade to a lighter shade of blue or sometimes acquire a purplish sheen. Modelers should be more concerned with simulating a dark blue suitable for their lighting conditions than with matching a "true" color sample. Out on the railroad, there were many shades of blue on B&O cabooses.

In 1972, the C&O created a holding company, Chessie System, Inc., to own the assets of the B&O, C&O, and affiliated companies. To emphasize the new consolidated corporate structure, Franklyn J. Carr and the staff of what would become the Department of Visual Media and Design (part of the Public Relations and Advertising Department) created a unified painting and lettering scheme for the equipment of the subsidiary companies. Chessie System chose primary or highly-visible colors (yellow, blue, and vermillion) and striking graphics both to make locomotives and cars more visible as a safety measure, and to advertise the new Chessie System to shippers and the public.

The Chessie System abandoned the letter style used by the B&O since about 1900 and the C&O's version of Railroad Roman for a clean, modern sans-serif letter form very similar to one used by the C&O at the turn of the century. Chessie retired both the Capitol dome heralds and the C&O for Progress logo. In their place, the railroad introduced the "Ches-C" as the official copyrighted trademark/logo, comprising the letter "C" outlining the silhouette of Chessie, the C&O Railway's sleeping kitten mascot. Because the B&O and C&O (and later, the Western Maryland Railway) continued to operate as separate companies for accounting purposes, equipment carried both the Chessie System name and logo, with the appropriate railroad's initials and car or locomotive number.

The railroad specified a particular shade of yellow, blue, and vermillion for repainting cabooses, but with use the color of the cars varied due to weathering. As the paint aged, the yellow frequently darkened from grime and oxidation. Often, the vermillion accents faded or changed color to a dirty orange depending on the particular paint and atmospheric or washrack chemicals. In a few cases, over-zealous washing almost completely removed the lettering and some of the yellow, exposing the previous paint job underneath. As the CSX merger progressed in the early 1980s, few cabooses received major maintenance or repainting, so that many cars in the Chessie scheme ended their service badly weathered, grimy, and in a variety of derivative colors.

The effect of sunlight and the atmosphere on caboose colors must not be underestimated. Even stable paints chalked, faded, and suffered a variety of color shifts at they aged. Again, there were variations in the ways paint from different manufacturers weathered. Some got lighter, some got darker, and some seemed to dissolve away. Sometimes the railroad washed cabooses, either by hand or by one of the mechanized "laundries" used to clean equipment. If the harsh acid or basic detergents commonly used were not proportioned correctly, even a few washings could destroy an otherwise sound paint job and alter the color of a car. Sometimes, it removed lettering.

Many cabooses carried coatings of soot, road grime, brake shoe dust, or the effects of operation in a specific environment. In later years, for example, cabooses at the end of coal trains were damaged by the abrasive action of coal dust blown back from the train. The powdered coal favored by utilities had the same practical effect at 45 miles per hour as an abrasive blasting rig, and for some years the B&O placed an empty, doorless boxcar between the last coal hopper and the caboose to protect the car and crew from the dust. The soot from steam and diesel locomotives settled on the roofs of cabooses, giving them a grimy, black finish. This black coating is frequently confused with the intentional black roofs of wooden cupola caboose cars with standing seam metal or canvas/composite roofs, which were painted black or sealed with tar to prevent leaking. In territories which required heavy braking, the minute iron particles ground off hundreds of hot brake shoes formed a cloud of dust which gave a brown, rusty cast to cabooses over time.

Even the air itself could have subtle effects on the color of equipment. For example, the sulphur-and-iron laden air around Pittsburgh acted differently on caboose colors than the salty maritime air of Baltimore, or the "acid rain" now known to have existed over parts of the railroad. These examples reinforce the point that just as cabooses would have displayed subtle color variations when freshly painted, natural processes gave them a "patina" in service which further altered their colors. When restoring an actual car or simulating the colors on a model of a B&O caboose, it is necessary to consider what it is that is to be reproduced. Is it to appear as if right out of the paint shop or is it to represent a caboose working around a steel mill? The modeler or restorer must be lead by what "looks correct" for the circumstances as well as by paint chips of "standard" colors. In the real world there was a rainbow of reds, blues, greens, and yellows at the end of B&O trains.

The lettering on B&O cabooses was also subject to wide variation. At different times, the B&O chose an understated scheme which included the minimum required information, and at other times the railroad regarded the sides of cabooses as billboards. Many variations resulted from periods of rapid change, when the "standard" lettering scheme changed every few years. Since the railroad repainted and lettered cars only as needed, upon major shopping, or at relatively long intervals, changing something as simple as the design of the B&O logo took many years to fully implement. Between 1940 and 1973, the logo changed so many times that numerous variations of caboose lettering schemes existed simultaneously.

Other "non-standard" decoration resulted when a repair track or shop either lacked the proper stencils, chose not to use them, or had outdated or incorrect information. The B&O tolerated a fairly high degree of autonomy and variety, so that if a car foreman at a far-away point simply liked one version of the Capitol dome logo more than another, he might apply it to a freshly painted car with reasonable impunity. Naturally, cars as-built or shopped together as part of a program showed the greatest degree of uniformity and compliance with painting and lettering standards. Older cars, ones far from Baltimore, and cars shopped individually showed the most variation. In later years, the addition of consolidation stencils (black rectangles as background for car and brake data), restriction codes, Automatic Car Identification system labels, and other supplemental lettering (radio, fuel fill, etc.) further "customized" the look of individual cars.

As many photographs in this book demonstrate, painting and lettering variations were common, widespread, and idiosyncratic. The very fact that so many cars carried them suggests that B&O management was satisfied if the cars carried the needed data, the form of decoration was somewhat less important. As stated before, the "rules" for painting and lettering cars are only guidelines, and individuals desiring highly specific details should consult photographs of the car they wish to simulate or restore.

PAINT SCHEMES

Caboose Colors - Prior to 1900

The earliest photograph in this book revealing information about caboose painting is that of B&O 1871 on page 30. This eight-wheel caboose was photographed in 1899, and carries the words BALTo & OHIO on a white panel centered on the side of the caboose with the number 1871 on a white panel below the road name. The panels seem to be white in the black & white photograph, but no documentation exists to confirm it. Similarly, it is not known if the words BALTo & OHIO were in black or some other dark color. It is reasonable to conclude that the basic carbody color of B&O cabooses at this time was red, but the shade could be any of the iron oxide colors. In cars without the white panel, the words BALTo & OHIO appear to be in white on the side of the caboose.

Caboose Colors - 1900 to 1916

No diagrams or detailed standards have been found for the period of the B&O's reorganization. However, B&O Painting Specification No. 7C-1, titled "Specifications for Painting Caboose Cars," dated November 10, 1905 states that the exterior body of the caboose is to receive 3 coats of paint with the third and final coat being red enamel. Further, all lettering is to be done in white and applied in such a manner that it has a solid white appearance. The specification also notes that the roof is to be painted with two coats of freight car paint which is referred to elsewhere as "brown paint of B&O standard shade." Finally, under the heading of interior paint it is noted that both sides of the window sashes were to be painted with "interior caboose enamel-dark shade." The exact shade is not specified, but may have been the dark green paint of later years. In summary, this evidence suggests that cabooses of this era were red with brown roofs (although the exact shades of red or brown are not known), the lettering was white and the window sashes were dark enamel (possibly dark green).

Caboose Colors - 1916 to 1941

The one reference available for this era is B&O Circular No. F-60-H, dated May 1, 1940, entitled "Repainting and restenciling of wood, steel underframe and all steel freight equipment." It provides instructions for the painting of wooden cars, which would include all cupola cabooses. Cabooses were to receive 3 coats of "B&O freight car brown" paint, and white stencil paste was to be used for stenciling white letters and figures on brown surfaces. Again, this description does not specify the exact shade of brown or how reddish this brown may have appeared on these cars. As in previous specifications, the window sashes continued to be "interior caboose enamel dark shade" on both sides, which may or may not have been the dark green shade of later years. Cabooses of this era were thus freight car brown with white lettering, the actual shades of which no doubt varied.

As there were just a few bay window cabooses built in this interval, it seems reasonable to assume that they also were painted according to the freight car specification. An exception was Class I-5B caboose C-2502, displayed at the 1939-1940 New York World's Fair (and at other locations) in a non-standard paint scheme which featured a silver or gray carbody with black lettering. As far as is known, this scheme was not applied to any in-service bay window cabooses.

Class K-1 C-1060 at Aldene, New Jersey was in use on the Staten Island Rapid Transit on December 18, 1939. It carried the 1916 lettering scheme still standard at that time. This scheme consisted of only the railroad name and the car number. The paint colors used on the C-1060 cannot be determined from this black & white photograph, but if painted according to specifications, the caboose had a freight car brown body and white lettering. The darker color of the window sashes might have been the same dark green shade used in later years. (George E. Votava, The B&O Railroad Historical Society Collection)

Above: This excellent photograph of Class I-5 C-2113 was taken at Baltimore, Maryland about September 1927, when it was less than five months old. It represents the original paint and lettering applied to the I-5 cabooses. The lettering scheme is the standard for the era, featuring the name "Baltimore & Ohio" in seven-inch letters along the top of the side, and the car number in seven-inch numerals centered along the bottom of the side. Although the photo is black and white, the window frames appear to be of a different color than the car sides. This suggests when the caboose was built it was given dark green window frames to contrast with the brown carbody. (Gary Schlerf Collection)

Left: The B&O displayed several pieces of equipment at the 1939-1940 New York World's Fair including one of its innovative wagon top caboose cars in a special silver (or gray) paint scheme. Class I-5B C-2502 was photographed at the Fair in Flushing, New York on August 6, 1939. (George E. Votava, The B&O Railroad Historical Society Collection)

Caboose Colors - 1941 to 1955

By 1941, the B&O's standard caboose color scheme can begin to be documented with color photography and some corporate records. The specific painting and lettering specifications have not yet been found in either B&O Railroad Historical Society or B&O Railroad Museum files, but company memoranda providing some useful information do exist and a B&O diagram concerning painting handholds has been found.

From photography it can be determined that the carbody was bright red with the lettering generally in white. Window frames and doors were dark green. Initially, hand rails and grab irons were black, but after 1945 most were yellow. The underbody of the car was black. A few color photographs show that some cars received yellow lettering during this period, but the extent of this practice is not known.

The only confirmed (by documentation) painting change to have taken place during this period was the conversion from black grab irons and handholds to yellow. Figure 41, page 120, presents the B&O's "Instructions for Painting Caboose Car Handholds." It was issued for the first time on August 17, 1945. This diagram indicates which safety appliances are to be painted yellow, but modifications to this drawing through revision "F" reflect painting changes up to the blue with yellow end "pool service" scheme of 1965. Initially, the grab irons were to be painted Signal Yellow but revision "B" of October 18, 1945 "changed the color from Yellow Signal Enamel (Stock No. 356) to Refrigerator Yellow paint (Stock No. 313)." Revision "C" on May 3, 1946 added the "entire end ladders, top of hand rail and edge of step treads" to those appliances to be painted yellow.

Among the useful painting information from company memoranda there is a May 11, 1946 statement that "safety appliances, on exterior of B&O Caboose Cars and indicated on print T-72781-C, will be painted with Refrigerator Yellow paint, Stock No. 313, in place of Devils Red." This memo confirms the yellow paint information showed in Figure 41 and suggests two other things. First, "Devils Red" was in use by 1946 as the name of the caboose red paint used by the B&O. (A 1947 standard diagram for a B&O Fire Hose House also specifies that the shed be painted Devils Red, B&O Stock No. F-151. Note that this is the same paint stock number indicated as Caboose Car Red in Figure 40, Diagram T-83278). Second, not all safety appliances on B&O cabooses were painted black prior to August 1945. Some at least were painted the same color as the body of the car as was the practice for freight cars.

Another fact related to the appearance of B&O cabooses and grab irons surfaced among these memoranda. An April 23, 1942 letter states the B&O had "decided to change the contour and eliminate the center support of the side curved handholds to be used at the four corners of Caboose Cars." This change is very apparent when comparing photographs from before and after the World War II.

Through the period, there was a variety of lettering schemes applied to caboose cars. Please see the lettering section for a detailed discussion of the lettering and markings used with this basic color scheme.

Above: This photograph of C-2352 taken at New Concord, Ohio on July 17, 1953 illustrates the 1948 scheme for wooden bay window cabooses. The body colors were most probably red with white lettering, black underframe, and the grab irons appear to be yellow. (Paul Dunn, Robert Hubler Collection)

Above: Class I-1 C-145 was photographed at Kane, Pennsylvania on March 10, 1946. While the car had been recently shopped and presented a neat appearance, obviously it had seen hard usage, judging from the sag in the end platform. The caboose was lettered in the 1941 scheme, but the line above the words "Baltimore & Ohio" is a non-standard variation. The colors cannot be discerned in this photo, but based upon later color photographs of similar cabooses, the colors were probably Devils Red with white lettering. Cabooses in this scheme have been noted with either black or yellow grab irons. Based on the lighter color in this photo, the C-145 probably had yellow grab irons. (J. W. Brauner, Robert Hubler Collection)

Caboose Colors - 1955 to 1965

Beginning in 1955, the standard red B&O caboose paint scheme can be completely documented with official company painting diagrams. Diagram T-83278 (see Figure 40, page 119) describes the painting instructions for B&O caboose cars. Although it is illustrated with a sketch of a bay window caboose, the text of the diagram is clear that it applies to all types of cabooses. The colors indicated are probably those applied to B&O cabooses for many years. This diagram, however, gives us the identification of all these colors for the first time. The caboose carbody was a bright red which the diagram identifies as "Caboose Car Red, Stock No. F-151". The exterior lettering was "white stencil paste, Stock number F-191" or, if sprayed, "Stock No. F-192 spray stencil paint." The underbody of the car was to be coated with black "Car Cement, Stock No. F-30," except for the trucks and air reservoir which were painted black with Stock No. F-40. Car Cement was a sealing and rust-inhibitive coating used to protect underframes and underbody parts where no lettering was required. No mention is made of the exterior doors or window frames being painted green, although this has been observed in numerous color photographs of this and earlier eras. However, notice that under the interior painting instructions, the window frames and doors are the dark green which is identified as "Stock P-206 Green Base Wall Gloss." Perhaps the shops interpreted this to mean that both sides of the doors and window frames were to be painted in dark green.

Cupola Caboose Colors - 1964 to 1969

On March 31, 1964, the lettering diagram for cupola cabooses was revised to add a 23.5-inch diameter capitol dome herald. Several photographs of cabooses in this lettering scheme show them with red window frames and doors rather that the dark green of previous paint schemes. However, we cannot determine if this was a change officially sanctioned or merely some local variation. It might have reflected a stricter interpretation of the interior painting instructions discussed in the previous section. Also during this period, a number of cupola cabooses were repainted with yellow ends. They were photographed primarily in Chicago or at the Chillicothe shops. This was not standard, but may have been a local adaptation for extra visibility in the Chicago area or a carryover from the pool service paint scheme.

Right: This view of Class I-16 C-2774 illustrates the 1955 paint scheme applied to wooden bay window cabooses. Although the lettering is slightly rearranged due to the configuration of the caboose, the colors were the same as applied to cupola cabooses during this era. The body of the caboose is red, the lettering white, the window frames dark green, and the underframe is black. The grab irons are yellow for increased visibility and safety. (S. P. Davidson, Robert Hubler Collection)

Figure 40

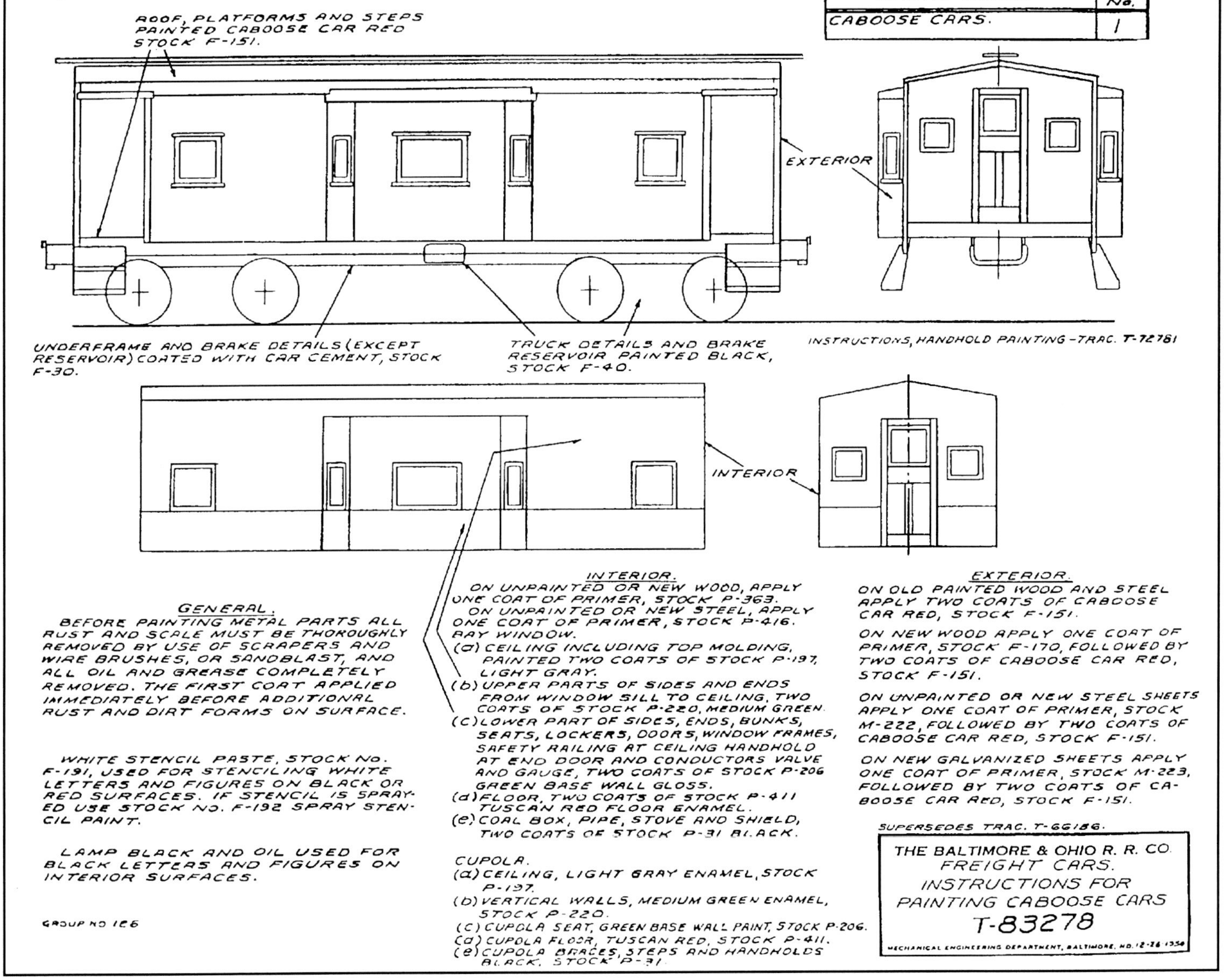

ROOF, PLATFORMS AND STEPS PAINTED CABOOSE CAR RED STOCK F-151.

WHERE USED	LINE No.
CABOOSE CARS.	1

EXTERIOR

UNDERFRAME AND BRAKE DETAILS (EXCEPT RESERVOIR) COATED WITH CAR CEMENT, STOCK F-30.

TRUCK DETAILS AND BRAKE RESERVOIR PAINTED BLACK, STOCK F-40.

INSTRUCTIONS, HANDHOLD PAINTING - TRAC. T-72761

INTERIOR

GENERAL.
BEFORE PAINTING METAL PARTS ALL RUST AND SCALE MUST BE THOROUGHLY REMOVED BY USE OF SCRAPERS AND WIRE BRUSHES, OR SANDBLAST, AND ALL OIL AND GREASE COMPLETELY REMOVED. THE FIRST COAT APPLIED IMMEDIATELY BEFORE ADDITIONAL RUST AND DIRT FORMS ON SURFACE.

WHITE STENCIL PASTE, STOCK NO. F-191, USED FOR STENCILING WHITE LETTERS AND FIGURES ON BLACK OR RED SURFACES. IF STENCIL IS SPRAYED USE STOCK NO. F-192 SPRAY STENCIL PAINT.

LAMP BLACK AND OIL USED FOR BLACK LETTERS AND FIGURES ON INTERIOR SURFACES.

GROUP NO 126

INTERIOR.
ON UNPAINTED OR NEW WOOD, APPLY ONE COAT OF PRIMER, STOCK P-363.
ON UNPAINTED OR NEW STEEL, APPLY ONE COAT OF PRIMER, STOCK P-416.
BAY WINDOW.
(a) CEILING INCLUDING TOP MOLDING, PAINTED TWO COATS OF STOCK P-197, LIGHT GRAY.
(b) UPPER PARTS OF SIDES AND ENDS FROM WINDOW SILL TO CEILING, TWO COATS OF STOCK P-220, MEDIUM GREEN.
(c) LOWER PART OF SIDES, ENDS, BUNKS, SEATS, LOCKERS, DOORS, WINDOW FRAMES, SAFETY RAILING AT CEILING HANDHOLD AT END DOOR AND CONDUCTORS VALVE AND GAUGE, TWO COATS OF STOCK P-206 GREEN BASE WALL GLOSS.
(d) FLOOR, TWO COATS OF STOCK P-411 TUSCAN RED FLOOR ENAMEL.
(e) COAL BOX, PIPE, STOVE AND SHIELD, TWO COATS OF STOCK P-31 BLACK.

CUPOLA.
(a) CEILING, LIGHT GRAY ENAMEL, STOCK P-197.
(b) VERTICAL WALLS, MEDIUM GREEN ENAMEL, STOCK P-220.
(c) CUPOLA SEAT, GREEN BASE WALL PAINT, STOCK P-206.
(d) CUPOLA FLOOR, TUSCAN RED, STOCK P-411.
(e) CUPOLA BRACES, STEPS AND HANDHOLDS BLACK, STOCK P-31.

EXTERIOR.
ON OLD PAINTED WOOD AND STEEL APPLY TWO COATS OF CABOOSE CAR RED, STOCK F-151.

ON NEW WOOD APPLY ONE COAT OF PRIMER, STOCK F-170, FOLLOWED BY TWO COATS OF CABOOSE CAR RED, STOCK F-151.

ON UNPAINTED OR NEW STEEL SHEETS APPLY ONE COAT OF PRIMER, STOCK M-222, FOLLOWED BY TWO COATS OF CABOOSE CAR RED, STOCK F-151.

ON NEW GALVANIZED SHEETS APPLY ONE COAT OF PRIMER, STOCK M-223, FOLLOWED BY TWO COATS OF CABOOSE CAR RED, STOCK F-151.

SUPERSEDES TRAC. T-66156.

THE BALTIMORE & OHIO R. R. CO.
FREIGHT CARS.
INSTRUCTIONS FOR
PAINTING CABOOSE CARS
T-83278
MECHANICAL ENGINEERING DEPARTMENT, BALTIMORE, MD. 12-26-1934

Figure 41

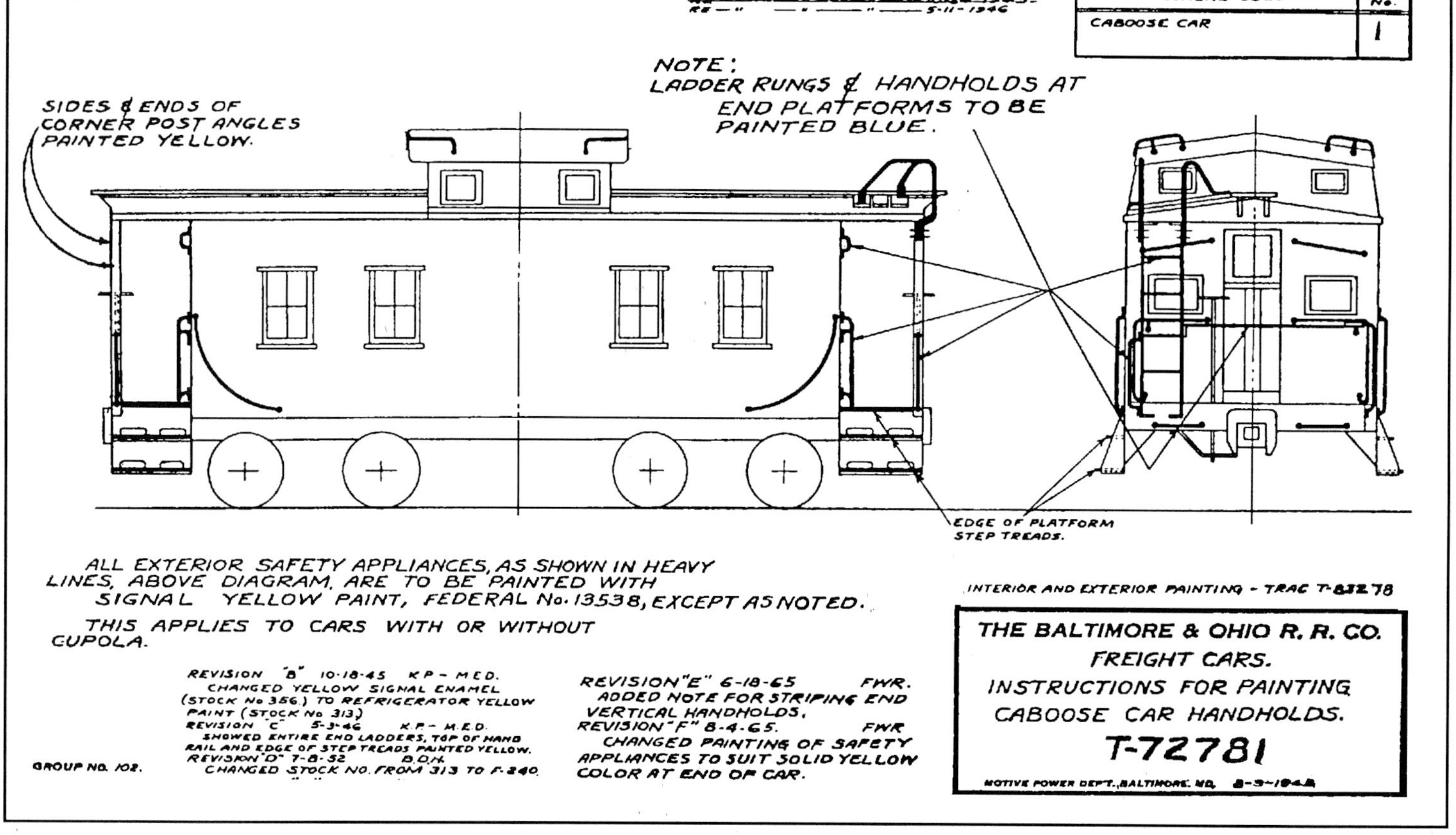

Diagram annotations:

- SIDES & ENDS OF CORNER POST ANGLES PAINTED YELLOW.
- NOTE: LADDER RUNGS & HANDHOLDS AT END PLATFORMS TO BE PAINTED BLUE.
- EDGE OF PLATFORM STEP TREADS.
- ALL EXTERIOR SAFETY APPLIANCES, AS SHOWN IN HEAVY LINES, ABOVE DIAGRAM, ARE TO BE PAINTED WITH SIGNAL YELLOW PAINT, FEDERAL No. 13538, EXCEPT AS NOTED. THIS APPLIES TO CARS WITH OR WITHOUT CUPOLA.

WHERE USED: CABOOSE CAR — LINE No. 1

GROUP NO. 102.

REVISION "B" 10-18-45 K.P — M.E.D.
CHANGED YELLOW SIGNAL ENAMEL (STOCK No. 356) TO REFRIGERATOR YELLOW PAINT (STOCK No. 313)
REVISION "C" 5-3-46 K.P — M.E.D.
SHOWED ENTIRE END LADDERS, TOP OF HAND RAIL AND EDGE OF STEP TREADS PAINTED YELLOW.
REVISION "D" 7-8-52 D.O.H.
CHANGED STOCK NO. FROM 313 TO F-240.
REVISION "E" 6-18-65 F.W.R.
ADDED NOTE FOR STRIPING END VERTICAL HANDHOLDS.
REVISION "F" 8-4-65. F.W.R.
CHANGED PAINTING OF SAFETY APPLIANCES TO SUIT SOLID YELLOW COLOR AT END OF CAR.

INTERIOR AND EXTERIOR PAINTING - TRAC T-83278

THE BALTIMORE & OHIO R. R. CO.
FREIGHT CARS.
INSTRUCTIONS FOR PAINTING CABOOSE CAR HANDHOLDS.
T-72781
MOTIVE POWER DEPT., BALTIMORE, MD. 8-3-1945

Below: The C-2438 exhibited the 1955 bay window caboose paint scheme. As with cupola cabooses, the body was bright red with white lettering. The underframe was black, and the grab irons were yellow. Note that the C-2438 is one of the I-12 cars with long side grab irons which extend to a point half way up the side window. It was photographed at Somerset, Pennsylvania on June 13, 1965. (J. W. Brauner, Robert Hubler Collection)

Above: Class I-1A C-498 illustrates the 1955 paint scheme as applied to a cupola type caboose. Badly in need of a paint job, the car has a faded red body with white lettering. The window frames are a dark green color and the underframe is black. Although the paint was badly worn, the grab irons were (or were supposed to be) yellow. The C-498 was photographed at Willard, Ohio on December 14, 1964. (Julian W. Barnard, The B&O Railroad Historical Society Collection)

Below: B&O C-1403 illustrates the 1964 paint scheme as applied to a Class I-1A caboose. The car displays a simplified Capitol dome herald and an interesting application of Gothic style numbers rather than the previously used Roman style. The colors applied are a bright red body with the lettering in white and the handrails and grab irons are yellow while the underframe is black. The C-1403 was photographed at Columbus, Ohio in September 1969. (Paul Dunn, Robert Hubler Collection)

Pool Service Caboose Colors - 1965 to 1969

In 1965, the B&O began to pool cabooses on its mainline trains. The surviving I-12, I-17, I-17A, C-15B and the new I-18 cabooses used in this pool service received new schemes. Both the paint and the lettering schemes are illustrated by diagram W-90699 (Figure 47, page 164). This diagram indicated that the sides, underframes and trucks were to be painted Enchantment Blue, the ends Signal Yellow, and the roof aluminum. The diagram also specified white lettering.

It should be noted the vast majority of the I-12 cabooses did not receive the aluminum colored roof in spite of the directions provided by this diagram. The author only observed one wagon top caboose on which the silver roof was attempted. As may be expected with a round roof car, the application of the silver paint was difficult and often sloppy, with no clear demarcation between the silver and the blue paint.

Left: B&O C-2868 illustrates the 1965 pool service paint scheme as applied to a Class I-17A. The previous lettering scheme which consisted of the 23.5-inch diameter capitol dome herald and the 18-inch B&O initials was retained, but the caboose colors were changed to a blue body with yellow ends and a silver roof. The C-2868 is seen at Willard, Ohio on December 3, 1966. (Julian W. Barnard, The B&O Railroad Historical Society Collection)

Below: An example of the second version of the 1965 pool service paint scheme is provided by this photograph of I-12 C-2815. In this version, the large "B&O" lettering on the bay window has been eliminated, but the sides are still blue, the ends yellow and the trucks and underside of the car black. Since this was a wagon top car, the roof was not painted silver (as on the I-17, I-17A and I-18 cabooses) but was blue like the sides. The C-2815 is sitting outside the DuBois, Pennsylvania shops on May 9, 1976, awaiting repairs just as the shops were about to be closed. The railroad subsequently sent the car in this condition to the C&O car shops at Raceland, Kentucky, which repaired and repainted it into the Chessie System scheme. (Robert Hubler)

Cupola Caboose Colors - 1970 to 1971

In 1970 and 1971, when a number of wooden cupola style cabooses were repaired at the Chillicothe shops for use in non-pool service, they were repainted in a scheme similar to the C&O caboose paint scheme. It featured a large 38-inch diameter capitol dome in black on a yellow carbody. The car number was also in black below the dome. There was a red stripe along the lower edge of the car, and the letters "B&O" did not appear on the car itself, only in the herald. The roof and grab irons were painted aluminum.

Right: Class I-5D C-2227 illustrates the yellow paint scheme applied to a number of wooden cabooses by the Chillicothe, Ohio shops in 1970 and 1971. In this color scheme, the sides and ends were yellow and the lettering was black with a red stripe along the bottom of the sides. The trucks and underframe of the car were painted black. The roof, handrails and grab irons were painted with aluminum paint, giving them a bright silver color. The C-2227 was at Grafton, West Virginia on September 4, 1977. (Robert Hubler)

Lower Right: The C-3820 displays a heavily weathered version of its original paint scheme at Cincinnati, Ohio on October 29, 1977. All Class C-26 cabooses were delivered in this scheme, featuring blue sides and ends. The striping, lettering and handrails were yellow, and the trucks were black. The ends of the roof were painted yellow with diagonal red stripes to enhance visibility. (Robert Hubler)

Non-Pool Service Bay Window Caboose Colors 1970 to 1971

At the same time wooden cupola style cabooses were repaired at the Chillicothe shops for use in non-pool service, at least four non-pool service bay window cabooses were also shopped (I-5BAs C-2502, C-2504 & C-2505 and I-13 C-1826). These were repainted in the same C&O style paint scheme. For these bay window cars, the large 38-inch diameter Capitol dome in black was placed to the right of the bay on the yellow carbody. The car number was in black below the window of the bay and a red stripe ran along the lower edge of the car.

Pool Service Caboose Colors - 1970 to 1971

Also in 1970 and 1971, the DuBois shops conducted a repair program on the I-17 and I-17A cabooses. These cars were repainted in a new scheme, which was also applied to some Class I-12 and I-18 cars. It was similar to the scheme for the non-pool bay window cars, but the colors were almost a mirror image. The colors of this paint scheme are documented in Figure 48 on page 168. The carbody was blue instead of yellow as on the non-pool cars, and the large Capitol dome to the right of the bay window was yellow instead of black. The car number was also in yellow below the window on the bay. The stripe along the lower edge of the car was yellow instead of red.

Above: This view of Class I-17A C-2942 shows the 1970 blue paint scheme applied to pool cabooses. All I-17 and I-17A cabooses received this scheme during an overhaul program at the DuBois, Pennsylvania shops in 1970 and 1971, and the C-26 cabooses were delivered in 1971 wearing these colors. Only about two dozen I-12 cars received this scheme, along with only one I-18 caboose. The body was solid blue with yellow used for the lettering, the stripe along the bottom of the side, and the vertical panel at the ends of the roof. Diagonal red warning stripes were also applied to this yellow panel at the ends of the roof. The trucks and underframe were black and the handrails and grab irons yellow. The C-2942 was photographed at Cincinnati, Ohio on January 2, 1978. (Robert Hubler)

Below: In early 1973, shops across the B&O began applying the Chessie System paint scheme to cabooses. It would be the middle of 1974 before the Chessie scheme appeared on wagon top cabooses. The C-2467 at Lima, Ohio in 1976 provides an example of this paint scheme as it appeared on a Class I-12 caboose. The basic color was yellow, applied to the sides, ends and handrails. This was accented with vermillion (red-orange) stripes along the top and bottom of the car and the ladders were vermillion as well. Blue was used for the lettering and the outside of the frame. The trucks were black, and silver paint was applied to the

roof, even on round roof cars like the wagon top cabooses. Below the "Ches-C" logo is the plate applied for the ill-fated Automatic Car Identification system, widely but unsuccessfully used in the 1970s. This railroad version of a bar code inventory system resulted in too many phantom, "missing," mislabeled, and duplicate cars to be reliable. The box underneath the floor below the toilet on C-2467 was part of a waste retention toilet system. Often, their installation required the relocation of the battery box to the other side of the car. (Robert Hubler)

Steel Caboose Colors - 1972 to 1981

In 1972, the Chessie System adopted a new paint scheme for B&O cabooses. See Figure 49, on page 171. The carbody was yellow and the lettering a dark blue. The roof was aluminum, with vermillion stripes along the top and bottom of the car sides. Some variations of this scheme had vermillion window frames. The Class C-27 and C-27A bay window cabooses delivered in this scheme also had a green "safety cross" superimposed on railroad track applied to the sides of the car.

Below: This photograph of the C-2873 provides an example of the Chessie System paint scheme applied to an I-17A. The carbody is yellow with blue used for the lettering and the frame stripe. Vermillion stripes were applied to the top and bottom of the sides with the top stripe extending around the end of the car. The end ladders were also vermillion. Black trucks and a silver roof rounded out this colorful scheme. The C-2873 was photographed at Cincinnati, Ohio on August 28, 1977. (Robert Hubler)

Below: The Class C-26A cabooses were delivered from the factory attired in the Chessie System colors, as illustrated by this view of the C-3910 at Cincinnati, Ohio on July 5, 1976. The colors were identical to those applied by the railroad to older cabooses and included a yellow body, vermillion stripes, silver roof and blue lettering. (Robert Hubler)

Left: The Class C-27 cabooses were delivered in the standard Chessie System paint, but with one addition. This photograph of the C-3958 displays this scheme and the new large safety cross emblem to the right of the bay window. The standard Chessie colors are unchanged, with yellow carbody, vermillion striping, blue lettering, and silver roof. The additional color is provided by the white and black railroad track emblem with a dark green safety cross in the middle. The C-3958 was at M&K Junction, West Virginia on April 14, 1979. (Robert Hubler)

Right: The last B&O cabooses ever built, the Class C-27A cars, came from the builder in the Chessie System scheme. Like the preceding C-27 class, the scheme included the safety cross emblem. This view of the 904078 shows the standard colors of yellow body and vermillion striping, blue lettering and silver roof. The safety emblem differs slightly from the previous C-27 cars. The black and white tracks are unchanged, but the safety cross is a much lighter shade of green. Notice how it appears almost white in this black and white photograph. The 904078 was photographed at Garrett, Indiana on September 13, 1981. (Robert Hubler)

Lower Left: At Holloway, Ohio, the first I-5B (converted to an I-5BA by this time) wears a non-standard version of the Chessie System paint scheme. The C-2502 has a yellow carbody, black roof and lettering and vermillion grab irons. It was painted at Grafton, West Virginia (a shop which did not normally paint cabooses), and this strange scheme probably reflects the lack of proper stencils. (Paul Dunn, Robert Hubler Collection)

"Safety" Caboose Colors - 1973 to 1974

In 1973 and 1974, the DuBois, Pennsylvania shops painted eight I-18 and four C-26 cabooses into a special variation of the Chessie System paint scheme. The purpose was to promote safety on the railroad. The cabs painted in this scheme had a silver roof and ends, and each had its sides painted in relatively exotic colors. The lettering was also a Chessie System variation, contrasting with the color of the side and including a safety slogan along the roof line and a green cross on white tracks safety emblem. The list to the right shows each of the twelve B&O safety cabooses, the color applied to the sides, lettering and the safety slogan. One final note concerning the light green safety caboose (C-3774). On more than one occasion, non-railfan friends have described this color as chartreuse. The author interprets this to mean that, if ever there was such a thing as the legendary chartreuse caboose, the B&O had one.

B&O Safety Cabooses

Number	Side Color	Letters	Slogan
C-3000	Dark Green	White	Be Alert, Don't Get Hurt
C-3003	White	Black	Long Chances Shorten Lives
C-3010	Yellow(Gold)	Blue	Safety Is A Full-Time Job
C-3017	Maroon	White	Safety & Service - We Work For Both
C-3025	Red	White	Your Family Needs You, Stay Safe For Them
C-3028	Dark Blue	White	Safe Today - Here Tomorrow
C-3035	Light Blue	Black	Keep Safety In Mind All Of The Time
C-3043	Orange	Black	Safety Is Of First Importance
C-3714	Brown	White	Chessie Has Nine Lives, You Have One - Be Safe
C-3718	Purple	White	Safety Is No Accident
C-3771	Tan	Blue	Safety Is Not A Part-Time Job
C-3774	Light Green	Black	Safety Is No Mystery Just Common Sense

Right: In 1973 and 1974, the B&O specially painted 12 cabooses in various bright colors. Each carried a different safety slogan. Eight of these "safety cabooses" were I-18s. This photograph shows the first I-18, C-3000, painted with a dark green body, silver roof and ends, and lettered in white with a variation of the standard Chessie System lettering. The Chessie logo is missing, but a safety slogan has been added, as has the green, black, and white safety cross emblem. The car was at Lima, Ohio on May 23, 1976. (Robert Hubler)

Lower Right: Another example of an I-18 decorated as a "safety caboose" was the C-3010. It had a dark yellow body, referred to as gold in railroad literature of the time. The caboose had a silver roof, frame and ends. The lettering is a light blue and the safety slogan is on a white band along the roof line. Again, the Ches-C logo is missing but the green, black and white safety cross emblem has been added. The C-3010 was photographed at Dayton, Ohio on July 16, 1976. (Robert Hubler)

Above: Four of the B&O's Class C-26 cabooses were painted as "safety cabooses." The C-3714 was at Dayton, Ohio on August 8, 1976 with dark brown sides, silver ends, a silver roof, white lettering, and the green, black and white safety cross. (Robert Hubler)

Below: This B&O C-26 caboose was at Cincinnati, Ohio on September 4, 1978. The C-3774 had light green sides, silver ends, silver roof and black lettering, along with the usual green, black and white safety cross. The safety slogan was on a white band along the roof of the caboose. Parenthetically, the railroad referred to this color as light green. Other non-railroad oriented people have referred to it as chartreuse. While the B&O was noted for its many accomplishments, perhaps it is just as well that we should not include among these that the B&O was the first railroad to actually have a chartreuse caboose. (Robert Hubler)

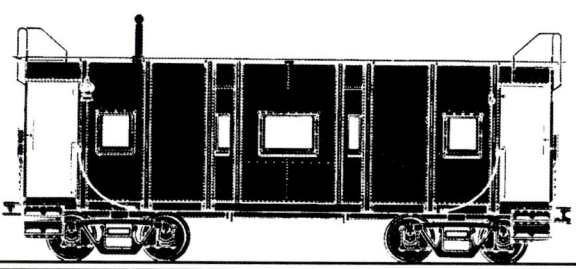

COLOR ALBUM

Above: This rare color view of B&O Class I-12 C-2806 at Eckington Yard, D.C. on June 6, 1948 shows the yellow lettering applied to some B&O cabooses in the 1940s. Also note the thick, black coating on the roof - reported to be a non-skid surface application. The cupola caboose to the right appears to be a freight car brown color. (Leonard W. Rice, John R. King, Jr. Collection)

Left: B&O Class I-16 C-2311 at Riverside yard in Baltimore, Maryland on January 28, 1950 illustrates just how bright and visible the "devil's red" paint scheme could be when fresh. Compare it with the sooty drabness of the cab coupled to it. (Charles T. Mahan, Jr.)

Above: B&O Class I-1 C-379 at Washington Court House, Ohio in July 1963 illustrates the 1955 "Billboard B&O" scheme but with red window frames. The bright red had faded to a shade similar to the color of the boxcars behind it. (G. McKay, Robert Hubler Collection)

Below: At Clarksburg, West Virginia, Class I-5D C-1929 trailed an eastbound freight. The caboose carried the 1955 cupola caboose lettering scheme, including the more common green window frames. A Sentinel Service boxcar was four cars forward. (Andy White)

Above: The "Billboard B&O" lettering style as applied to a bay window caboose is illustrated by Class I-12 C-2822 at Benwood, West Virginia in August, 1957. The enthusiastic painter even gave the smoke jack and coupler a coat of red paint. The latter was contrary to AAR regulations which prohibited the painting of couplers or wheels (paint could hide cracks). (Al Chione Slides, used with permission.)

Below: The B&O's only Class I-5A caboose was photographed at Huntington, West Virginia in May 1965. (Ed Kirstatter)

Above: B&O Class I-17 C-2858 stood in fresh paint at Mt. Clare shops in Baltimore, Maryland on November 21, 1964. Note the simplified dome herald, the small electric marker lights, and the newly applied rock screens. (Charles T. Mahan, Jr.)

Left: In the heart of the Pittsburgh steel district, C-1827 and C-2413 pass in the shadow of the Jones and Laughlin blast furnaces at Laughlin Junction in this circa 1962 photograph. Both cars show the patina of soot and road grime typical of equipment used in heavily industrialized areas. (B&O Railroad Museum Collection)

Below: B&O Chicago Terminal C-1896 is a B&O Class I-1A (former B&O C-478) which retains its original steps and platforms. It was photographed in Chicago, Illinois on June 15, 1969. (The Houser Collection)

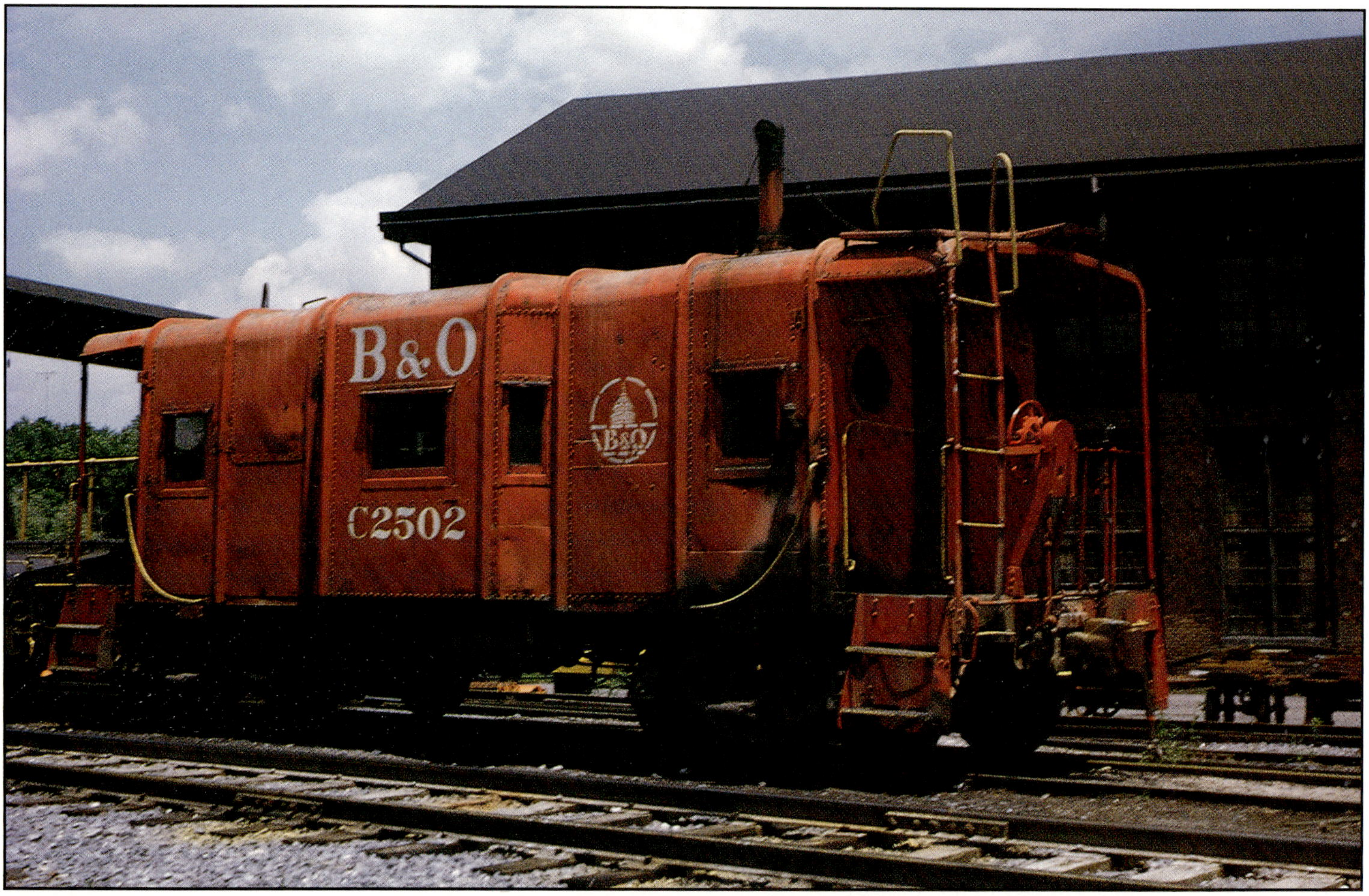
B&O
C2502

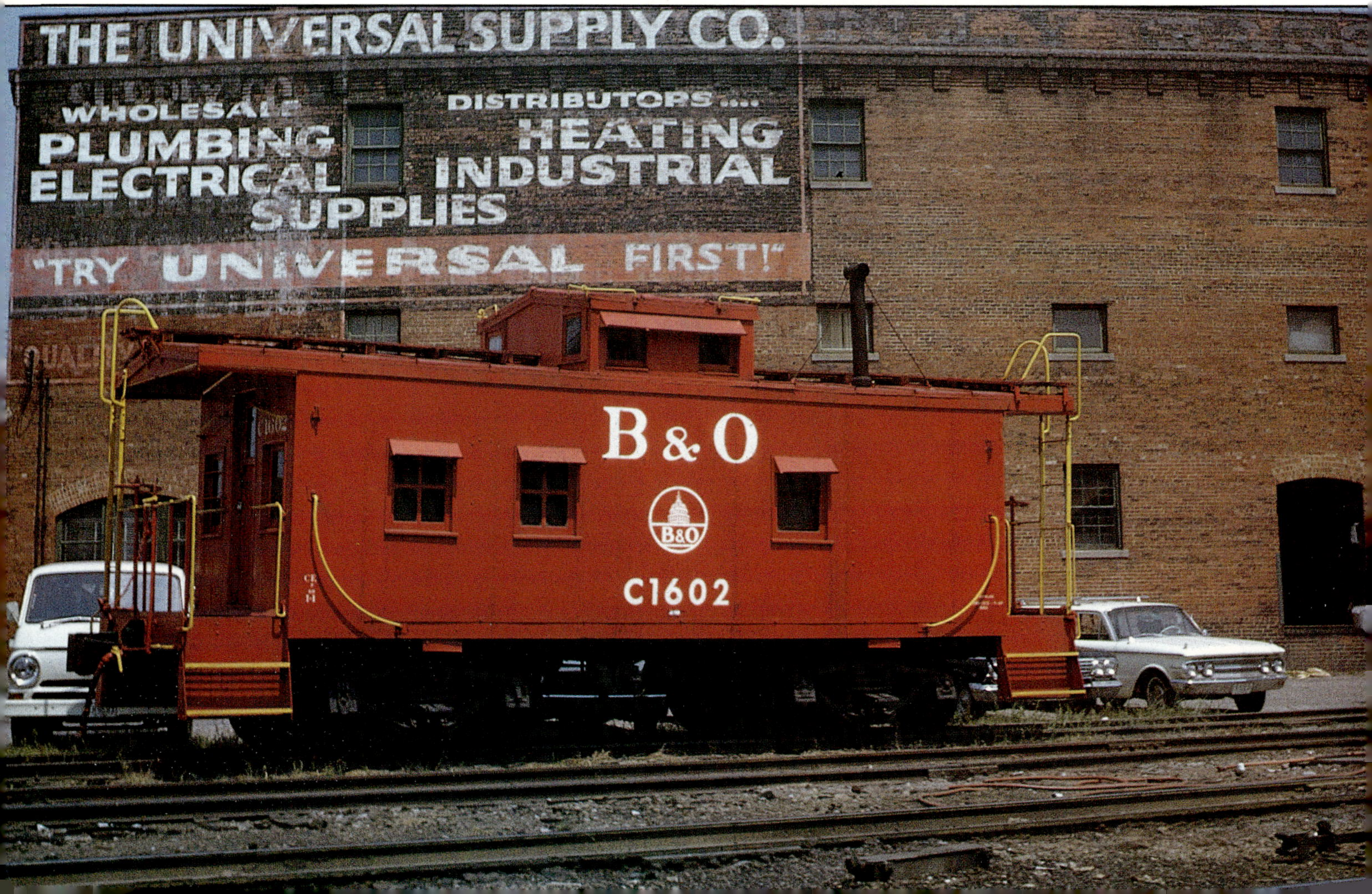
THE UNIVERSAL SUPPLY CO.
WHOLESALE
DISTRIBUTORS ....
PLUMBING
HEATING
ELECTRICAL
INDUSTRIAL
SUPPLIES
"TRY UNIVERSAL FIRST!"
B&O
C1602

Right: Class I-5C C-1953 at Chicago, Illinois displayed a black roof on March 30, 1968. The railroad had also stencilled "Watch Your Step Safety First" in yellow on the step backs above the top tread. (Al Chione Slides, used with permission.)

Top Left: Photographed at Martinsburg, West Virginia in June 1970, Class I-5BA C-2502 is showing its over thirty years of service on the B&O. (John Schletzer)

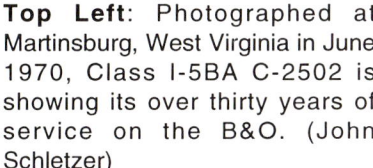

Center Right: Although marked as an I-5, the C-2089 obviously has had its truck centers expanded. It displayed the last lettering scheme used on red B&O cupola cabooses. Photographed at Brunswick, Maryland in July 1972. (Gary Schlerf)

Lower Left: B&O C-1602 was a relatively rare Class I-3, fresh from the Chillicothe shops, wearing the 1964 cupola caboose lettering scheme with C&O-style Gothic numbers. Note that it had been sheathed in plywood and the window frames were red. It was photographed at Parkersburg, West Virginia in August 1969. (John Schletzer)

Right: This November 7, 1971 photograph of C-2168 in Chicago, Illinois illustrates the unusual yellow ends applied to some wooden cabooses used in the Chicago area. The treatment of the windows is also interesting. (The Houser Collection)

Above: Class I-12 wagon top C-2457 illustrated the 1965 "pool service" paint scheme of blue with yellow ends but without the "B&O" above the bay window. The Capitol dome herald on this car was an alternative design used only briefly in the mid-1960s. The car was photographed at Wheeling, West Virginia on August 16, 1966. (Carl Stillwell, The Baltimore & Ohio Railroad Historical Society Collection)

Below: The Class I-18 cabooses were delivered in the 1965 blue pool service colors as illustrated by the C-3014 at Brunswick, Maryland on July 27, 1966. A combination of fading, and a light coat of road grime had lightened the blue considerably. The C-3014 is now at the B&O Railroad Museum in Baltimore, Maryland and has been restored to this paint scheme. (Carl Stillwell, The Baltimore & Ohio Railroad Historical Society Collection)

Right: At Holloway, Ohio on September 3, 1977, Class I-5D C-2198 wore 1970 yellow scheme as applied to cupola cabooses. The R indicates that the car was fit only for restricted service. The safety appliances were painted aluminum, and the car bore both an ACI label and a consolidation stencil. Even a simple color scheme could become complicated. (Robert Hubler)

Left: The 1970 yellow paint scheme as applied to a B&O Class I-10 (former BR&P) caboose is shown at Johnsonburg, Pennsylvania on May 9, 1971. (The Houser Collection)

Below: The only Class I-13 to receive the 1970 yellow paint scheme was the C-1826, photographed at Cincinnati, Ohio in August 1971. The plywood sheathing made it resemble a steel car. (Charly's Slides, B&O Railroad Historical Society Collection)

Above: In the early 1970s, the Chillicothe shops repainted several non-pool service wagon top bay window cabooses in the C&O style yellow scheme. Class I-5BA C-2502 was one of these and was photographed at Grafton, West Virginia in December 1975. (John Schletzer)

Below: B&O Class I-12 C-2803 illustrated the 1970 blue-with-yellow-lettering paint scheme as applied to a wagon top caboose. Photographed at Dayton, Ohio June 4, 1976. The almost uniform coat of road grime gave the car an almost greenish-gray cast. Note the high-cube boxcar ahead—ample validation for the B&O's choice of bay window cars. (Robert Hubler)

Above: B&O Class I-17A C-2899 was photographed at Johnsonburg, Pennsylvania on May 9, 1971 fresh out of the DuBois shops in the 1970 pool service scheme. (The Houser Collection)

Below: Class C-26 caboose C-3809 was still in its original paint scheme at Dayton, Ohio on June 18, 1978. This class was the last to carry a B&O paint scheme, as all future cabooses were delivered in the Chessie System paint scheme. Both the fenders on the rear platform and their reason for being were evident in this photograph. (Robert Hubler)

Below: The 903050 was a former C&O caboose acquired by the B&O in September 1967 to meet pool service requirements. It was eventually classed C-15B and operated on the B&O for many years. Photographed in August 1984 at the Cumberland car shop, it is seen with faded blue lettering. (John Schletzer)

Above: The oddest of all B&O cabooses was the one-of-a-kind C-3051, rebuilt at the DuBois shops in 1976 from a boxcar. It was the railroad's attempt to construct a caboose suitable for yard and transfer service. Eventually assigned Class C-28, it was in Baltimore, Maryland on November 13, 1976. (Charles T. Mahan, Jr.)

Top Left: Fresh from the paint shop, Class I-12 wagon top C-2822 shone in its new Chessie System paint at Dayton, Ohio on August 28, 1977. The railroad's intent was not to produce a pretty car, but to highlight key features of the car for trainmen and hopefully decrease injuries. The aluminum paint on the roof reduced the interior temperature by several degrees on sunny days. (Robert Hubler)

Below: The Class C-26A cabooses were the first to be delivered in the Chessie System colors. C-3863 trailed a B&O freight through Dayton, Ohio on July 4, 1976. Note the four reflectorized disks on the end platform railing, and the light gray coating of road dust on the underbody. (Robert Hubler)

Left: One of the first of the so-called "safety cabooses" was the red and silver Class I-18 C-3025. The car was heading north through Dayton, Ohio on September 11, 1977. Some of the safety slogans were blatant appeals to employees' sense of guilt and responsibility to others. (Robert Hubler)

Above: Another of the vividly colored safety cabooses was C-3718, a Class C-26, featuring purple sides and silver ends. This cab was at Brunswick, Maryland in November 1981. Note how different the lettering was from the C-3025. (John Schletzer)

Left: This brown Chessie safety caboose was photographed at Riverside yard in Baltimore, Maryland in April 1976. (John Schletzer)

Above: The last B&O cabooses built were the Class C-27A cars. They carried Chessie System colors modified with the addition of a large green, black and white "safety cross". An example is the 904013 at Brunswick, Maryland on March 1, 1981. The cars had white safety appliances, rather than the orange appliances of many repainted cars. (Robert Hubler)

Below: In 1982 the railroad implemented a "Careful Car Handling" program and painted six cabooses in this orange scheme to promote it. Class C-26 903747 was photographed just after leaving the Brunswick, Maryland car shop in November 1982. (John Schletzer)

Above: In 1985 the Cumberland shops repainted a surplus B&O Class I-17A caboose into a green safety scheme for use around the locomotive shop. While it was also used to promote safety at other locations on the division, it was never used in revenue service. The 902884 was photographed at Cumberland in November 1985. In 1994 it was added to the B&O Museum's collection and repainted in blue as C-2884. (John Schletzer)

Below: The CSX paint scheme was applied to former B&O caboose Class C-27A 904038. The company's intent was to call attention to two longstanding safety programs, Operation Redblock and Operation Lifesaver. The car was photographed at Maysville, Kentucky in October 1991. (John Schletzer)

Cupola Caboose Colors - 1975

Between 1975 and 1977, a few wooden cupola style cabooses were repaired at the Chillicothe shops and repainted in a simplified scheme consisting of the letters "B&O" and the car number in black on a yellow carbody. The roof was painted aluminum. Some of the cars received a red stripe along the bottom of the side, while others did not. This was the last paint scheme applied to B&O cupola caboose cars.

Steel Bay Window Caboose Colors - 1982

During the summer of 1982, the railroad began to paint a series of three C&O and three B&O cabooses in a special bright orange scheme to promote "Careful Car Handling." The freight damage prevention and hazardous materials management departments sponsored the program to heighten employee awareness of the need to move and couple freight cars carefully to reduce damage. As part of this promotion Chessie employees were advised they would receive an orange baseball cap with the "Careful Car Handling" logo if they phoned in sightings of the specially painted cabooses.

The Brunswick, Maryland car shop repainted the three B&O Class C-26 cabooses in this scheme. The 903747 and 903758 were repainted in November 1982, and the 903820 in April 1983. The carbodies were bright orange with yellow stripes at the bottom of the body and at the roof line. The roof, frame, and underbody were blue, while the safety appliances were white.

Bay Window Caboose Colors - 1991 to 1992

In 1991, CSX Transportation began to refurbish a number of cars for continued service on those trains that still required cabooses. Some of these cabooses were former B&O cars and were painted in a CSX paint scheme. They were given gray sides and red reflective panels on the yellow ends. Both sides of the caboose had a blue and yellow diagonally striped band with the words "CROSS TRACKS SAFELY" in yellow on the top edge of the band. Most of the lettering was blue, with one side of the car featuring the "Operation RED BLOCK" anti-drug logo. The opposite side had an "Operation Life Saver" grade crossing safety logo. The handrails and grab irons were painted white to contrast with the rest of the colors.

Upper Right: B&O I-5D caboose C-2292 sat on the caboose track at the Chillicothe, Ohio, yard on December 26, 1977. It carried the 1975 cupola caboose paint scheme applied at Chillicothe in February of that year. The spartan scheme consisted of a yellow carbody, minimal lettering done in black paint, a silver roof, silver handrails and black trucks. (Robert Hubler)

Lower Right: B&O Class C-26A caboose 903918 was at the B&O Railroad Museum in Baltimore on December 29, 1993. This caboose illustrates the CSX Transportation paint scheme applied to a few former B&O cabooses beginning in 1991. The sides were grey with yellow ends. Most of the lettering is blue. One side of the car featured the "Operation RED BLOCK" anti-drug logo, while the opposite side carried the "Operation Life Saver" grade crossing safety logo. Both sides of the caboose carried a blue and yellow striped band with the words "CROSS TRACKS SAFELY" in yellow on a blue band. (Robert Hubler)

LETTERING SCHEMES

Caboose Lettering - Prior to 1900

The earliest B&O caboose lettering diagram available was issued in 1916 (see Figure 42). Therefore, photographs provide the primary evidence for earlier lettering schemes. The oldest photograph with visible lettering in this book is of B&O caboose 1871 on page 30. This eight-wheel caboose was photographed in 1899, and carried the words BALTo & OHIO in a white panel centered on the side of the car. The number 1871 was also in a white panel below the road name. Other photographs from this era show such white panels applied to boxcars, hoppers and gondolas. Only a few photographs of eight-wheel cabooses from this era have been found, most without visible lettering. It is impossible to state with certainty whether this scheme was intended to be applied to all cabooses, only eight-wheel cabooses or was a "standard" caboose lettering scheme. A photograph of two four-wheel cabooses from this era with the words BALTo & OHIO and the number on the sides of the caboose, but without the white panel is shown below.

Caboose Lettering - 1900 to 1916

Photographs taken between 1900 and 1916 show cabooses with the number in white centered along the lower edge of the car side. The only railroad identification consists of the letters "B&O" directly above the number. Some early photographs suggest that this may have been the lettering scheme applied to the first Class I-1 cabooses when they were built. Comparisons with photos of later lettering schemes indicate that the car side numbers used in this scheme may have been 7 inches in height.

Upper Right: Class I caboose C-24 illustrates the lettering scheme which was applied to B&O cabooses until about 1916. This consisted of the "B&O" initials and the car number centered along the lower edge of the carbody. The C-24 was a former B&OSW caboose but matches none of the other B&OSW cabooses shown on page 30. It was renumbered to C-1810 in 1925 and was wrecked at Hamden, Ohio on December 7, 1926. (Roger Kirkpatrick Collection)

Above: This undated and somewhat distorted photograph of two Class K-1 cabooses at the Cumberland, Maryland shops illustrates the pre-1900 lettering scheme without a large white panel. (The B&O Railroad Historical Society Collection)

Right: B&O Class K-1 caboose 100777 was built in 1899 as 1730, renumbered 100777 after 1900, and again renumbered C-777 after 1907. The photograph illustrates the turn-of-the-century lettering scheme, with the letters "B&O" above the car number and both centered on the side. The B&O adopted a series of standard letter and number forms shortly after its take-over by the Pennsylvania Railroad in 1901, and continued to use these distinctive forms, loosely described as a thick "Railroad Roman," until the mid-1960s and coordination with the C&O Railway. (John Malone Collection)

Cupola Caboose Lettering - 1916 to 1941

This is the first of the B&O caboose lettering schemes for which the Society or the B&O Railroad Museum has documentation. By examining B&O Diagram W-33265 (Figure 42), and the other diagrams in the series, it is possible to follow the evolution of B&O cupola caboose lettering schemes. This tracing was originally issued May 15, 1916, and the lettering consisted of the words "Baltimore & Ohio" in 7-inch letters centered along the top edge of the caboose. The number was also in seven-inch numerals and centered on the side of the car 12 inches from the bottom edge of the side. In addition, the tracing shows the size and positioning of the various servicing stencils as applied to cabooses.

Bay Window Caboose Lettering - 1931 to 1941

In 1931, the first bay window caboose appeared on the B&O in the form of the Class I-7 C-2500. Due to the nature of the bay window carbody, the lettering scheme had to be modified from that used on the cupola cabooses. Specifically, the words "Baltimore & Ohio" were in two lines along the top of the bay window instead of being centered in seven-inch letters along the top edge of the caboose as on the cupola cars. The caboose number was applied in standard 7-inch numerals centered on the bottom of the bay window. This lettering is illustrated by the photograph of the C-2500 on page 69.

Above: At Parkersburg, West Virginia on February 5, 1934, Class K-1 C-1290 was less than one month out of the B&O shops at Gassaway, West Virginia and presented a very clean appearance. This photograph illustrates the 1916 caboose lettering scheme consisting of the railroad name and the car number. Close inspection of the letters and numbers reveals overspray from the spray painting process widely used by the B&O by this time. The dark lines and broken appearance of the letters indicate that the painter did not touch up the lines and areas masked by the wires used to hold the stencils together. In the depths of the Depression, painters had no doubt been furloughed at Gassaway, and the remaining men did what they could to get the work out the door. (S. P. Davidson)

Cupola Caboose Lettering - 1941 to 1948

On October 2, 1941, the lettering diagram for cupola cabooses was revised to incorporate a 24-inch Capitol dome herald, which was centered on the side of the caboose 5" below the words "Baltimore & Ohio." The size and placement of all the other lettering remained the same. See Figure 42 below.

Figure 42

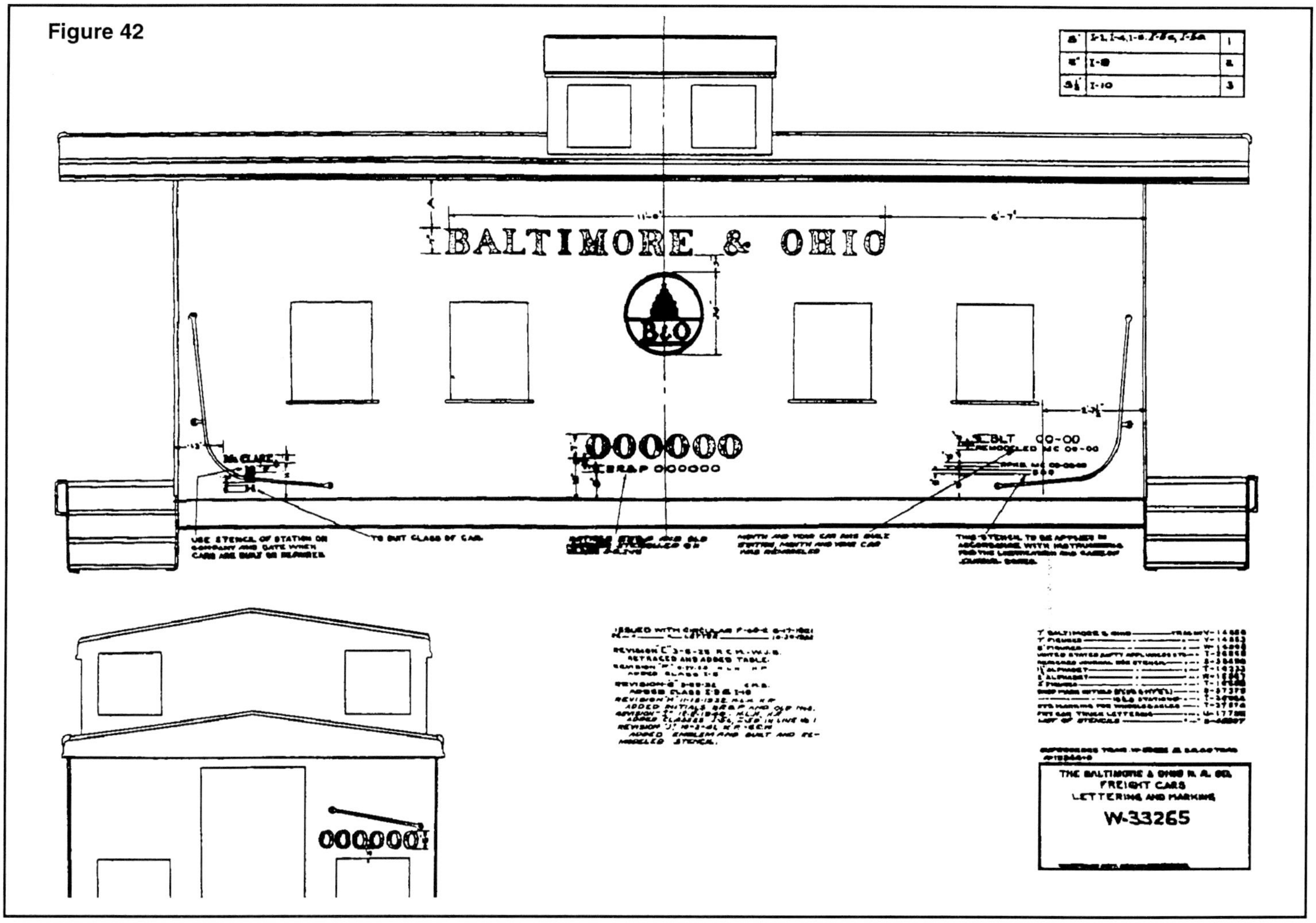

Right: In the fifteen years since it was built, little had changed on Class I-5 C-1977 shown at Galeton, Pennsylvania on May 25, 1941. One anomaly is that the lettering scheme includes the Capitol dome herald. The caboose lettering diagram for this scheme was not revised to show the addition of the herald until October 2, 1941, nearly 5 months after this photograph was taken. It would appear that at least some shops received orders to add the Capitol dome several months before the lettering diagram was revised to incorporate the change. (J. W. Brauner, Robert Hubler Collection)

149

Steel Bay Window Caboose Lettering
1941 to circa 1945

When the Class I-12 wagon top cabooses were built, they received a lettering scheme differently arranged from that applied to the wooden Class I-13 bay window cabooses or to cupola cabooses. As in the previous scheme used on steel bay window cars, the lettering had to be modified due to the nature of the carbody. The words "Baltimore & Ohio" were in two lines along the top of the bay window. The number was applied using standard 7-inch numerals centered on the bottom of the bay window. The I-12 cars also had the 24-inch diameter Capitol dome herald applied to the left of the bay window, since the bay's window prevented it from being centered on the car.

Wooden Bay Window Caboose Lettering
1941 to 1948

The I-13 and I-16 caboose conversions of 1941 through 1943 were lettered in two variations. On the I-13 cars, the words "Baltimore & Ohio" were spelled out in a single line to the right of the bay window while the 24-inch Capitol dome herald appeared on the left of the bay window. The caboose number was in the standard seven-inch numerals centered on the bottom of the bay window. On the I-16 cars, this scheme was reversed with the words "Baltimore & Ohio" spelled out in a single line to the left of the bay window while the Capitol dome herald appeared to the right of the bay window. The caboose number was in the standard seven-inch numerals and centered on the bottom of the bay window. The I-13 lettering is illustrated by the photograph of C-1800 on page 81.

Cupola Caboose Lettering - 1948 to 1955

On September 14, 1948, the lettering diagram for cupola cabooses was revised to incorporate the 36-inch diameter "Linking 13 Great States" herald replacing the 24-inch Capitol dome herald (see Figure 43). The size and placement of all the other lettering remained the same. As noted in the following paragraph, while the 1948 date is the revision date given on the diagram for cupola cabooses, photos of the second group of Class I-12 wagon top cabooses show that the "Linking 13 Great States" herald was used on these cabooses when they were built in 1945.

Above: At Baltimore in the late 1940s, I-16 caboose C-2702 still carried its original 1941 lettering scheme with the small Capitol dome herald. The "fishbelly" underframe characteristic of these cabooses is apparent in this photograph, and the light caused the grooves of the car siding to stand out in particularly sharp relief. C-2702 was equipped with an experimental train radio, and the antenna is visible on the roof. (Carl Gerber, The Baltimore Chapter NRHS Collection)

Figure 43

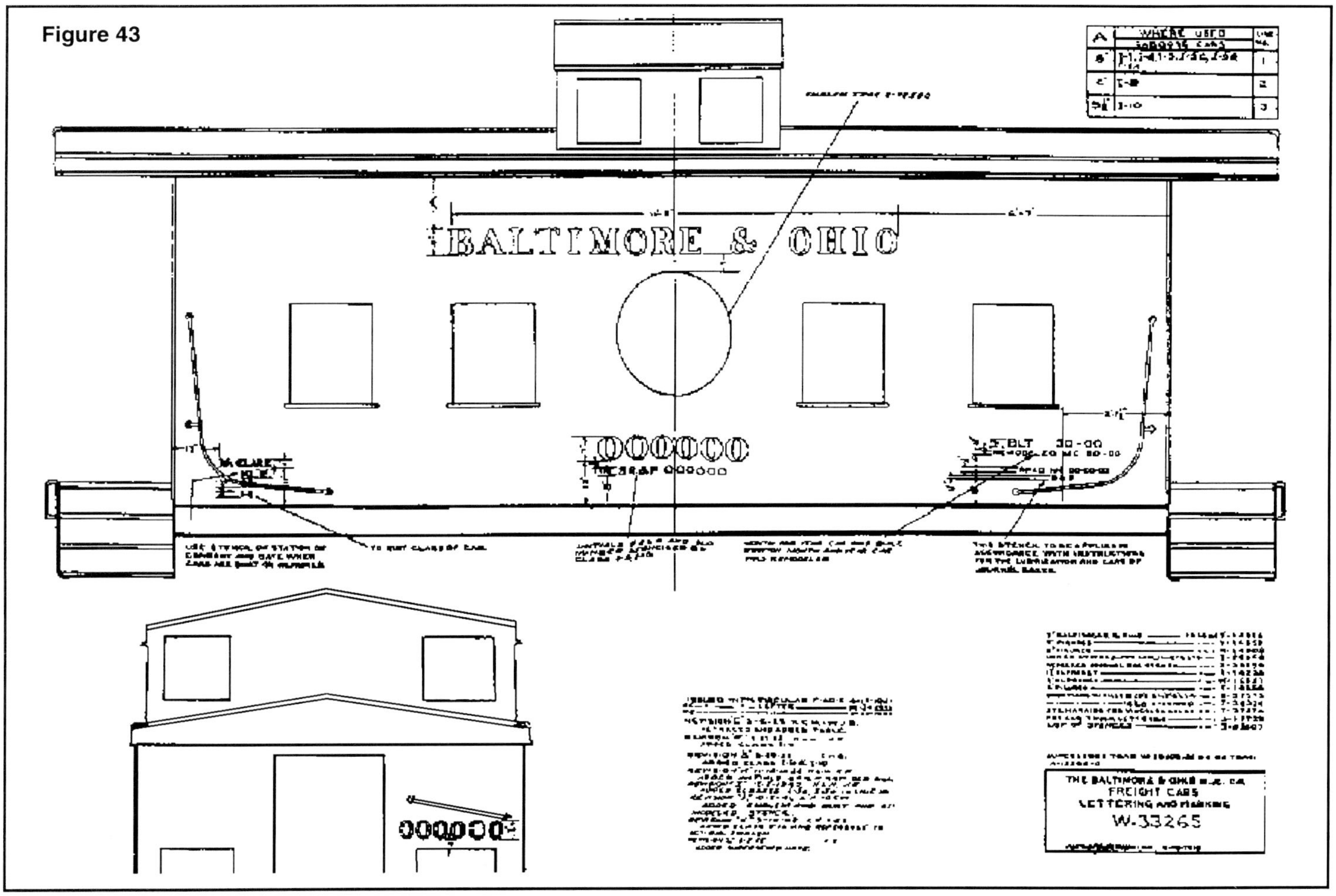

Above: This curious photo of Class I-1 caboose C-84 was taken at Benwood, West Virginia on June 18, 1946. This effectively illustrates the 1948 cupola caboose lettering scheme, something of an anomaly since the railroad's lettering diagrams were not revised to include the 36-inch "13-states" herald until almost two years after the photograph was taken. The herald is much brighter than the rest of the lettering, suggesting that it was applied some time after the caboose was repainted. (Paul Dunn)

Above: B&O I-5C caboose C-2138 was at Garrett, Indiana on March 13, 1965. Even at this late date this car carried the 1948 lettering scheme with the words "Baltimore & Ohio" spelled out along the top of the sides. However, instead of the large 36-inch diameter "13-states" herald which was normally used with this lettering scheme, the smaller 25-inch diameter herald used with the later billboard B&O lettering scheme had been applied. Because the stencil lines were not touched up, the logo had an "ad-hoc" appearance. Such variations were common, especially at the far reaches of the system where smaller car shops performed routine maintenance for a modest number of cabooses. (Julian W. Barnard, The B&O Railroad Historical Society Collection)

Left: Former CI&W caboose 10, seen as B&O C-1685 at Connersville, Indiana on April 24, 1949, appears to have changed little since it was acquired by the B&O in 1927. This photograph illustrates the application of the 1948 lettering scheme to an I-6 caboose. Note that the 36-inch diameter "13-states" herald barely fits between the two middle windows and the words "Baltimore & Ohio" have been separated in order to clear the tall windows. (J. W. Brauner, Robert Hubler Collection)

Steel Bay Window Caboose Lettering
circa 1945 to 1955

When the second group of I-12 wagon top cabooses were built in 1945, they received a lettering scheme different from that applied to the first group of I-12s (see Steel Bay Window Caboose Lettering, 1941 to 1945 on page 150). As in the previous scheme used on steel bay window cars, the lettering had to be modified due to the nature of the carbody. The words "Baltimore & Ohio" were in two lines along the top of the bay window as before and the number was in the standard 7-inch numerals centered on the bottom of the bay window. However, this group of I-12 cars had the 36-inch diameter "Linking 13 Great States" herald applied to the left of the bay window rather than the plain 24-inch diameter Capitol dome herald used on the first group of I-12 cabooses. This is interesting, since the "Linking 13 Great States" herald would not be specified for cupola cabooses until 1948 (see Cupola Caboose Lettering, 1948 to 1955, on page 150).

Wooden Bay Window Caboose Lettering
1948 to 1955

As with the cupola cabooses, sometime around 1948 the 36-inch diameter "Linking 13 Great States" herald replaced the plain Capitol dome herald as standard on the I-13 and I-16 bay window cabooses. This scheme was different from that used on the I-12 wagon top cabooses. While the I-12 cabooses had the words "Baltimore & Ohio" in two lines along the top of the bay windows, the I-13 and I-16 cabooses had the words "Baltimore & Ohio" in a single line along the lower edge of the carbody. In some cases the words "Baltimore & Ohio" were to the right of the bay window and the herald was to the left, and in other cases the scheme was reversed. Photos of I-13 and I-16 cabooses show each class of caboose with both variations. The number was in the standard seven-inch numerals and centered on the bottom of the bay window.

Above: The company photographed I-12 C-2819 at Mt. Clare in the late 1940s, possibly to show the installation of an experimental radio setup (notice the "radio" stencil just under the number). Although not a builder's photo in the usual sense, it does illustrate the original lettering scheme as applied to the second series of I-12 cabooses, featuring the 36-inch diameter "13-states" herald and the words "Baltimore & Ohio" in two lines above the bay window. (Carl Gerber, The Baltimore Chapter NRHS Collection)

Above: I-13 caboose C-1820 (former B&O Class L-6 stock car 13028, nee CI&W stock car 679) carries the 1948 paint scheme as applied to I-13 cabooses, with the words "Baltimore & Ohio" spelled out to the right of the bay window and the large 36-inch diameter Capitol dome herald to the left of the bay window. The C-1820 was photographed at Indianapolis, Indiana in the 1950s. (S. P. Davidson, Robert Hubler Collection)

Cupola Caboose Lettering - 1955

On April 5, 1955 the lettering diagram for cupola cabooses, W-33265, was superseded by diagram W-84674 (Figure 44, page 157). In the lettering scheme specified by this diagram, the words "Baltimore & Ohio" were replaced by the letters "B&O" in 18-inch letters. The 36-inch diameter "Linking 13 Great States" herald was reduced in size to 25 inches in diameter. The size and placement of all the other lettering remained the same. This lettering scheme is illustrated by the photograph of C-1411 on page 155.

Bay Window Caboose Lettering - 1955

In 1955, the B&O also issued a new lettering diagram for bay window cabooses. The words "Baltimore & Ohio" were replaced by "B&O" in 18-inch letters. The 36-inch diameter "Linking 13 Great States" herald was reduced to 25 inches in diameter. The size and placement of all the other lettering remained the same.

Cupola Caboose Lettering - 1955 to 1961

On October 26, 1955, just six months after the previous lettering diagram was issued, the lettering diagram for cupola cabooses was revised to change the size of the car number from seven inches in height to nine inches. The size and placement of all other lettering remained the same.

Upper Right: This photograph of Class I-1A caboose C-1411 illustrates the 1955 lettering scheme as applied to a cupola caboose. Notice how the use of the 18-inch "B&O" has lessened the space available for the herald, thus causing the railroad to reduce the size of the "13 States" herald to a diameter of 25 inches. This view of the C-1411 was taken at Zanesville, Ohio in August 1969. (Paul Dunn, Robert Hubler Collection)

Lower Right: At Willard, Ohio on January 3, 1965, C-2021 provided an example of the 1955 lettering scheme for cupola cabooses as applied to a Class I-5D car. This caboose was rebuilt with sanitary facilities at Dubois in August 1961. As a result it lost two windows on this side and all four on the other side. It also received an AAR vertical hand brake wheel, replacing the original stem brake. (Julian Barnard, The B&O Railroad Historical Society Collection)

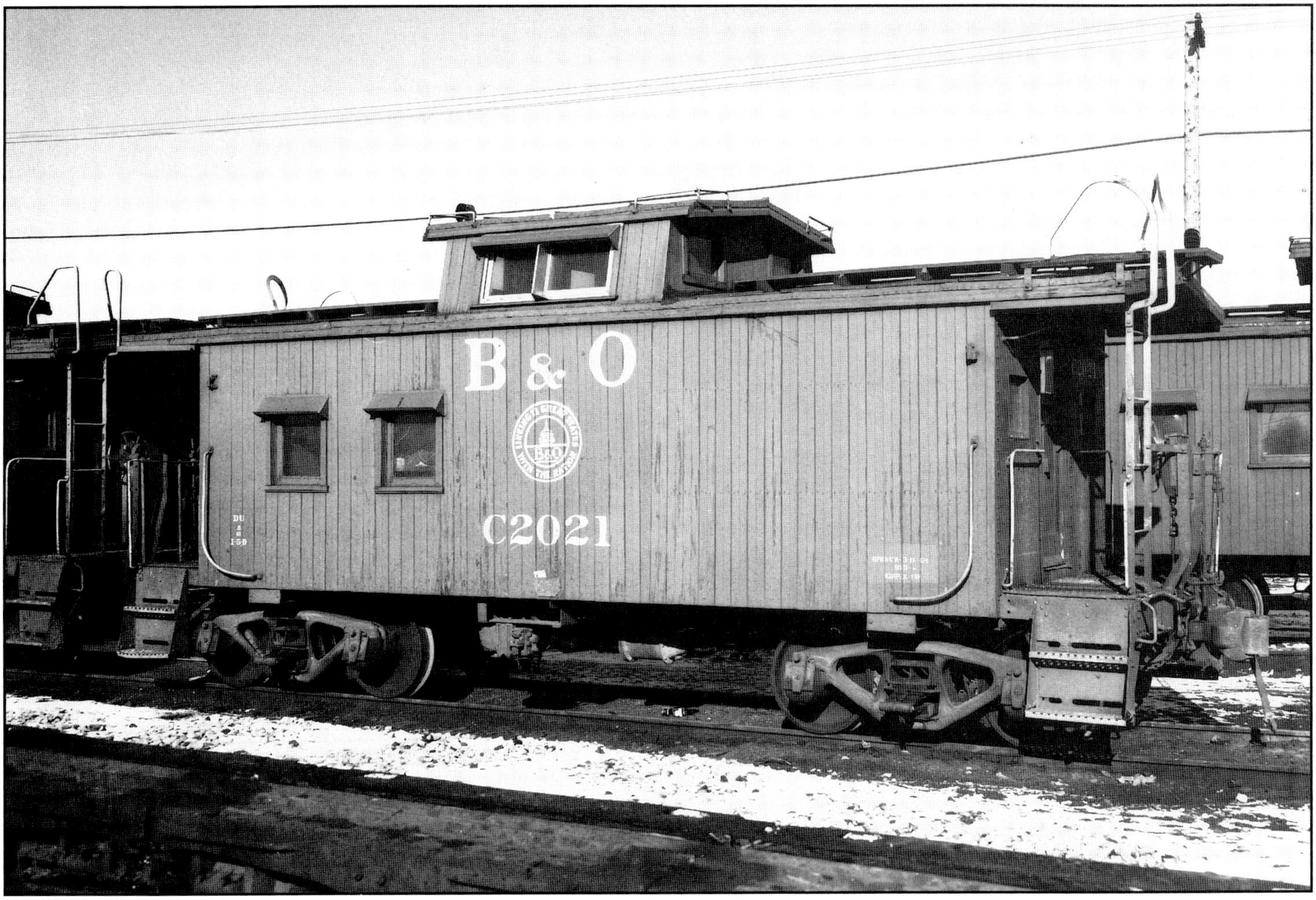

Above: I-5D, C-2001 was photographed at New Castle, Pennsylvania on February 14, 1965. It was equipped with the relatively uncommon "J" shaped side grab irons. Modelers should pay particular attention to the car number, because the DuBois shop used different lettering styles for each of the zeros as shown by "C-2001." Ordinarily, few modelers would dare do this. (J.W. Barnard, The B&O Railroad Historical Society Collection)

Below: This lettering scheme exhibits an anomaly. During the era in which this photograph was taken, the lettering scheme included a "13 States" herald which was not applied to the C-409. Either this was an oversight on the part of the shop crew, or perhaps the proper stencil was unavailable at the time the C-409 was painted. Despite some effort by the company to enforce lettering standards, many cabooses (and locomotives, especially in later years) wore non-standard decoration for substantial portions of their service. (Paul Dunn, C. W. Abbot Collection)

Above: B&O Class I-13 caboose C-1813 was photographed at Indianapolis, Indiana in the mid-1950s. It carries the typical 1948 paint scheme with the words "Baltimore & Ohio" spelled out and the large 36-inch diameter Capitol dome herald, but with a variation. Notice that unlike other I-13s pictured in this book, the words "Baltimore & Ohio" are to the left of the bay window and the herald is on the right. The B&O rebuilt this caboose from Class L-6 stock car 13019, originally CI&W stock car 670. (S. P. Davidson, Robert Hubler Collection)

Figure 44

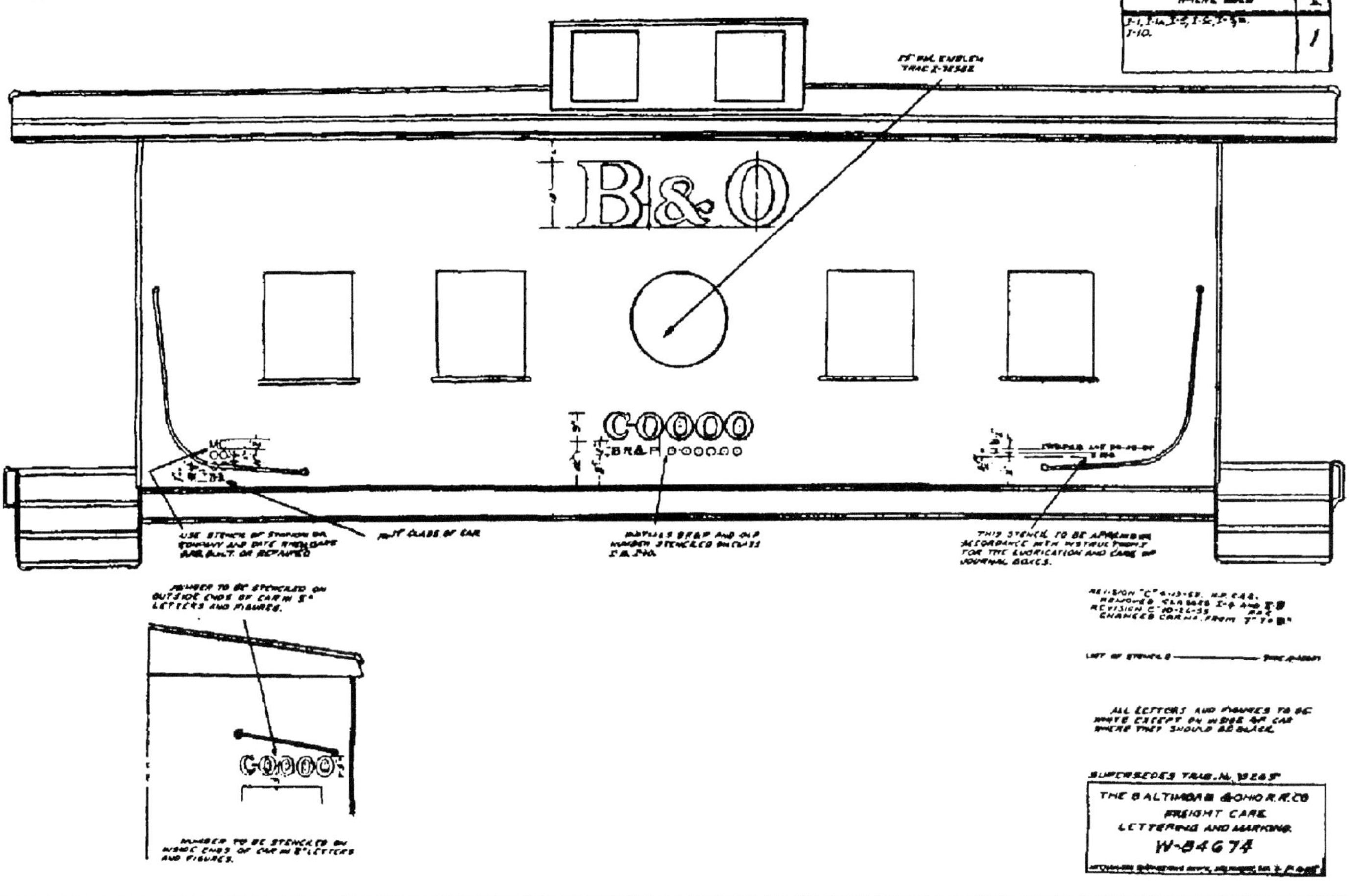

Bay Window Caboose Lettering - 1955 to 1962

On October 26, 1955, the lettering diagram for bay window cabooses was revised to change the size of the number from seven-inches in height to nine-inches. The size and placement of all other lettering remained the same.

Upper Right: B&O Class I-16 caboose C-2779 at Whiting, Indiana on November 6, 1965, had been leased to the B&OCT. As it was used for transfer service, its bay window was removed and the opening simply covered over with no additional windows. It displayed an interesting variation of the billboard B&O scheme, having the older 36-inch "13 States" herald instead of the 25-inch version normally used with this paint scheme. (Eileen Wolford Barnard, the B&O Railroad Historical Society Collection)

Above: B&O C-2465 is an example of a Class I-12 caboose in the 1955 lettering scheme with the billboard B&O initials and the small 25-inch diameter "13 States" herald. Note the C-2465 has the shorter style side grab iron extending only to the bottom of the side window. The raking light clearly shows how the sheets between the ribs have begun to flex and deform slightly. It was photographed at Willard, Ohio on July 10, 1966. (Julian W. Barnard, The B&O Historical Society Collection)

Left: Looking a bit the worse for wear, Class I-17A caboose C-2946 was at Willard, Ohio on July 9, 1966. It was from the second to the last group of I-17A cabooses, built at the B&O's Washington, Indiana shops in February, 1961. This photograph shows the original paint scheme carried by this class of car, the 18-inch "B&O" initials and the 25-inch diameter "13 States" herald. At this time, the window screens have yet to be applied and the trucks still had leaf springs. (Julian W. Barnard, the B&O Railroad Historical Society Collection)

Cupola Caboose Lettering - 1961 to 1964

On July 7, 1961, the railroad revised the lettering diagram for cupola cabooses to eliminate the "Linking 13 Great States" herald. No herald of any type was supposed to be applied to cabooses during this period. The size and placement of all the other lettering remained the same. It should be noted that some shops continued to paint cabooses in the "no herald" scheme after 1964, either through error or lack of proper stencils (see Cupola Caboose Lettering, 1964 to 1968, on page 161).

Bay Window Caboose Lettering - 1962 to 1965

On May 4, 1962, the lettering diagram for bay window cabooses was revised to change the 25-inch diameter "Linking 13 Great States" herald to a 23.5-inch simplified Capitol dome herald. See layout in Diagram X-84671, Figure 45. The size and placement of all the other lettering remained the same.

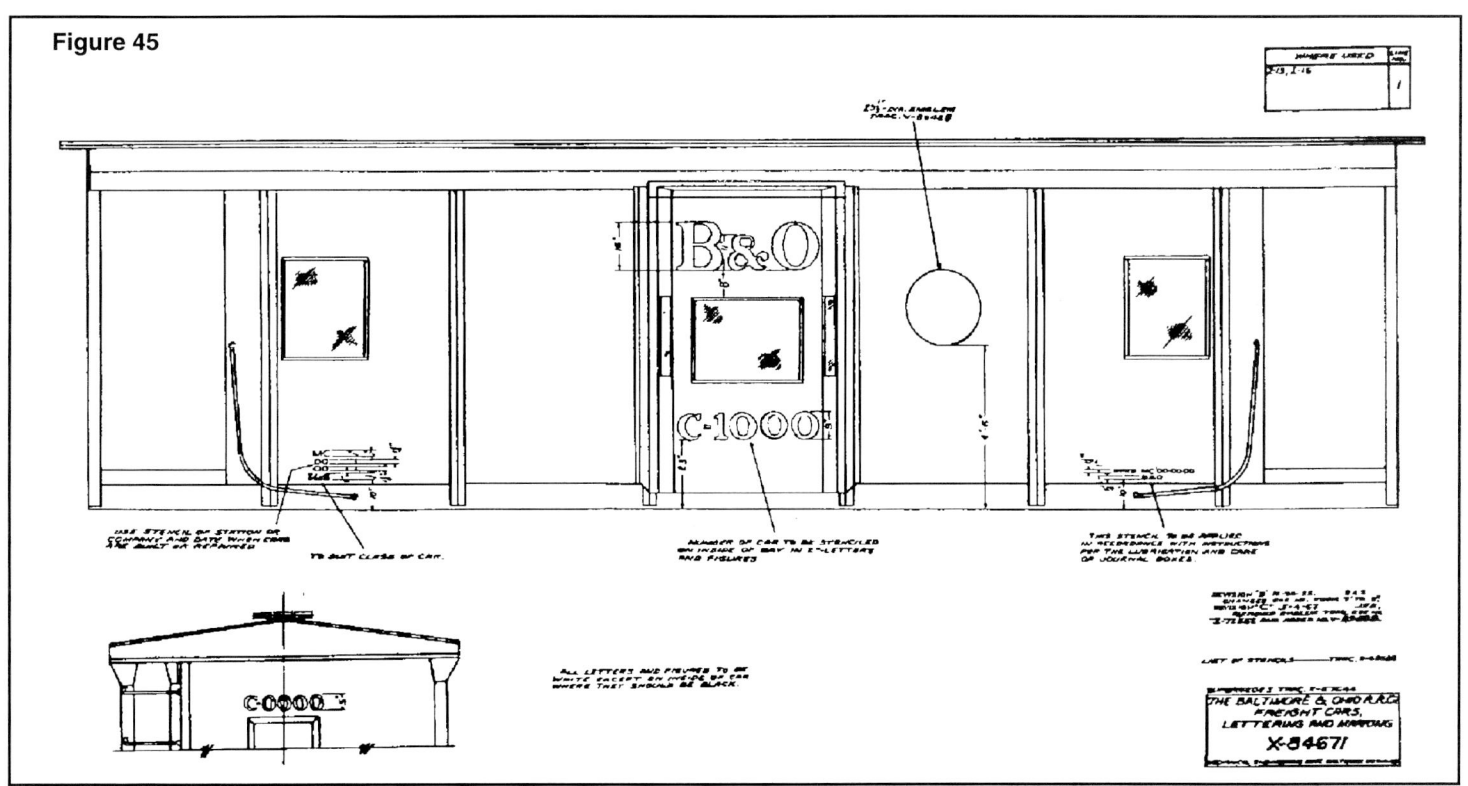

Figure 45

Above: The 1962 painting and lettering scheme remained red with white lettering, but the "13 States" herald was replaced by the simplified Capitol dome herald. I-12 caboose C-2417 was at Willard, Ohio on March 5, 1966 in this scheme. (Julian W. Barnard, The B&O Railroad Historical Society Collection)

Below: B&O caboose C-2871 illustrated the 1962 bay window caboose red paint scheme as applied to an I-17A. The 25-inch diameter "13-states" herald was replaced by the 23.5-inch diameter capitol dome herald, but all the other lettering remained the same. The C-2871 was at Cumberland, Maryland on January 1, 1966. This same lettering scheme was used with different car body colors on cabooses converted to pool service in 1965 and 1966. (Julian W. Barnard, The B&O Railroad Historical Society Collection)

Figure 46

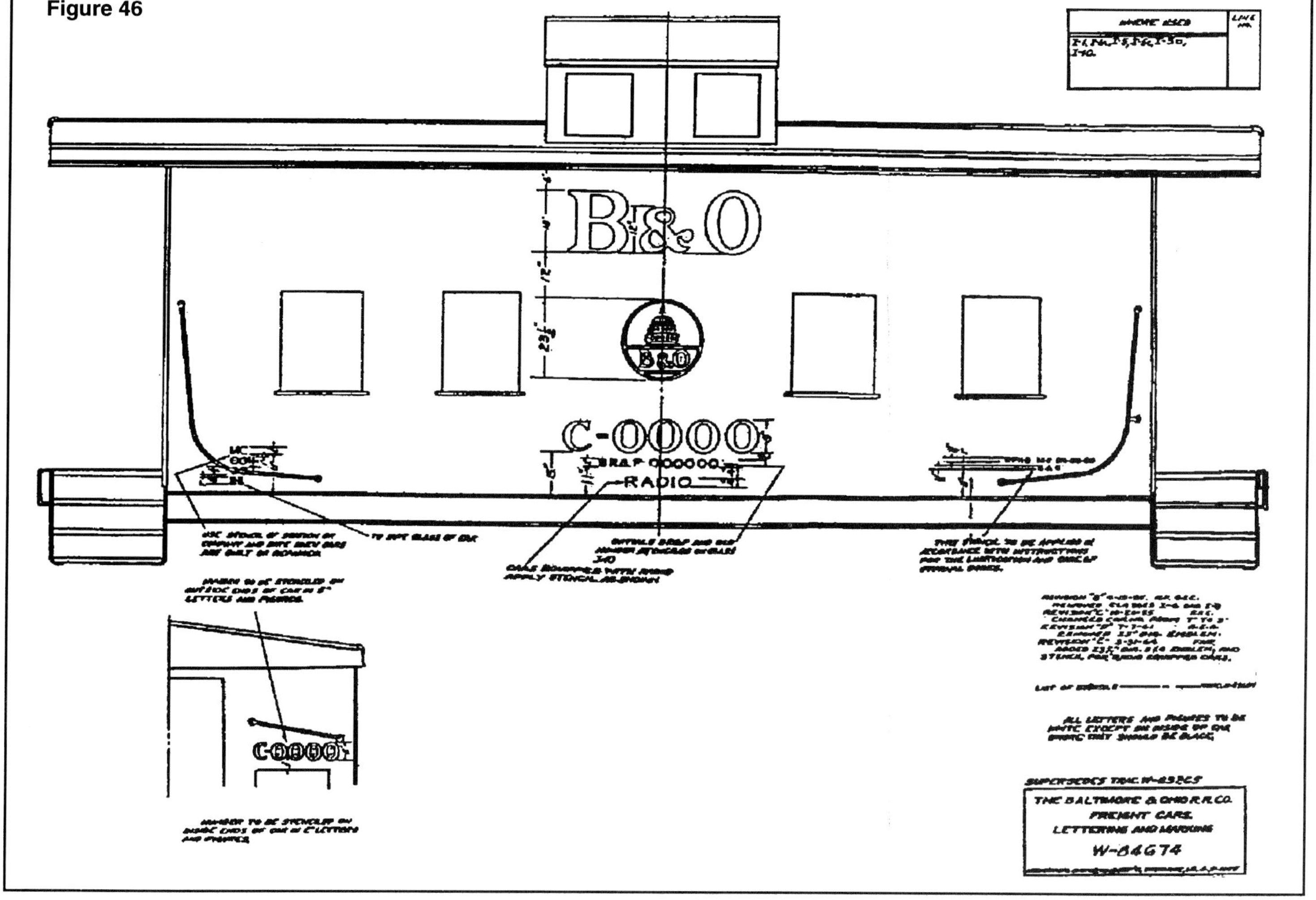

Cupola Caboose Lettering - 1964 to 1968

On March 31, 1964, the lettering diagram for cupola cabooses was revised to add a 23.5-inch diameter simplified Capitol dome herald in place of the "Linking 13 Great States" herald of previous year (see Figure 46). The size and placement of all the other lettering remained the same. As noted above, a few shops continued to paint cabooses in the "no herald" scheme after 1964, either through error or lack of proper stencils (see Cupola Caboose Lettering - 1961 to 1964, on page 159).

Right: This view of B&O I-1 caboose C-375, taken at DeForest Junction on July 2, 1966, illustrates the 1964 lettering scheme as applied to a Class I-1 caboose. It featured the large "B&O" and the 23.5-inch diameter Capitol dome herald. (Julian W. Barnard, The B&O Railroad Historical Society Collection)

Above: In this photograph, Class I-5 caboose C-2291 is in fresh paint at the Chillicothe, Ohio shops in August 1966. The lettering scheme applied to this car is curious. If one follows the B&O lettering diagrams, by this date, the 23.5-inch Capitol dome herald should have been applied to the caboose. Clearly, this has not been done. Were the Chillicothe shops still following the 1961 lettering diagram which specified no herald? Or, was the photograph taken before shopping was completed and the herald had yet to be applied? (Paul Dunn, Robert Hubler Collection)

Below: This Class I-5D caboose features the late 1960s lettering scheme with the 23.5-inch Capitol dome herald. The car also displays C&O inspired Gothic style numbers and the 18-inch "B&O" rather than the more common Roman style lettering. The C-2031 was photographed at Columbus, Ohio in September 1969. (Paul Dunn, Robert Hubler Collection)

Pool Service Caboose Lettering - 1965 to 1969

In 1965, the B&O began to pool cabooses on its mainline trains. The surviving I-12, I-17, I-17A and the new I-18 cabooses were used in this service. A new scheme was developed for these pool cabooses, illustrated by diagram W-90699, (Figure 47, on page 164). It was identical to the lettering scheme applied to bay window cabooses just prior to the implementation of the pool concept. The only difference is in the colors applied to the pool service cabooses. After June 1966, the large "B&O" stenciled above the bay window was dropped from the scheme, but this change does not appear to have been reflected by a change to the lettering diagram.

Above: Class I-12, C-2473 was only three months out of the DuBois, Pennsylvania shops when it was photographed at Willard, Ohio on July 10, 1966. After making repairs in April, 1966, DuBois repainted the car in the pool service colors of blue with yellow ends, with the large B&O initials above the bay window. (Julian W. Barnard, The B&O Railroad Historical Society Collection)

Below: For some reason (perhaps to repair wreck damage) I-12 caboose C-2473 was sent back to the DuBois, Pennsylvania shops in November 1966, only seven months after it had previously been shopped there. For a second time, it was repainted the blue with yellow ends pool service colors, but by this time, the large B&O initials above the bay window had been dropped from the lettering scheme. This photograph was taken at Rowlesburg, West Virginia, on July 27, 1974. (Robert Hubler)

Above: Most of the I-18 cabooses went directly from their original paint to the new Chessie System colors beginning in 1973. Very few ever received a second coat of blue paint in the interval. B&O C-3013, at Somerset, Pennsylvania on November 8, 1970, was one of the exceptions. Apparently, it suffered some form of damage and was repaired and repainted at DuBois, Pennsylvania in January, 1969. Note the absence of the B&O initials (which had been dropped by this time) and the fact that the caboose had been stenciled for the nonexistent "I-18A" class. (J. W. Brauner, Robert Hubler Collection)

Upper Right: B&O caboose C-2857 wears the 1965 pool service colors as they were applied to an I-17 car. This scheme featured the large "B&O" initials and the 23.5-inch diameter capitol dome emblem of the previous lettering scheme, but the colors were quite different. The body was blue, the ends yellow, the lettering white and, at least on the I-17, I-17A, and I-18 cars, the roof was silver. This photograph of C-2857 was taken at Willard, Ohio on August 12, 1966. (Julian W. Barnard, The B&O Railroad Historical Society Collection)

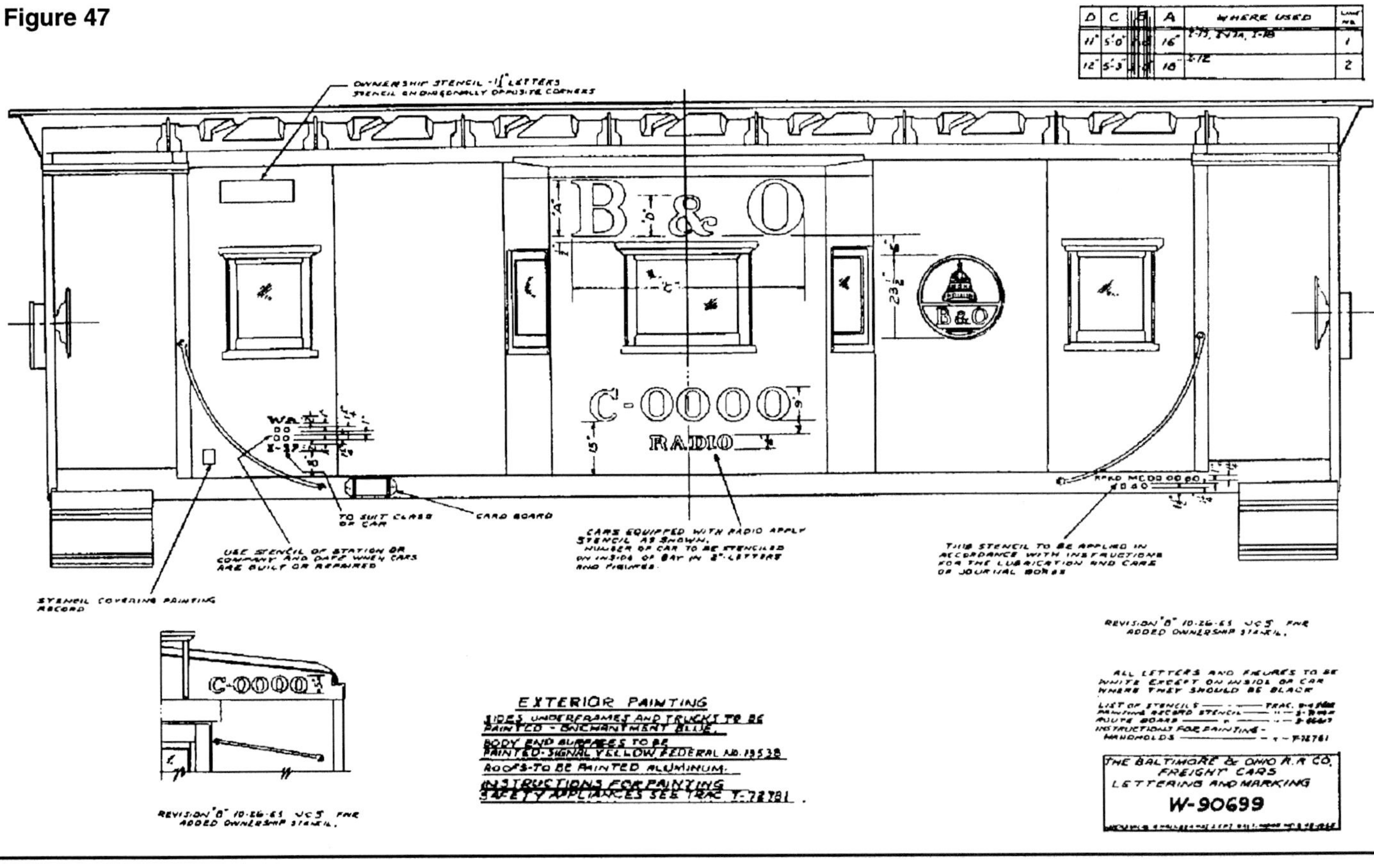

Cupola Caboose Lettering - 1969

About 1969, the railroad repainted a few of cabooses in a manner which previewed the lettering scheme adopted with the "yellow caboose scheme" the following year (see Cupola Caboose Lettering , 1970 to 1971, on page 166). This scheme featured a Capitol dome herald (various sizes were used) painted in white on a red carbody. The car number was also in white below the dome. The letters "B&O" did not appear on the car itself, only in the herald.

Below: The author took this photograph of I-5D, C-2141 at Rowlesburg, West Virginia on July 25, 1973. It provides an example of the relatively rare 1969 scheme, consisting only of the Capitol dome herald and the car number in white on a red carbody. This was the last red paint scheme applied to B&O cupola cabooses and omitted any railroad identification except for the herald. The Brunswick, Maryland shops applied this scheme and used the large 38-inch diameter capitol dome herald. This is the herald which would be used in the 1970 yellow caboose paint.

Cupola Caboose Lettering - 1970 to 1971

In 1970 and 1971 a number of wooden cupola style cabooses were repaired at the Chillicothe shops for use in non-pool service. Cars which went through this program were repainted in a scheme inspired by the C&O caboose paint scheme, and featured a large 38-inch diameter Capitol dome herald in black on a yellow carbody. The car number was also in black below the herald and was applied using the C&O Gothic style numerals. There was a red stripe along the lower edge of the car, and the letters "B&O" did not appear on the car itself, only in the herald.

Non-Pool Service Bay Window Caboose Lettering 1970 to 1971

At the time the wooden cupola style cabooses were repaired at the Chillicothe shops for use in non-pool service, at least four non-pool service bay window cabooses were also shopped (I-5BAs C-2502, C-2504 & C-2505 and I-13 C-1826). These were repainted in the scheme inspired by the C&O caboose paint scheme. For these bay window cars, the large 38-inch diameter Capitol dome in black was placed to the right of the bay on the yellow carbody. The car number was in black below the window of the bay window. There was a red stripe along the lower edge of the car and the letters "B&O" did not appear on the car itself, only in the herald.

Upper Left: This photograph of Class I-5 C-2212, taken in Dayton, Ohio on May 19, 1973, illustrates the 1970 lettering scheme for cupola cabooses. The 38-inch diameter herald is in black on a yellow body. The 9-inch car numbers were also black, and were in the C&O-inspired Gothic style as opposed to the Roman style of numbers previously used. This lettering scheme was applied only to cabooses which were repaired at the Chillicothe, Ohio shops in 1970 and 1971. Note that the car's class is incorrectly shown as I-5D since the truck centers have not been lengthened. (Robert Hubler)

Lower Left: Only one I-13 caboose ever received the 1970 yellow caboose paint scheme. (Chillicothe - October, 1970). It was C-1826 (formerly B&O Class L-6 stock car 13035, originally CI&W stock car 686). The C-1826 is now owned by C. W. Abbott of Newark, Ohio and was photographed there on February 15, 1975. (Robert Hubler)

Pool Service Caboose Lettering - 1970 to 1971

In 1970 and 1971 the DuBois shops conducted a repair program on the I-17 and I-17A cabooses. They were repainted in a new scheme also applied to Class I-12 and Class I-18 cabooses. It was similar to that applied to the non-pool bay window cars, but the colors were almost a mirror image. The carbody was blue instead of yellow, as on the non-pool cars. The large Capitol dome to the right of the bay window was in yellow instead of black, while the car number (in the C&O-style Gothic font) was also in yellow below the window on the bay. The stripe along the lower edge of the car was yellow instead of red. The lettering diagram for this scheme is shown in Figure 48 on page 168.

Above: This is a beautiful view of I-17A C-2944 in the late afternoon sun at Dayton, Ohio on August 28, 1977. The C-2944 illustrated the 1970 lettering scheme for pool service cabooses. This scheme consisted of a blue carbody with a 38-inch diameter herald in yellow to the right of the bay window, 9-inch numbers and a 3-inch yellow stripe along the bottom of the car. It was applied to all surviving I-17 and I-17A cabooses when they received program repairs at DuBois, Pennsylvania in 1970 and 1971. (Robert Hubler)

Right: The 1970 pool service lettering scheme was also applied to some of the I-12 wagon top cabooses. An example is the C-2496, photographed at Dayton, Ohio on December 7, 1975. (Robert Hubler)

Figure 48

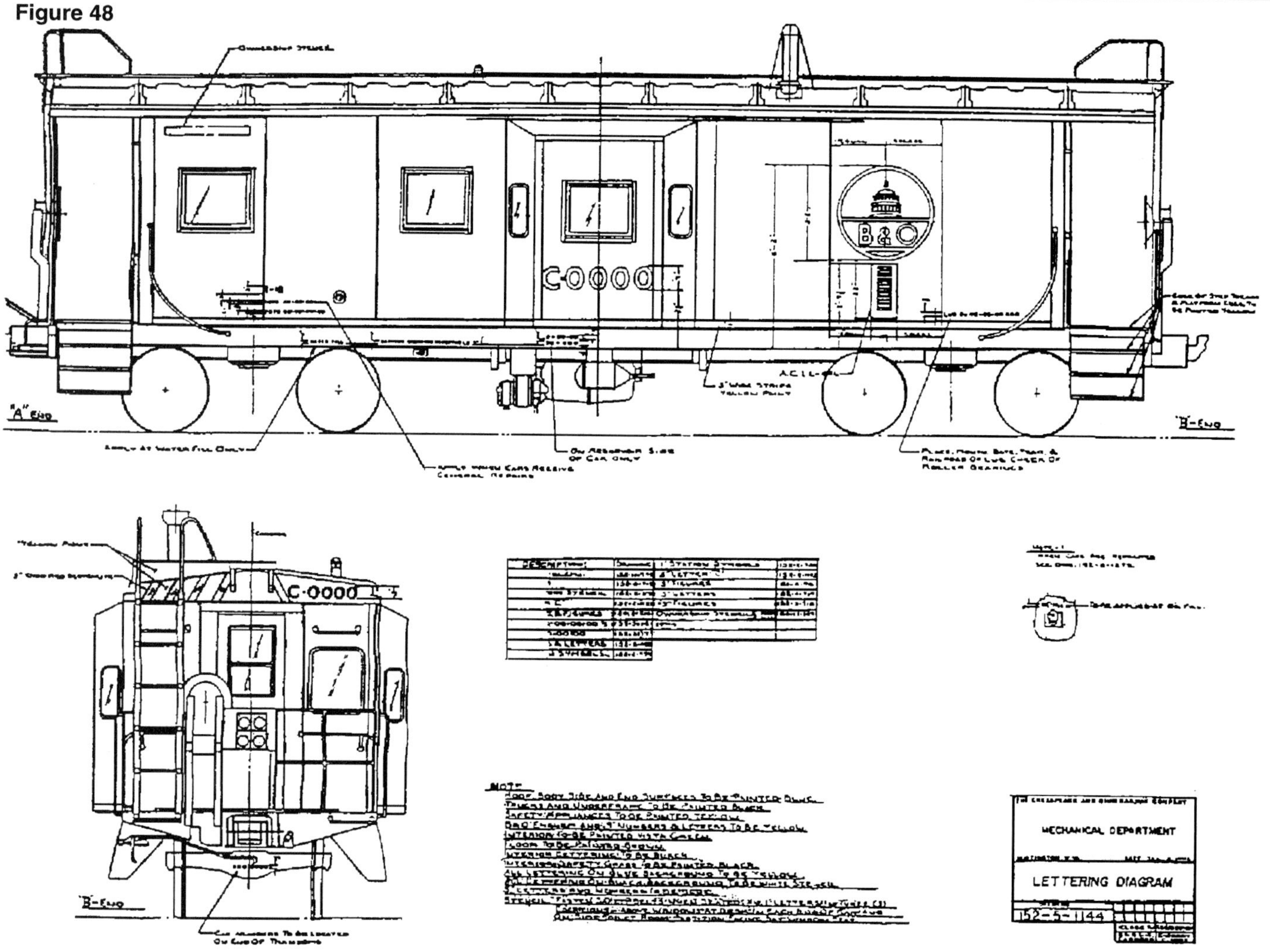

Below: When the C-26 cabooses were built in 1971, the 1970 blue with yellow lettering scheme was current for pool cabooses. All C-26 cabs were delivered in this scheme, which is illustrated by this photograph of C-3711 taken at Chillicothe, Ohio on December 26, 1977. The C-26 class cabooses were the only cars to be delivered with this lettering scheme. (Robert Hubler)

Caboose Lettering - 1972 to 1981

In 1972, the Chessie System came into being and shortly thereafter introduced a new paint scheme ultimately applied to most B&O cabooses remaining in service. The letters "B&O" appeared on the top of the bay window with the number on the bottom. The Ches-C logo appeared to the right of the bay window, while the words "Chessie System" were along the lower edge of the car to the left of the bay window. In some variations of this scheme, the "C" in Chessie System was replaced with the Ches-C logo. The lettering diagram for the Chessie System scheme is illustrated in Figure 49 on page 171.

Above: This photograph of C-2437 taken at Dayton, Ohio on May 21, 1977 illustrates the Chessie System lettering scheme applied to an I-12 caboose. The scheme called for a Chessie logo to the right of the bay window, the B&O initials above the window on the side bay, and the car number below with the words "Chessie System" to the left of the bay window. On shorter cars, such as the I-12, I-17 and I-17A classes, the words "Chessie System" were scaled down to fit the available space. (Robert Hubler)

Right: One of the first of the Class I-17A cabooses to be repainted with the Chessie System colors was C-2884, refurbished at DuBois, Pennsylvania in November, 1973. The B&O Railroad Museum acquired this caboose for display and had it repainted in the blue pool service scheme. The author photographed the car at Dayton, Ohio on December 31, 1976.

Above: This is an example of a C-26 caboose repainted into the Chessie System scheme at the DuBois shops. The C-3824 was photographed at Cincinnati, Ohio on October 29, 1977. (Robert Hubler)

Below: The C-26A cabooses were the first to be delivered from the builder in the Chessie System scheme. An example is provided by the C-3835 at Cincinnati, Ohio on July 5, 1976. All C-26A cabooses carried the standard Chessie System lettering, and none ever received special Chessie System safety caboose lettering. (Robert Hubler)

Above: All Class I-18 cabooses were painted into some form of the Chessie System scheme. Eight cars were lettered into special safety caboose schemes, while the rest of the class received the standard Chessie System lettering. The C-3019 was one of the cars which carried the standard scheme. It was at Cincinnati, Ohio on July 5, 1976. (Robert Hubler)

Figure 49

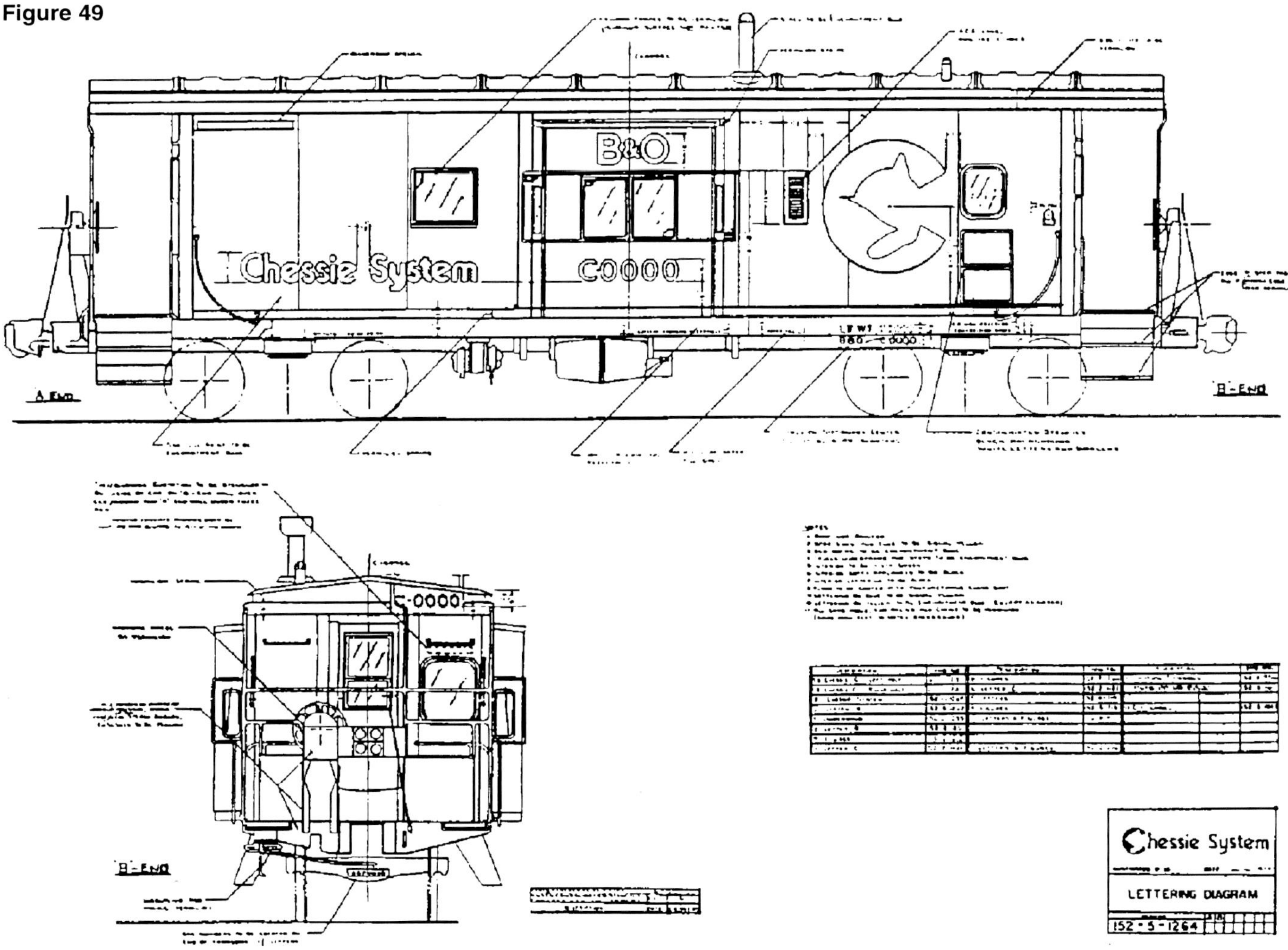

Above: The C-27 cabooses also were delivered from the builder with the Chessie System lettering scheme, with addition of the safety cross emblem which first appeared on 12 safety cabooses painted by the railroad in 1973 and 1974. The application of this safety emblem displaced the large Chessie logo to the left of the bay window. The C-3966 was photographed at Willard, Ohio on September 9, 1978. (Robert Hubler)

Below: The C-3930 was the only caboose to have its safety cross emblem repainted with white tracks on a black background during a shopping. All the other emblems were done with black tracks on a white field. (See page 108) The C-27 was photographed in New Castle Jct., Pennsylvania on September 2, 1979. (D. H. Hamley, John C. La Rue, Jr. Collection)

Above: The Class C-27A cabooses were delivered with the same variation of the Chessie System lettering scheme as used on the earlier C-27 cabooses. The most prominent feature of this scheme was the large safety cross emblem. On the three window side of the caboose there was no space for the large Chessie logo. As seen in the photograph, this caused the replacement of the "C" in the Chessie System name with a small version of the Chessie logo. The 904013 was photographed at Garrett, Indiana on September 13, 1981. (Robert Hubler)

Below: B&O Class I-5D caboose C-2248 was operating in mine run service out of Cowen, West Virginia on September 4, 1977. It was repaired at Chillicothe in April of that year, and received a patchwork version of the last B&O wooden caboose paint scheme. The center panel has been repainted, covering the large Capitol dome herald. It is interesting to note that, in one touch of color, the red stripe along the side was renewed in this partial repainting. (Robert Hubler)

Cupola Caboose Lettering - 1975

Between 1975 and 1977, a small number of wooden cupola cabooses were repaired at the Chillicothe shops in order to squeeze a few more months of service from them. Cars which went through this program were repainted in an abbreviated lettering scheme featuring only the letters "B&O" and the car number in black on a yellow carbody. This was the last paint scheme to be applied to B&O cupola caboose cars and, except for the colors, it was reminiscent of the scheme applied to cabooses from 1900 to 1916 (see Caboose Lettering - 1900 to 1916, on page 146).

Bay Window Caboose Lettering - 1982

In 1982, the railroad painted three B&O Class C-26 cabooses in a special bright orange scheme to promote "Careful Car Handling." The lettering for cabooses 903747, 903758, and 903820 was white and followed the standard Chessie lettering scheme for bay window cabooses except for a special "Careful Car Handling" logo to the right of the bay window. The logo was a graphic of two boxcars slamming together inside of a crossed out circle with the words "Handle With" above and "Care!" below the circle. The letters "B&O" appeared above the bay window with the car number at the bottom. The words "Chessie System" were along the lower edge of the car to the left of the bay window with the "C" in Chessie System replaced with the Ches-C logo. See page 143.

Caboose Lettering - 1991 to 1992

In 1991, CSX Transportation began to remodel a number of B&O bay window cabooses for use on those trains which still required this equipment. These cars received a complex lettering scheme. Both sides of the caboose carried a diagonally striped band bounding each side with the words "CROSS TRACKS SAFELY" in the middle of this band along the top edge of the car. The initials "CSXT" and the number were to the left of the bay window. One side of the car had the "Operation RED BLOCK" anti-drug logo to the right of the bay window. On the opposite side, the "Operation Life Saver" grade crossing safety logo was to the right of the bay window, with the words "Look Listen Live" stacked above the CSXT reporting marks. The CSXT scheme is illustrated by the photographs of 904038 and 903918 on pages 144 and 145.

Above: This circa 1911 view looking east in Willard, Ohio shows the east bound hump yard scale house and caboose track. Two of the cars have an extended height cupola with a door to allow direct access from the cupola to the roof walk. The middle caboose is the X-3002, one of a small number of "Service" cabooses on the B&O roster during this era. (B&O Railroad Museum Collection)

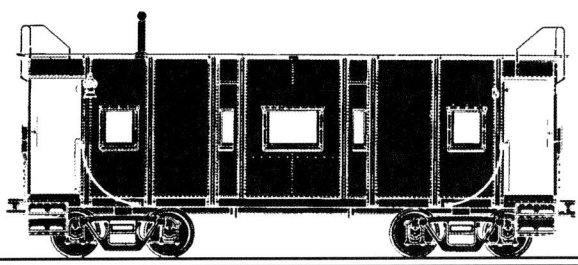

INDEX OF PHOTOGRAPHS

Class C&C	
C1703	45
C1707	46
C1709	45

Class C-5	
90369	99

Class C-8	
90771	100
90855	99

Class C-9	
90631	101

Class C-15B	
C3050	97
903050	140

Class C-26	
C3711	168
C3714	128, 142
C3718	142
C3753	103
C3754	22
C3774	128
C3809	139
C3820	123
C3822	103
C3824	170
903747	143

Class C-26A	
C3831	105
C3835	170
C3844	14
C3863	141
C3866	105
C3910	125
903918	145

Class C-27	
C3930	108, 172
C3934	107
C3954	107
C3958	126
C3966	172

Class C-27A	
904013	143, 173
904022	110
904031	110
904038	144
904054	111
904078	126
904093	111

Class C-28	
C3051	107, 141

Class I	
Unknown	29
C24	147
C1599	30
1871	30
C1856	30
X3002	174

Class I-1	
C84	151
C145	118
C189	37
C220	38
C242	39
C275	38
C307	39
C356	38
C372	37
C374	35
C375	161
C379	130
B&OCT C1895	39

Class I-1A	
C409	156
C474	49
C490	49
C498	121
C1402	50
C1403	121
C1411	155
C1425	50
C1432	44
B&OCT C1896	133
B&OCT C1906	50

Class I-2	
CH&D 30	42
CH&D 92	42
C1568	41

Class I-3	
C1602	43, 134
C1603	44
C1611	44

Class I-5	
C1900	14, 53
C1952	54
C1977	149
C2050	51
C2063	52
C2064	54
C2087	52
C2113	116
C2204	54
C2212	166
C2245	55
C2282	53
C2291	162

Class I-5A	
C2501	56, 57, 131

Class I-5B	
C2502	116

Class I-5BA	
C2502	126, 134, 138
C2504	59
C2505	60
C2507	60

Class I-5C	
C1915	61
C1949	61
C1953	135
C2138	152
C2214	62

Class I-5D	
C1901	65
C1926	65
C1929	130
C1934	65
C1994	64
C2001	156
C2021	155
C2031	162
C2074	63
C2089	135
C2101	Front Cover
C2141	165
C2168	135
C2198	137
C2203	20
C2227	123
C2239	63
C2248	173
C2277	8
C2283	64
C2292	145

Class I-6	
CI&W 17	66
CI&W 19	67
C1676	67
C1685	152
C1689	67
C1692	66

Class I-7	
C2500	68, 69

Class I-8	
BR&P 38	71
Unknown	70

Class I-10	
BR&P 285	73
C2601	75
C2602	15
C2621	75
C2623	137
C2626	23
C2639	74
C2646	75

Class I-11	
C1774	76
C1775	76
C1776	76

Class I-12	
C2407	23
C2413	132, Back Cover
C2417	160
C2426	19
C2433	78
C2437	1, 169
C2438	120
C2448	78
C2457	136
C2465	158
C2467	124
C2473	163
C2478	80
C2481	23
C2485	79
C2496	167
C2802	79
C2803	138
C2806	129
C2807	78
C2815	122
C2819	153
C2822	131, 140

Class I-13	
C1800	81
C1813	157
C1818	83
C1820	154
C1824	81
C1826	137, 166
C1827	132

Class I-14	
SF43 (C1652)	84

Class I-16	
C2306	88
C2311	129
C2352	117
C2363	88
C2701	87
C2702	150
C2774	119
C2779	159
C2784	88

Class I-17	
C2853	5
C2855	90
C2857	165
C2858	89, 133
C2861	91

Class I-17A	
C2868	122
C2869	93
C2871	160
C2873	125
C2884	169
C2889	93
C2890	93
C2899	139
C2939	92
C2942	124
C2944	167
C2946	158
902884	144

Class I-18	
C3000	127
C3010	127
C3013	164
C3014	96, 136
C3019	171
C3025	142
C3031	95
C3045	96

Class K-1	
B&O Unknown	146
P&C Unknown	9
C721	34
C754	34
C845	31
C1060	115
C1145	33
C1180	33
C1290	148
B&OCT C1725	32
B&OCT C1741	32
100459	176
100656	19
100714	32
100777	147
100941	33

Class M&K	
Unknown	46

175

A B&O crew shows off its K-1 caboose, which appears to be in its original condition. The photograph's date of November 14, 1901 does present a mystery since available records indicate that the 100459 was not built until September 1902. In any event, it became C-459 and served the B&O until 1916 when it was destroyed in a collision. (Roger Kirkpatrick Collection)

Additional Information Needed

The information, photographs and diagrams presented in this book have been assembled over many years of effort and with the assistance of numerous people. The B&O Railroad Historical Society, the B&O Railroad Museum, and colleagues throughout the field have gathered and reconstructed a great deal of data, but more is needed to present a complete history of B&O cabooses. Constructive criticism is always welcome, and anyone who has additional factual information or corrections is asked to contact the author via The B&O Railroad Historical Society. Corrections and additions will be incorporated in future additions to this book or presented in other B&O Railroad Historical Society publications.

In particular, the Society needs diagrams of cabooses from railroads acquired by the B&O. These include the Coal & Coke, Morgantown & Kingwood, Cincinnati Indianapolis & Western (Class I-6), and Buffalo & Susquehanna (Class I-11 and I-12 (1st)). Additional painting and lettering diagrams are needed as well, especially for the pre-World War II era. Photographs of older B&O cabooses, particularly those carrying the 1400 to 1999 or 100000 to 101134 series numbers, would be extremely useful, as would stories, anecdotes, and souvenirs of life aboard the cars themselves. Please contact the Society if you have any additional information to share.

About the Society

Throughout its 160 years, the B&O Railroad enjoyed a rich and varied history. It survived to become one of the world's oldest railroad companies through a combination of skill, foresight, and chance. Its importance to the cultural and economic history of the United States is indisputable. The Baltimore and Ohio Railroad Historical Society exists to help assemble, interpret, and share that history.

The B&O Railroad Historical Society is an independent non-profit educational corporation with a membership of approximately 1,800 spread throughout the United States and numerous foreign counties. The Society's purpose is to foster interest, research, and publication concerning the B&O. Through the Society, members may participate in an annual conference, field trips, research projects, equipment restorations, and local meetings. An all-color calendar and a bimonthly magazine are products of the program. Nominal yearly dues of $20 make it all possible. Your participation is invited.

The Baltimore and Ohio Railroad Historical Society, P.O. Box 13578, Baltimore, Maryland 21203

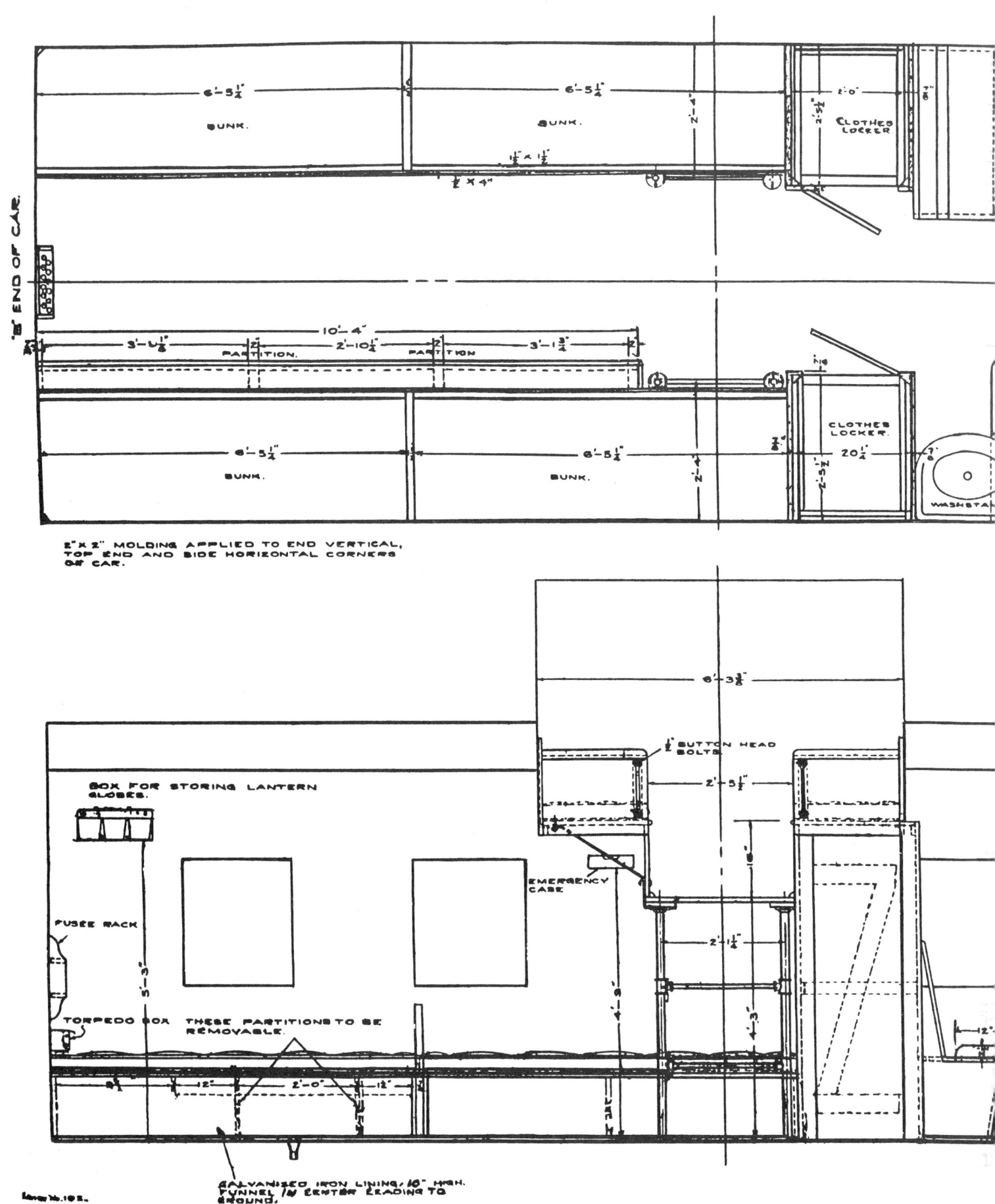